True Pros

of

Commercial Real Estate

Jake James

Published by True Pros Media LLC
Washington, DC
truepros.media
ISBN 979-8-9925115-0-5

First Edition
Printed in the United States of America

Contents

Part Three
Developers

To all those striving to reach the next level.

You're not alone. Don't ever give up.

Acknowledgments

First and foremost, I have to thank Jack Schwager. His *Market Wizards* books were the main source of my inspiration. He was gracious enough to discuss this idea, provide insights into his experience, and answer my many questions. Thank you, Jack.

Next are Chris Powers and Moses Kagan. These were the first two individuals I reached out to. This book might never have been written if they had ignored me or declined. Their responsiveness and support from the beginning gave me the momentum to move forward and contact others. Thank you both.

Then there's Bob Knakal. He gets a special shout-out because, unbeknownst to him at the time, his was the first interview I'd ever conducted in my life. His graciousness throughout the process and our meeting in The Knakal Map Room gave me the confidence to pursue the rest of these interviews. Thank you, Bob.

And of course, the rest of the True Pros I interviewed in this book. I could go on and on about each and every one of you. You were all supportive, responsive, and incredibly gracious in carving out time to fit me into your schedules. Thank you all.

Now, for the ones who carried me through, starting with Duke. My little buddy never failed to tell me when it was time to take a break from editing to give him some belly scratches. Thanks, pal.

Alexandra, you bring me boundless pride and love that words can't fully express. You're my favorite little girl in the whole entire world. I love you more than you'll ever know.

And lastly, I have to thank Elizabeth more than anyone. Your love and support throughout this project have been incredible. Thank you for your encouragement, your reviews, and your understanding. Not many women would cancel a two-week European trip so I could travel around the country and interview a bunch of strangers. I love you. Thank you for believing in me.

Preface

Why I Wrote This Book

The idea for this book emerged from an unexpected parallel between two seemingly different fields: trading and commercial real estate (CRE). I spent ten years working in trading, during which time I read extensively on how successful traders thought and operated. Years later, as I began exploring CRE as a side interest, I noticed striking similarities between these two worlds. Both require practitioners to read markets, manage risk, and make high-stakes decisions with imperfect information. Both reward those who can maintain discipline while seizing opportunities. And in both domains, the best among them seem to develop an almost intuitive sense for their markets and a pattern recognition ability that comes from years of experience.

When I started learning about CRE, I found myself wondering: Who owns all of these buildings? How did they come to own them? How do developers decide which projects to pursue? Who determines what gets built where, and why? Where does all the money come from? What makes some brokers so much more successful than others? Why do some players make it through market cycles and others don't?

While there are many excellent books about real estate investment strategies, property development techniques, and market analysis, few capture the human element of the industry. The relationships successful professionals build, their decision-making processes, how they got into the business, how they overcame mistakes, and what separates the best from the rest.

What stood out most in these interviews was how different each journey was. Success came in many forms, and often from unexpected directions. While some interviewees started with more resources than others, they each forged their own path, seeking out mentors, pursuing education, or building their foundation from the ground up.

My hope is that this book will serve as both a practical resource and a source of inspiration, showing not just what is possible in CRE but how to achieve it. Whether you're just starting your career, a seasoned professional, curious about business and CRE, or seeking cross-industry insights, I believe you'll find valuable lessons in these conversations with some of the industry's most accomplished pros.

Looking Forward

These interviews lay the groundwork for a larger vision. As I developed this concept for CRE, I realized how beneficial similar collections would be for other sectors. If this book resonates with readers as I hope it will, I may expand True Pros into a broader series, each volume focusing on a different field. From the trades to oil and gas, small businesses to healthcare, adventure sports to technology.

Beyond books, I envision True Pros growing to include newsletters, podcasts, resources, and a community where professionals can share insights across disciplines. Every industry has exceptional professionals whose hard-won wisdom deserves to be captured and shared. This first volume, focused on commercial real estate, lays the foundation for what I hope will become a much larger body of work.

Learn More and Get Involved

For additional commercial real estate resources and updates, visit the True Pros community online or sign up for our newsletter. This is a completely independent project. Self-funded, self-published, and built from scratch. To learn more about how this book came together, including notes on the editing process, AI assistance, and privacy considerations, see the How This Book Was Made section at the back of the book.

Scan to explore True Pros and join the newsletter at ***truepros.media***

Introduction

Every building has a story.

That luxury high-rise cutting through the downtown skyline? Behind every inch of glass and steel lies a story of vision, calculated risk, and skillful execution. The neighborhood strip mall where you grab that coffee every morning? It exists because someone made a series of countless decisions, negotiations, and strategic bets on that corner's future. Even that unremarkable warehouse at the edge of town is the product of sophisticated market analysis and careful financial engineering.

The commercial real estate (CRE) industry shapes our cities, influences how we live and work, and drives significant portions of the global economy. With a market value exceeding $20 trillion in the United States alone and over $33 trillion globally, CRE represents one of the world's largest asset classes. It accounts for approximately 6 to 7 percent of GDP in most developed economies and employs millions of professionals across a spectrum of specialties.* Yet for most people, including even some within the industry, the inner workings of CRE are still a mystery.

* *Nareit, "U.S. Commercial Real Estate Market," 2021, https://www.reit.com; Savills, "Global Real Estate Value," 2017, https://www.savills.com.*

Who decides what gets built and where? How do deals actually come together? What separates the outstanding from the merely ambitious in this high-stakes world?

This book pulls back the curtain on CRE through in-depth conversations with a diverse array of distinguished professionals who have mastered different aspects of the industry. From veteran brokers who've orchestrated billion-dollar deals to visionary developers who've transformed entire neighborhoods, from sharp-eyed investors who've built generational wealth to innovative fund managers who've weathered multiple market cycles, each interview offers distinctive perspectives on how the industry really works.

The core idea for this book was inspired by Jack Schwager's *Market Wizards* series, a classic collection from the trading world that reveals how elite traders approach markets, risk, and opportunity through intimate conversations. Like those books, this one aims to capture how successful CRE professionals think about opportunities, risk, and value creation. Jessica Livingston's *Founders at Work* was another source of inspiration. Her interviews with tech startup founders capture the raw, early stages of company-building in a way textbooks never could.

Inspired by these works, I sought to fill a gap in real estate literature, where few books document the firsthand experiences and perspectives of the industry's most accomplished professionals. To bring these stories to life, each chapter follows a simple format: a snapshot of the professional highlighting key achievements, an introduction setting the stage for the interview, the interview itself—the core of the chapter, and a brief conclusion with key takeaways. Links to learn more about each professional and their business are provided at the end of each chapter.

These profiles present not just career stories, but a behind-the-scenes look at how excellence is built in commercial real estate. You'll learn:

- How top brokers build and leverage their networks
- How investors think about value creation
- How fund managers structure deals and raise capital
- How developers evaluate opportunities and manage risk

- How these professionals charted their particular paths in the industry

The interviews delve into pivotal career moments, key decisions, and the lessons learned from both triumphs and failures.

These conversations reveal that while CRE can seem dauntingly complex from the outside, certain fundamental principles consistently emerge:

- The importance of market expertise
- The power of strong relationships and networks
- The interplay of timing, execution, and attention to detail
- The delicate balance between calculated risk-taking and prudence

What stands out across these conversations is not just professional accomplishment, but the sincere enthusiasm and satisfaction these individuals find in their work. Whether they're discussing complicated deals, market challenges, or daily operations, an unmistakable passion animates their stories. Some seemed destined for the industry from an early age, while others discovered it through serendipitous encounters or career pivots. This raises an interesting question: Do these professionals thrive because they found an industry that perfectly suits their talents and interests, or did their commitment to mastering their craft lead to the fulfillment they now experience? The answer likely varies for each individual, but what's clear is that true expertise and genuine enjoyment seem inextricably linked in these success stories.

Throughout this book, you'll encounter industry-specific terminology, vernacular, and acronyms commonly used by CRE professionals. When industry terms or acronyms are first mentioned in the text, you'll find their definitions or explanations in footnotes at the bottom of the page. For even more clarity, I've provided a comprehensive Glossary at the end of the book that defines these terms. Appendix A offers a CRE Primer with foundational concepts and frameworks for readers new to commercial real estate or those seeking a refresher. Additionally,

Appendix B contains three detailed case studies that illustrate key industry processes and decision-making in action. These resources will help you maximize your learning from the interviews while gaining practical knowledge of how the industry works.

Whether you're an industry veteran, a young professional starting your career, someone seeking business principles that apply across fields, or simply curious about how the built environment around you comes to be, these interviews offer valuable lessons in one of the world's most consequential and enduring industries.

The following chapters are more than just stories of achievement. They're a collective wisdom highlighting the paths to success in commercial real estate. Through these conversations, we'll explore not just what these professionals have achieved, but how they think, how they make decisions, and how they've built their careers in an industry where the stakes can be extraordinarily high and the lessons often expensive.

Welcome to an insider's view of commercial real estate. The stories you're about to read will change the way you look at every building you encounter.

Part One
Brokers and Advisors

In commercial real estate, the best brokers do far more than just close deals. They've evolved beyond transaction facilitators into strategic partners who blend market intelligence with relationship capital. The professionals in this section work across investment sales and tenant representation but share one defining trait: they see opportunities others miss.

What distinguishes these professionals is their commitment to putting clients' long-term interests first. Their market knowledge runs deep. Not just property values and cap rates, but the intangible factors that truly drive decisions. Through their stories, you'll see how they've transformed what was once a purely transactional service into something much more valuable: strategic counsel that shapes portfolios and influences entire market segments.

Bob Knakal

Chairman and CEO, BKREA

New York City

- Founded BKREA in 2024, leveraging four decades of expertise in New York City's commercial real estate market.
- Closed over 2,342 commercial property transactions as of December 2024, including a landmark $179 million portfolio sale that helped finance the acquisition of an iconic Manhattan office building.
- Created The Knakal Map Room, a comprehensive, physical mapping of Manhattan development sites built through 220 hours of fieldwork, an unparalleled market intelligence resource.
- Co-founded Massey Knakal Realty Services in 1988, growing it from a startup to the city's dominant property sales firm before selling to Cushman & Wakefield in 2014 for approximately $100 million.

Since first hearing about The Knakal Map Room, I had always wanted to go and see it in person. When the invitation came to conduct our interview there, I couldn't believe my luck. I wasn't quite sure what to expect, but when I walked in, I saw a giant map stretching across a huge conference table and the rest covering a wall that must have been 30 feet long and 10 feet high. As you look closer, you realize it's a physical representation of the entire city of New York, all color-coded to decipher the status of each individual parcel and every potential development site.

During COVID, Bob recognized the unique opportunity to walk around the city with hardly anyone around so that he and his team could note every single site on every single block. The project would end up taking them over 220 hours on foot, cataloging properties across the city. The map isn't just a visualization tool; it's the physical embodiment of his approach to real estate.

Regarded by many to be a legend in New York real estate, he's personally brokered over 2,300 properties worth roughly $22 billion. Yet despite this stature, Bob answered my cold call in two rings, a testament to the accessibility and work ethic that has fueled his success since 1984.

Taking the train up from DC for our meeting, I watched Manhattan's iconic skyline emerge on the horizon. I couldn't help but wonder how many of those buildings were ones Bob had sold.

After starting college at the Wharton School of the University of Pennsylvania, Bob entered real estate fortuitously. He walked into Coldwell Banker's Hackensack office thinking it was a bank. That chance encounter led to a summer internship, which became a full-time role four years later in the firm's Manhattan office. Four years after that, in 1988, he co-founded Massey Knakal Realty Services with Paul Massey, introducing a territory-based model that divided New York City into specialized zones. The strategy proved transformative: from 2001 to 2014, the firm sold more than three times as many properties as its nearest competitor. All the while, the local boutique company was competing with much larger national and global commercial real estate firms.

Following the firm's acquisition by Cushman & Wakefield in 2014, Bob continued as Chairman of New York Investment Sales, consistently ranking among the top brokers globally. He then became the Chairman of New York Investment Sales at JLL, bringing 53 colleagues from Cushman in one of the largest mass transitions in CRE history. In 2024, he launched BKREA (BK Real Estate Advisors), a new venture blending decades of experience with emerging tools like AI.

Beyond deal-making, Bob has contributed to the industry through teaching, media appearances, and thought leadership. He's also active in philanthropy, supporting organizations such as The Prescott Foundation for Children, Ice Hockey in Harlem, Ronald McDonald House, and Shema Kolainu.

Sitting in The Knakal Map Room for our interview—my first interview ever—Bob's warmth and enthusiasm quickly put me at ease. We ended with an unplanned adventure when I helped him reattach a dangling piece on the highest corner of the wall map. I watched anxiously as he balanced between a windowsill and a folding desk to place it perfectly, hoping my first interview wasn't going to end with me participating in putting one of the real estate community's most beloved members in the hospital. Luckily, we both walked away unscathed. The next day, I shipped a step-stool to his office, equal parts thank-you gift and safety precaution.

Bob's four decades in commercial real estate show what happens when someone commits fully to knowing a market inside and out. His work has helped alter New York City's landscape while setting standards that continue to shape how the next generation approaches this business.

Date of Interview: October 1, 2023

Bob, thank you so much for taking the time to speak with me today. Being here in the Map Room is amazing. I wanted to start off at the beginning. You've been in the business a long time, and your career has gone through multiple real estate cycles, and New York itself has gone through so many changes. Could you take us back to how you first entered the real estate industry?

In my freshman year at Wharton, I wanted to be an investment banker. I thought I needed a summer job that would look good on my resume, so during spring break, I made up a list of all the investment banks and commercial banks in Bergen County, where I grew up in Maywood, New Jersey. I drove around dropping off my resume at every bank on my list.

I walked into Paine Webber's Hackensack office, gave them my resume, came out, and saw Coldwell Banker right across the hall. I thought it was another bank, so I walked in and gave them my resume, too. They called me later that day and set up an interview for the following day. I went to the library to look up this bank and discovered it was actually a real estate company. I almost didn't go to the interview, but they were the only ones hiring college kids for the summer. I took the job, and the rest is history.

What was that first experience like in the industry?

That first summer was eye-opening. The internship was in market research. We were tracking office buildings, retail properties, and industrial properties. I had no idea about any of this before. I didn't even really know what a retail building was. I'd go to stores, malls, and office parks. Some buildings would be full; others, 10 percent occupied. It didn't occur to me that a mostly vacant building might have trouble paying its taxes or mortgage.

I asked tons of questions. Josh Levering, who gave me my first job, probably thought, "What's with this kid?" But I found it fascinating. I went back the second summer to run the market research internship program, and my third summer, I got my salesperson's license and worked as an assistant to an industrial broker named Tom Mallaney, who's still a good friend. Then, I started full-time with Coldwell Banker in New York when I graduated in 1984.

What drew you to the sales aspect versus other areas of real estate?

That's a great question. It was definitely a combination of things. I liked both the selling aspect and the buildings themselves. That first summer, driving around looking at buildings, identifying properties, writing down information about tenants. I really got into it. I've always been someone who dives headfirst into things.

The environment at Coldwell Banker in that Hackensack office was fantastic. I met great people who were smart, hardworking, and making money. They were incredibly welcoming to me as just a college kid by inviting me out for drinks on Fridays and treating me like part of the team. Several of those folks are still friends of mine today.

There was still some doubt initially about whether to go into investment banking instead. What really pushed me toward real estate was an entrepreneurial management class at Wharton. A guy running a pet food company came in and said, "Find something you love and do that. I sell dog food, and I'm the happiest guy in the world." That really hit home. I loved what I'd done that summer at Coldwell Banker, so I went back again instead of looking for investment banking internships.

You've mentioned there's been a highly correlated relationship between baseball and real estate throughout your career. Did your background in sports help prepare you for the business?

Absolutely. Having played sports my whole life, basketball through school and baseball through college, being part of teams was very important. It taught you competition, working with others, and getting along with different personalities. We actually told our HR folks to look for people who participated in team sports when hiring. If you played sports, you're competitive, and real estate is a very competitive business. Team sports particularly show that you can work with others, as teamwork is a characteristic that must be embraced.

We also looked for excellence in any competitive environment. Could have been captain of the debating team or publisher of the school newspaper. Just something showing you excelled in a competitive setting. These characteristics significantly increased the odds of success, though nothing was a perfect correlation.

What made you choose New York over other markets?

When I was a kid, my paternal grandparents lived on East 73rd Street in Manhattan. We'd visit every couple of months, and coming down FDR Drive, you'd see these huge buildings. Even just seeing the buildings along First and Second Avenue was incredible. I always had a fascination with New York. Plus, it was the major leagues. I figured if I'm going to try this, let me try it in the Big Apple. I had nothing to lose, and I absolutely fell in love with the city.

When you walk around the city now and see buildings you've been involved with, is there a certain pride in that?

Yes, this is particularly true when we sell the land on which new towers are built. While the developer builds the building, when you sold the land and see a new building there, you feel like you had a small hand in making it happen. You live and die with these deals so much. I can still walk through buildings we sold in the 80s in my mind and see what was on every floor. I remember them so vividly because each one was so important. I might not remember what I had for breakfast today, but ask me about a deal from 1993, and I'll tell you all about it. That's one of the cool things, you remember all these deals because they meant so much.

Those early years at Coldwell Banker seemed to shape your future approach. How did you and Paul decide to team up?

When we started at Coldwell Banker, the experienced guys were like, "I've sold a lot of buildings. Who are these young kids? What do they know?" But we just did basic fundamental things really well. After six months, the company saw the types of listings we were getting, and they were having people come in from all over the region to meet with us asking, "How are you guys doing this? You're young kids in New York City, which is really competitive, and you're doing really well."

Our second year, we were the top salespeople in the office. That's when they made us the bosses of the group. I'm sure it pissed those other guys off, but we made more money than them. It's very much a results-oriented business. That is one of the aspects of the business I love the most. It is one of the purest forms of meritocracy there is. You get out of it what you put into it.

What was your approach in those early days?

We had a prospecting plan that worked. We approached it very methodically. Back in the '80s, publicly available information was very opaque. I remember plenty of times calling up tenants in a building and saying, "Hey, this is Joe McCluskey from the New York Fire Department. You've got some massive fire violations on this building. I've got to speak to the owner right away." And they'd give you his phone number.

We were very methodical about getting ownership information on every single building, on every block in our territories. We took a very fundamental proof-stacking approach where we did market reports before people were doing market reports. We talked about how many buildings were in the area, how many sold last year and the year before, what the average prices were. We became experts in a very tiny pocket of the city, but we knew that pocket better than anybody. Even the folks who were doing it for decades.

It's very easy in this business to run for the shiny new toy. You're selling a building over here, then they want you to sell a building over there, then someone says, "Could you lease my building for me?" You think, "I could make money doing that," but we always focused on doing things that would help us get the next one.

What ultimately led you and Paul to leave Coldwell Banker and start your own firm?

We didn't have significant non-compete agreements back then. But more importantly, we saw an opportunity in the market. Coldwell Banker was predominantly focused on office leasing. They had about fifty or sixty guys leasing office space, about 20 people in retail leasing, and only four people in the sales group. We knew we could do something different by focusing entirely on sales and really owning specific neighborhoods.

We also wanted to build something of our own. We were young, ambitious, and figured if it didn't work out, we could always go back to working for someone else. We had very little to lose and everything to gain.

How did you approach differentiating yourselves in the market?

When we started out on our own, we had a very simple value proposition. Our territories were very small. We spent a couple of months studying everything about the area, then started calling clients. I remember giving a presentation to an owner on East 58th Street. We had sold three buildings at the time, and they were interviewing several firms. The owner said, "Look guys, you have virtually no experience. Why should I hire you? I'm interviewing these other firms that have years of experience."

We said, "Yeah, you're absolutely right, we've sold three buildings. But one was down the block, one was across the street, one was right next door to you. We know this neighborhood better than anybody and we can be a better advocate for you." We got the assignment. That approach snowballed.

Our value proposition was straightforward: we only sell buildings, we only represent sellers, we only work on exclusives, and we only work in your neighborhood. That took eight seconds to say, nothing ambiguous about it. It resonated with people. Then we started growing like a jigsaw puzzle, putting somebody to the north of us and the south and the east and west. Within the first week of starting Massey Knakal, we had three or four new listings from folks we had worked with in the past.

Were there challenging times in those early days?

There are always challenges in commercial brokerage. However, there is one that changed everything for us. There was a watershed moment involving Rosenthal & Rosenthal, a factoring company in the garment center. This was probably 1990–91, when we were struggling and running the business on credit cards. We had the credit lines maxed out. About $60,000 on cards, plus a $75,000 loan from Jack Holler. We were out of money with nowhere to go.

We had these three buildings on East 50th Street under contract with Fred Shalom as the buyer, but the deal wasn't supposed to close for another sixty days. I'm sitting at my desk at 226 East 54th Street when Stephen Rosenthal calls: "Bob, where are you?" "Sitting at my desk." "Get over here, we're closing 50th Street. I have a check for you!" Shalom had decided to close early, which rarely ever happens.

I ran out of the office, running down 54th Street. I get to Third Avenue, and Paul Massey just happens to be coming down the street. I said, "Paul, you'll never believe it—50th Street's closing!" We were literally hugging each other, jumping up and down on the corner. Went over, picked up the check—$90,000 commission. That was unbelievable, as it represented six months of our operating expenses and provided some breathing room for us. Things really started picking up from there, and we were able to climb out of that debt.

I love that story. It feels like something out of a movie. Did that success give you the opportunity to push your marketing

approach further? It seemed incredibly innovative for the time. Can you talk about that?

It was just wanting to let people know what we had done. We sold our first building at 1421 Third Avenue, and we thought, "Let's put up a 'just sold' sign." The sign stayed up for nine months before they started work on the building. Then we said, "We should let everyone in our territory know we sold this building." So we put together a little tombstone announcement and mailed it out.

In the real estate business, particularly in the private capital world, it's not who you know, it's who knows you. We understood the concept of market presence but didn't call it that back then. Today people study it as a science with terms like "market presence" and "proof stacking," but we were doing these activities naturally because they made sense. We were "creating content" before that term was ever coined.

How did you measure the effectiveness of these marketing efforts?

It's always very difficult to determine exactly what works and what doesn't. We looked at ROI as two different things: return on investment and return on involvement. When a client calls and says, "I'm thinking about selling my building," they don't say, "I called you because I saw your ad." It's a collection of everything. The calls, texts, emails, hard mail, speaking events, networking events, client lunches.

I always said hard mail is more effective than email. If somebody deletes your email, they're deleting it in a split second with no impression made. But with hard mail, they have to pick it up, look at it, see what it is before throwing it out. If you do that month after month, your name and company name keep going into their head. When something happens that catalyzes a transaction—death, divorce, taxes, partnership dispute, any of the number of things that induce someone to sell—you want them to think, "Let me call that guy or gal who's been sending me that mail all the time."

As a top sales broker, why have you never purchased properties for your own account?

There are several factors. If we had been property buyers ourselves, every potential buyer would have asked, "If this is such a great deal, why didn't you buy it?" Second, we wanted to create a valuable company and stay completely focused on that goal. If we were purchasing properties, it would have taken time away from making the company valuable. Third, if we had invested in real estate while running a brokerage business, we'd be doubly exposed during market downturns. Not only would our income be negatively impacted, but the value of our investments would have been negatively impacted as well.

How did you and Paul divide responsibilities as the company grew?

The management aspect was never my favorite. That's why Paul and I were a good team. He liked to manage people, I liked to sell. When we started Massey Knakal, we did everything together—the books, interviewing, taking out garbage, painting offices. It wasn't until the late '90s that we started adopting separate focuses.

I liked the strategic aspects of owning the business and the camaraderie we could create, but I didn't enjoy things like having to cut staff or negotiating with suppliers over paper clip prices. During the Global Financial Crisis (GFC)*, we had to fire 25 percent of our people. By 2011, we started climbing out of that hole and hiring people back. The market was taking off by 2014, which proved perfect timing for our sale.

What was your approach to hiring and building the team?

We actually prefer to hire people with no experience because if they have experience, they were probably trained improperly. We looked for

* **GFC** (Global Financial Crisis): The 2007–2008 global financial downturn caused by the collapse of the U.S. housing market and widespread institutional failures.

passion. Why are they interested in real estate? Why do they want to work here? We need good answers to those questions. Then we looked for something competitive in their background, like team sports, and evidence they've demonstrated excellence somewhere.

But there's a crucial distinction between passion and desire. Passion is enjoying what you're doing, while desire is the magnitude of effort you'll put into it. You can have passion for something but not be willing to work hard at it. In interviews, we try to differentiate between how badly someone wants to get the job versus how badly they want to succeed at the job.

Sometimes people want the job because they think they should have it. That's not compelling. They'll flame out when things get tough. We want people who have a burning desire to succeed. I ask them: Who do you want to be a hero to? Why are you doing this? Who are you trying to impress and why? It throws people off, but you want answers that show deep motivation.

We also told our HR people that this is fundamentally a people business. If you interview someone and don't feel like you'd love to have lunch or a beer with them, don't offer them a job. Some people look great on paper, but if you wouldn't want to hang out with them, move on.

James Nelson is a perfect example. We interviewed him back in the early '90s along with another kid from Colgate. Paul hired the other kid first, who flamed out in six months. I needed to hire someone and didn't feel like interviewing more people, so we hired James even though I thought he didn't really check all of the boxes. But he was very likable, and I wanted to work with him. He turned out to be one of the best brokers in the city. His deep-rooted tenacity did not come through in the interview. Then we hired a Harvard valedictorian who flamed out in six months. You never know.

Let's talk about how you eventually sold the company. What drove that decision?

When we started the company, we did it with the intention of selling it one day. We didn't grow up wealthy and thought this was a way to get rich. We flirted with selling several times over the years. We almost sold to Marcus & Millichap in the early 2000s. They offered $6 million. We wanted $7 million. George Marcus said, "We're earning twenty-five percent on our dot-com investments, why should we pay more for you guys?" The dot-com bubble burst but our business kept flourishing. Then we nearly sold to Coldwell Banker for $50 million in 2007. That deal fell through for a variety of reasons, but we learned we'd need to sign five-year service contracts with any buyer.

Paul was turning 55 in 2015, and we realized our contracts would be perceived to be more valuable if we were in our 50s rather than our 80s. So in 2007, we said, "If the market's good in 2014, let's sell." When we got there, we'd come through the GFC, rebuilt the team, and the market was booming. That year, 5,534 buildings sold, which was an all-time record by more than 10 percent. The timing couldn't have been better.

I was really happy when you suggested meeting in The Knakal Map Room. It's become something of a legend in real estate circles. I was hoping to get to see it somehow. What inspired you to create such a detailed visualization of the city's real estate landscape?

The maps were always an integral part of what I did. I've used Sanborn tax lot maps since the mid-1980s. But The Knakal Map Room came about because a growing percentage of my practice has been development site sales. To evaluate development sites, you need to know the pipeline of competing projects. Both what's under construction and what's planned to be under construction. Unfortunately, that information is quite opaque in the city. The residential brokers publish reports on the condominium pipeline, but they're all different and there's virtually nothing on residential rental units, hotel rooms, or office space. I needed to produce that information and going out to look at buildings under construction was the best way to do that.

During COVID in March 2020, when the city was empty, it was the perfect time to do a physical count. We went out into the field with Sanborn maps and highlighters, marking everything under construction or that had been demolished in green, potential development sites in orange, and potential assemblage sites in yellow. This took 220 hours in the field over four months, followed by thousands of hours of research. The result was a twenty-four-foot by ten-foot map that became too unwieldy to carry around, so I rented a separate office to display it.

The Knakal Map Room has become a place clients love to visit to talk about the market. It provides a very different perspective on real estate development. For real estate nerds, it's sensory overload. There's so much information on that map and in the data we've extracted from it. It's been incredibly effective in showing clients that we know the development site market better than anyone else.

Your expertise in development sites often involves complex zoning and air rights transactions. Could you break down how air rights work in New York and why they're so crucial to development deals?

Air rights are fairly unique to New York because we're an as-of-right zoning jurisdiction. Every site is pre-entitled. With any parcel, you know three things: what type of building you can build, how much you can build, and what shape it can have. The key factor is floor-area-ratio (FAR), which tells you how many square feet of building you can have for every square foot of land. These ratios range from 0.5 up to 33 in some areas.

The first aspect tells you if you can have commercial, manufacturing, or residential uses in the building you are constructing. Then there is a density factor telling you how big the building can be. This is articulated in terms of "Transferable Development Rights," or "air-rights."

Think of it like one square foot Lucite blocks, potentially piled up on top of a building. If you have a five-story building in a district zoned for ten stories, you theoretically have five more stories of "air rights" that you can actually sell to adjacent properties. You need at least ten feet of contiguous property line, and you can transfer rights up to several buildings away if you have consecutive properties in the chain.

The third aspect is contextual zoning, which determines building shape through setback requirements for light and air. Some districts have height restrictions, others don't. That's why you see these extraordinarily tall buildings on 57th Street today—1,200 feet, 1,400 feet—because there's no height restriction and they can accumulate air rights.

Can you give an example of how this works in practice?

Look at what Donald Trump did with Trump World Tower on First Avenue. It's an extremely tall building because he bought air rights from several properties all the way down the block. He created a chain of consecutive lots and transferred all those air rights to enable that height. But you can't skip properties, it has to be continuous.

I once sold a building at 236 West 56th Street for $1.1 million, and they sold just the air rights two years later for $1.9 million. The owner made an $800,000 profit and still owned the building. That shows how valuable these rights can be. Interestingly, sometimes they have no value and sometimes, like in the 56th Street example, they have significant value.

With all these complex regulations, how do you stay on top of everything?

Because of my work in development, I maintain close relationships with zoning attorneys and elected officials, especially city council members who influence approvals. The zoning resolution has thousands of pages with various nuances and interpretations. Even the best zoning experts often need to look things up.

The community board meetings are crucial. You get incredibly detailed information about what's happening. What people are proposing, what they're thinking about, what kinds of deals are in process. When I started Massey Knakal, each territory agent had to attend their local community board meetings. You'd learn about new development proposals before they hit the market, understand neighborhood concerns, and spot emerging trends.

Can you share an example of how zoning complexity has impacted a deal?

I recently sold a site at 78th and First that perfectly illustrates why this expertise matters. The owners made what seemed like a minor technical decision that proved devastating. They incorporated a building into their zoning lot that was in a different zoning district. This triggered what we call "tower-on-base" zoning requirements.

Without getting too technical, they would have had to set back thirty feet from that building, which killed the project's viability because you need more than 50 percent of your square footage below a certain height in tower-on-base zoning. To fix this, they had to extract that building from the zoning lot. But because there were three air rights parcels to the south, included in the zoning lot, they needed approval from those three owners.

This single mistake cost them four years and $40 million. We had an offer that much higher when we started. The tragic part is they didn't want to pay $5,000 for a massing study upfront. They kept saying, "We'll figure it out later." The first two potential buyers walked away without even telling us what the problem was because it became so obvious to them after they did their homework.

What is a massing study?

A massing study is a graphical interpretation of the contextual aspect of the zoning, showing what you can build, how much you can build, and the shape of the building you can have. And that is critically important.

What a painful lesson. On a somewhat related note, when you're looking at assemblage sites, how do you evaluate them?

It's really about probability and patience. If you have ten buildings with ten different owners, you could still do an assemblage, but it's much harder than if two people own five buildings each. I assembled the land at the southeast corner of 55th and Second, which took nine years with all individual owners. There was one key piece, but we had to do several property sales and air rights deals.

It's almost more of a consulting assignment than a brokerage assignment after the first couple transactions. You get paid as each transaction closes. If there are nine properties, you might do one deal per year. The key is showing owners the development potential. If someone has a 25,000-square-foot building but you could build 100,000 square feet there, the development value should far exceed their current building's income value. Though sometimes people still hold out and end up with less than they could have gotten.

You've navigated multiple market cycles since the '80s: the Savings and Loan Crisis (S&L Crisis)*, the post-9/11 slump, the GFC, what you've termed "The Great Slog" from late 2015 through early 2021, and now. How does this current market environment compare to previous downturns?

There are fundamental differences now. Two major ones stand out. First, lender behavior is very different. Second, property sectors are performing differently than they would in typical downturns.

Our current downturn started in 2022 as the Fed started to raise interest rates in March. They increased at an unprecedented rate and to unprecedented magnitude.

In previous downturns like the S&L Crisis, early 2000s, GFC, and the Great Slog, all property types declined together, just to varying degrees. Today's market is much more segmented. Retail properties in New York are on the upswing after years of challenges. Hotels are on fire, indus-

* **S&L Crisis** (Savings and Loan Crisis): A financial crisis in the 1980s and early 1990s caused by widespread failures of savings and loan institutions, due to deregulation, risky lending, and fraud.

is strong and land is recovering. Multifamily and Class B & C office remains challenged as interest rates remain high and refinancing requires infusion and mortgage rates have doubled. This is forcing many owners to sell their assets.

Lender behavior is also notably different. During the S&L Crisis, lenders went through a two-to-three-year foreclosure process, took title, and hired brokers exclusively to sell properties. During the early 2000s and GFC, they didn't want to go through that lengthy foreclosure process, so they hired brokers to sell notes. This time around, they're operating very covertly. They don't want to air their dirty laundry in front of a lot of people, so they're either giving extensions or going directly to their own customers trying to make deals without putting properties out on the open market.

How are you analyzing these trends?

I've always tried to connect dots between macroeconomics, public policy, and real estate. I've written about the market my whole career. Weekly messages to clients, my blog, columns for Commercial Observer and Real Estate Weekly (back in the old days). Every day I look at what the 10-year Treasury and Secure Overnight Financing Rate (SOFR) rates are doing to understand where things are heading.

We're also using new tools. I've hired two data scientists to build an algorithmic neural network analyzing fluctuations in land value against macroeconomic metrics. AI can do millions of calculations in a second, but you need good data. Most real estate datasets are terrible. If you put garbage in, you get garbage out. I've personally verified thousands of sales to ensure our analysis has integrity.

Market insights are crucial right now, as many market participants are trying to figure things out. Look at what's happening. The government printed trillions of dollars, suspended student loan payments, flooded the system with money. Of course inflation kicked in. Now they're raising rates aggressively to put out the fire they started. The collateral damage is tremendous disruption in the real estate industry.

Some say it's mostly newer investors getting hurt, but the impact is much broader. People who've been investing for thirty to forty years are getting wiped out because of interest rate policy. We went through twelve to thirteen years of extraordinarily low rates. Could you blame people for operating within that framework? Sure, you could say, "Well, people should have known that over fifty years, the average 10-year rate was 5.4 percent." But when rates stay that low for that long, that becomes the operating environment everyone knows.

Looking at opportunities in this environment, private debt funds are going to be significant winners. A lot of principals who used to only buy property are now starting debt businesses. It's very lucrative because there's less debt available than typical. There's still plenty of debt out there, but it's very expensive. Anyone with dry powder and the ability to provide creative financing solutions is well-positioned.

Looking at the future of the industry, how do you see technology reshaping the fundamentals of the business?

Technology will profoundly change brokerage but not eliminate or even marginalize it. There are two main functions where technology will make a difference: finding buyers and negotiating deals. The buyer-finding part will be largely automated, but buildings aren't widgets, and negotiating is not formulaic or empirical. You'll always need human negotiation.

I think instead of getting a 1 percent commission on a $100 million sale, sellers will use some platform to get their top three bids, then come to a broker saying, "Here are my bids, negotiate this for $50,000 or $100,000." It becomes more of a consulting fee than a traditional commission.

During the dot-com boom, thirty-three companies launched claiming they would replace commercial brokers. All thirty-three failed. The business will change but not disappear. Looking back fifty years from now, I think 1993 to 2019 will be seen as the golden age of investment sales brokerage. I'm glad I'm in the back half of my career rather than starting out, because the business is going to change dramatically with technology.

How are you adapting to these changes?

I'm constantly trying to adapt and incorporate new tools. I'm using AI now for prospecting and enhancing our data sources. You have to keep pushing yourself to try new things, even if you're not naturally tech-savvy, like me. I am a guy who is glad my cell phone goes on each morning, but we are probably using AI more effectively than most companies. I have hired an AI guru to be my new COO, and this is such exciting stuff!

We create our own datasets. I have forty-six different mailing lists that I'm constantly adding to. If you're specializing in retail properties, you need to know who the key attorneys are, who's advising the major players, what services they use. You need to understand all the participants in that sector and build relationships with people you can rely on for information. We do a ton of land sales in NYC so that's where most of our research is focused.

And now with social media, it's another layer of market presence. I think the idea behind market presence is a misunderstood thing. The calls, mailings, speaking events, networking, and social media are about positioning yourself to become aware of information that other people don't have. People can look at all of those things, see you putting yourself out there, and think you're an egomaniac, but that's not what it's about. All of the market presence activities are about getting in the way of information, and that helps you do a better job for your clients.

You can have all the market presence in the world, but if you're not doing great work for your clients, you won't get more business. So at the end of the day, it's all about doing a great job for your clients. And however you do that, whether you are doing one activity or every activity, if it allows you to understand something better than your competition does, that's going to help your client. And that's the ultimate goal of everything.

How have you restructured your time to adapt to these changes?

I've restructured based on some ideas from Dan Sullivan and Benjamin Hardy's books. Monday is now completely dedicated to planning. Meetings from nine to four with different team members, reviewing last week's accomplishments and setting new priorities. Tuesday and Thursday, I'm in The Knakal Map Room prospecting the whole day. Wednesday and Friday are for everything else. But Tuesdays and Thursdays, I'm just prospecting. I used to feel stressed about not making client calls during planning time, but now I'm fully focused on each day's purpose.

I've always been active with working out too. In college, I worked out to play sports better. In my twenties and thirties, I worked out to look and feel good. When my daughter was born, I worked out to stay healthy for her. I started late in life and wanted to be around for a long time. Now I work out because I want to sell buildings for another twenty or thirty years.

What would you tell someone starting out in the business today?

Focus on developing skills that technology can't easily replace. Understanding deal structuring, negotiating, building relationships. The part that will be marginalized is finding buyers. But the human elements of putting deals together, that's not going away.

When we started Massey Knakal, the lack of publicly available information made our neighborhood territory system work really well. Today, with so much information available, product specialization works better. Brokers have two main assets: knowledge and time. You can't make more time, so you have to use it effectively.

Think about it. If I'm a generalist selling an office building, retail property, and apartment building this week, and next week I'm pitching an apartment building, the owner only cares about the apartment building I sold. Two-thirds of my recent experience isn't relevant. But if I sold three apartment buildings and I'm pitching another one, 100 percent of my recent work helps get the next assignment.

I'm increasingly focused on development sites and value-added redevelopment properties. If I get office or retail listings, I hand them off to others in our group. The more I read about effectiveness, the clearer it becomes: you make most of your money from 20 percent of what you do. Focus on that 20 percent and either delegate or stop doing the other 80 percent.

Have you ever considered crossing over to development or private equity?

I've been offered those opportunities many times, but I love what I do. It's not manual labor. I talk for a living, and I find it intellectually stimulating. It's both my job and my hobby. I've never woken up and thought, "Oh shit, I gotta go to work today." Instead, it's always been, "All right, we've got lots to do today, let's get at it." That puts you in a great spot in life. The biggest problem we have is that the days go by too fast, and I can't get as much done as I want to get done.

Again, the baseball analogy. I'm at 2,342 sales now, and I'd love to get to 3,000. That might take another ten to fifteen years, but you've got to have something to shoot for.

Let's talk about work-life balance. How do you approach that?

It's fascinating because things evolve over time. There's no perfect formula. It's different for everybody because it comes down to your priorities and how you want to live your life. I've found that the best way to figure out the right work-life balance is to pretend you just dropped dead and write the eulogies you want five different people to give at your funeral: a family member, your spouse, your best friend, a work colleague, someone from your religious community or social circle.

Those eulogies become a blueprint for how you want to live. We all have limited time and a million things we'd like to do, but you can't do everything. Those eulogies help you figure out what to prioritize. It forces you to think deeply about what matters most to each important relationship in your life.

This is not a complicated business. It's a very, very simple business. But it's a very hard business. It's day after day, week after week, month after month, year after year. In my case, decade after decade. You just have to keep doing those fundamental things. A lot of the brokerage business involves doing mundane stuff: reading articles, making calls every day, things that get monotonous. But you need to use discipline to continue doing it consistently.

Everyone's different. Things make different people tick differently. That's what makes people and relationships interesting. You have to understand yourself and what drives you, but also understand how that affects the people around you. Balance isn't about perfect equality of time; it's about being fully present and intentional about your choices.

From walking into Coldwell Banker thinking it was a bank, to more than 2,300 transactions totaling nearly $22 billion, Bob Knakal's career shows what's possible when you master your market, block by block. His approach combines high-profile deals with a methodical discipline, built transaction by transaction over decades.

The baseball analogies that appeared throughout our conversation are fitting. His success comes from consistency, preparation, and execution. Like a veteran player who studies every aspect of the game, Bob built systems to track ownership patterns, market trends, and zoning shifts. These tools gave him an edge in what many consider the ultimate real estate arena in the world. When it comes to commercial real estate in New York City, if you can make it there, you probably really can make it anywhere.

From all his experience, Bob has the ability to see patterns across New York's complex real estate landscape. He doesn't just track transactions; he understands how zoning changes ripple through neighborhoods and how ownership patterns shift over time. Bob built systems to capture these insights decades before data analytics became fashionable.

When he speaks about the market, there's genuine excitement in how he breaks down air rights deals or explains policy implications. After thousands of transactions, he still approaches each property with curiosity and analytical precision, treating buildings less as assets and more as pieces in a constantly evolving urban puzzle.

And for me, his perspective on marketing and social media was eye-opening. Looking at it as the ultimate goal of it all, boiling down to doing the best possible job for the client, was something I hadn't considered before. Of course, you do it because you want to generate more business, but that's not really the goal. If you're not producing results for the client, it's meaningless. "So at the end of the day, it's all about doing a great job for your clients."

For newcomers to commercial real estate, Bob's career offers a valuable lesson: market tools and technology will change, but deep market knowledge, relationship-building, and consistent execution remain the foundations of lasting success.

Connect

- Websites:
    - bkrea.com
    - BobKnakal.com
- X: @BobKnakal
- Instagram: @BobKnakalNYC
- LinkedIn: Bob Knakal

Bethany Babcock

Managing Broker and Co-Owner, Foresite Commercial Real Estate

San Antonio, TX

- Founded Foresite Commercial Real Estate in 2014, which now employs 37 people and manages over 90 properties.
- Created a sought-after industry training program that expanded from supporting students during COVID to a multi-city curriculum serving companies across the industry.
- Built a company culture focused on work-life balance, allowing herself and team members to prioritize family while still doing exceptional work.
- Navigated from property management to investment sales to founding a full-service brokerage firm.
- Transformed challenging retail properties into successful investments through creative leasing strategies and tenant relationships.

Bethany Babcock's path to becoming a leader in commercial real estate began with a temp agency mix-up. Instead of sending her to the insurance agency she was supposed to visit, it landed her an interview at a family office managing properties. Amazingly, this happenstance mistake would be the start of what would become an impressive professional career. From that unexpected start at age 18, after growing up in Chile as a missionary's daughter, she built Foresite Commercial Real Estate into a thriving full-service brokerage and property management firm in San Antonio, Texas.

Since founding Foresite in 2014, Bethany has grown the company to manage over ninety properties with a team of thirty-seven people. She has also received national awards in both leasing and investment sales. Like others in this book, I had been following her on social media and was looking forward to meeting her. She has a knack for writing and puts out a lot of great posts that I always look forward to reading. And when it comes to writing about real estate, she clearly knows her stuff. I flew to San Antonio to meet Bethany at her office on a Saturday. As we toured the space, Bethany shared that her husband had crafted much of the wood furniture himself, adding a personal touch that reflects the care she puts into every aspect of her business.

We settled into one of the offices for what became a three-hour conversation. Bethany speaks with quiet confidence about all that she has accomplished, but is quick to acknowledge the guidance and support system that helped her along the way. She started with no industry connections or family wealth and worked full-time while completing her degree debt-free through night classes. This work ethic served her well during the three years she spent in investment sales without a significant paycheck. She credits that time with teaching her persistence and how to cultivate a professional network.

From the beginning, Bethany built her company with a clear personal goal: to create a successful business that would allow her to pick up her son from kindergarten at 3:30 p.m. This philosophy of "front-loading" hard work to gain flexibility later has shaped Foresite's culture. The office includes a dedicated kids' room, and many team members follow similar schedules. Picking up their children from school, bringing them to the office if needed, and resuming work after bedtime. This approach has proven particularly attractive to her team of young parents and veterans starting second careers.

Bethany's approach to business growth is people-centric. Rather than setting geographic expansion targets, she grows "at the rate of people," developing new service lines and locations based on the distinct talents she discovers in her team. This philosophy extends to her training program, the *CRE Launch Program,* which began as an internal resource but expanded during COVID to help students complete internship credits. The program now serves professionals from across the country, attracting both young graduates and mid-career professionals looking to enter commercial real estate.

In this conversation, Bethany shares her journey from administrative assistant to industry leader, the challenges of building a business while raising a family, and her philosophy on creating meaningful work in commercial real estate. Her story highlights how faith, determination, and a commitment to helping others can create significant impact within the commercial real estate profession.

Date of Interview: January 13, 2024

Bethany, thank you for having me here at the Foresite office. Before we dive into your company's growth and operations, I'd like to hear about your path into the industry. From what I understand, it was totally by accident, is that right?

That's right. I had just moved to the United States when I was eighteen. My family was still in Chile, and I needed work quickly. I had asked around about what a good college job would be, and people would tell me Target, Costco, Home Depot. I tried them all, but no one wanted me. They wouldn't call me back. Nobody was hiring. I had no work experience and little self-confidence.

I found a temp agency and told them I just needed a paycheck by Friday. They sent me on what was supposed to be an interview at an insurance agency, but they gave me the wrong information sheet. It was actually for a temporary admin position at a family office that owned office buildings and shopping centers.

I walked in looking like a fourteen-year-old, and everyone was confused. But the interviewer said, "Well, you're here anyway, let's talk." When he asked about my experience, I just said, "Nothing, I'm eighteen." For whatever reason, he took a liking to me. He brought in another manager to interview me, and they hired me. It was just a temp position, so low risk for them.

I ended up staying with that company for five years, growing from entry-level admin to property manager while taking night classes in college. I had no idea what commercial real estate even was, but I fell in love with it. I remember when I first got the job and told my dad, he was like, great, maybe you'll get into real estate. But I thought, gross, open houses and cookies. I had no idea this whole industry existed with all the numbers and analysis. I just loved everything about it and became focused on building my career in that.

We're going to dive deeper into your career, but first I wanted to hear more about your background. It's got to be one of the more

unique stories I've heard. Can you tell me more about that and how you ended up in San Antonio?

Yeah, my father was pastoring at a small church in Sweeny, Texas, when I was about five. Eventually, he felt a calling to go build up ministry work in Chile. When he nervously told my mom about moving overseas, she said, "Finally! This is what I've been wanting to do my whole life too."

When I was seven, we moved to Costa Rica for a year to learn Spanish. It was easy for us kids but challenging for my parents to build connections without speaking the language. Then we moved to Chile, where I lived until I was eighteen. We only came back to the States once when I was fourteen.

When I was in high school, it was expected that I'd move back to the States at eighteen. My extended family was spread throughout the United States, mostly in California, but I didn't have strong connections there. My mom, who homeschooled me during my senior year, made researching where to live part of my final project. I had to research everything: potential jobs and their pay, apartment costs, car expenses, insurance, and education options.

I looked into community colleges and discovered there was a one-year waiting period before qualifying for resident tuition rates. I had to create a complete budget I could live on without financial support, as my parents weren't in a position to help. After all this research, I chose San Antonio.

Why San Antonio specifically?

My parents had briefly lived there when they were missionaries because it was centrally located for their church visits. During that time, I connected with the local church community. They were incredibly welcoming, would visit us in Chile, and we maintained strong relationships. Texas offered great cost of living, and I felt I could afford community college while working. The church community even offered me housing for my first few months until I could get on my feet.

I've heard you talk about these strong church connections before.

That's an interesting thread throughout your life. Was that also how you ended up meeting your husband?

Interestingly, though we kept crossing paths, we didn't meet until later. His parents were missionaries in Argentina, similar to my parents' work in Chile. We both attended the same Thanksgiving gathering at Winter Park, Colorado, for four years, at an event for kids whose families were overseas. We finally connected on our fourth year. We joke that we wouldn't have gotten along earlier. I was too nerdy. He was far too outgoing.

Anyways, we met during my last year of college. He had gone to seminary school up until that point, and then he went to college and used the same formula as I had, and we were both able to finish school debt-free.

I'm glad you brought that up. What advice would you give young people about avoiding student debt?

Yeah, I feel like it was a key factor to my success in starting this business because I wasn't burdened with student loans. My cost of living was lower than most. It was also what made it possible for me to go into investment sales, because I didn't have that burden of student loans. And so we've always operated our lives in that manner. The main reason and impetus for me wanting to go to school debt-free was largely based on fear, if I'm being honest. There was a fear that I wouldn't be able to finish college and I'd be burdened with debt. I wanted to make sure that that would never happen. So I was determined to pay as I went. That stress made me think very creatively, and I'm very grateful for that.

There's a very simple path for a very normal student like myself, that's not exceptional, that's not overly intelligent with great scores and all these things. Anyone with no financial support can do this. And that formula is simply to work full-time and take night classes at community college.

Take CLEP (College-Level Examination Program) tests at the university where you plan on getting your degree so they count as transfer credits, and then transfer to the most economical state school you possibly can.

Don't change your degree. Don't be bouncing around and taking unnecessary classes. Stick to the degree plan, and you can graduate debt-free, and that is still possible today. I know this was fifteen or twenty years ago, but it's still possible today.

I think people look at college so differently, and I think there's a trend to view it as an extended summer camp to experience life, to become an adult, and to learn. That's great. Just do it at community college and then go to the expensive school. Just don't take out debt to try to figure out who you are, because in the end, that debt will burden you from being able to become who you decided you wanted to be.

Looking back, what degree would you recommend for someone interested in commercial real estate?

Accounting. I think accounting is really beneficial for commercial real estate. Being able to understand the numbers behind it is something very few in our industry have. But you see a wide variety of degrees in our industry. I mean, you'll have people with history degrees, you'll have people with psychology degrees, and teaching degrees, and all these different things. I feel like the people who have a really good understanding of accounting tend to have a competitive advantage, especially if they're gonna go into the investment sales side of this business.

Going back to the CRE job you accidentally landed, how did you transition from administrative work to property management in those early years?

It started with Excel. When I first started, I didn't even know what Excel was. When the controller asked if I knew it, I said, "Is that the one with little lines?" After she walked away frustrated, I bought an Excel book and committed to becoming the office expert. This led to creating reports for the owner, who had seventy-five properties and hated computers. He needed clear, simple executive summaries.

As I got better with Excel, I started getting cooler projects and more data access. I always tell students: learn Excel. The Excel wizard always gets the best projects. This gave me a regular audience with the owner, who saw I had more potential. He recognized I was better suited for sales than administrative work and gave me a shot at property management.

I guess I was always a little bit of a salesperson but didn't realize it. So when we were leasing spaces, it was oh, you said no. Well, why? Let's figure it out. And there was never a "no," it was always "not that way." And so I was always trying to figure out, well, which way would get me to a yes, and let me creatively structure this. So I really found out that I enjoyed that kind of selling. That's when I really started to fall in love with the industry. It was like, okay, you said no to what I gave you. What can I create that you'll say yes to?

But one thing I think is really important about sales is that people assume that you have to be really outgoing. I'm still shy and awkward. I think a better skill set, or a better personality trait, is empathy. And being able to understand why someone can't do what you're proposing, and what they're telling you, and having a deep understanding of the why behind the "No". And I love to ask questions. I love to understand why someone might not be able to do it or why it's not working. And I think that that really helps to have as a skill set. The key is figuring out what way will work.

Property management taught me that you need to be available around the clock. When emergencies happen, you can't just clock out at 5 p.m. But it also taught me about building value through consistent operations and maintenance. These lessons became invaluable later when evaluating properties for investment sales and understanding what makes a property truly successful.

Let's talk about your next transition from property management to investment sales. What led to that change?

In 2008, during the financial crisis, I lost my job. While this coincided with the economic downturn, the actual circumstances were more complex. I found myself without work just as the industry was freezing all hiring. The experience I was so proud of suddenly seemed worthless because no one was hiring.

The only opportunity I could find was a commission-only position at an investment sales firm. Nobody wanted to work there because transactions had ground to a halt. The lending markets were essentially frozen. But I didn't want a gap in my resume, and I'd always thought I might want to try brokerage someday.

That must have been scary, especially with your husband still in college?

It was terrifying. I was very risk-averse and desperately wanted a salaried position. I initially saw it as temporary until I could find a W-2 job. I was receiving unemployment for a few months, which helped, but I reached a critical moment when I realized I wanted to commit to investment sales long-term. This meant I needed to stop collecting unemployment, even though we were still about $1,000 short each month in our budget.

Every week when filing for unemployment, I faced this question: "What jobs are you planning to apply for?" I couldn't answer honestly anymore because I had decided to commit to investment sales. Even when the unemployment office told me I could keep collecting if I just declared my commission income, I said no. The lady tried to convince me, saying, "I really think you're overthinking this." But I felt it wouldn't be honest since I wasn't actually looking for a job anymore. It was a tough decision because we really needed that money, but it didn't feel right.

The timing was remarkable. The same week I decided to stop collecting unemployment, my mentor, Chad, approached me about working together permanently as a team. He offered to give me a $1,000 monthly advance against future deals. It was too perfect to ignore. I had been very wary of brokers after past experiences, but this felt like clear divine guidance.

What incredible timing. How did you and Chad initially connect at the firm? Was it a formal mentorship program?

When I started, I wanted to work in office properties since that's where my experience was. The firm was good about pairing people with mentors, but they didn't have anyone local for office properties. The closest person was in Dallas. I knew that wouldn't work since San Antonio is such a relationship-driven market.

I noticed Chad in the office. He was different, very quiet and humble. He talked about his wife and family, and I felt comfortable around him after my previous negative experiences with brokers. One day, he came to my desk and said, "I know you want to do office, and that's considered the cool thing, but if you need help, I'm here." He was doing retail.

The more I observed him, the more I saw how everyone respected him. He set the tone for the office without trying. People came when he came and left when he left. I loved the way he talked to his clients. He was calm, he was articulate, and he was very empathetic, especially during the financial crisis. I decided to switch to retail to work with him.

How did you add value to the relationship with Chad? What's the day-to-day like for a new investment salesperson?

The first few months are spent building your database. You have to research properties, verify ownership, and collect phone numbers. Most firms don't provide this information. The goal is typically to gather 500 to 700 contacts, which takes about three to four months of full-time work. Then it's pure cold calling during business hours, 7 a.m. to 7 p.m.

All the other work—meeting preparation, property analysis, creating marketing materials—had to be done after hours. This was the expectation for the first three to five years until you could generate enough income to hire help. Different firms have different cultures, but that's generally how it works for new agents who aren't on teams.

The market conditions were incredibly challenging. We were in the midst of the financial crisis, and deals were scarce. Most properties were underwater on their loans, and banks weren't lending. We had to get creative with owner financing and other alternative structures just to keep transactions moving.

I looked for things Chad didn't enjoy doing and tried to take those off his plate. I learned marketing, created aerials from Google Maps, and took property photos. Anything to make myself valuable. Remember, this was during the recession when no one was making money. I was living off $1,000 a month from him, plus my husband's salary.

You went three years barely making anything. What kept you going?

Candidly, lack of options. The market was terrible. But I recognized the incredible experience I was getting. I was having conversations with sophisticated investors that someone my age normally wouldn't have access to. Even if investment sales didn't work out, I knew this experience would be valuable.

What's interesting is that most people in the office stayed too. We'd look around and say, "Is Chad still here? Okay, we'll show up tomorrow." He had a family to feed, and if he believed the market would turn, we believed too. Even our spouses would ask, "Is Chad still there?" When we'd say yes, they'd say, "Okay, stick it out a few more weeks." We just kept doing that.

I think about those years now when I talk to young professionals about work-life balance. I tell them that sometimes you have to front-load your effort in your twenties. Yes, I missed out on some social activities and worked incredibly long hours, but that investment created options for better balance later. The hustle isn't just about money, it's about building a foundation that gives you control over your time later.

Looking back, those difficult years were crucial. The relationships we built during the downturn became the foundation for our business. Clients remembered how we helped them through tough times, and that created lasting loyalty. Plus, learning to do deals in a challenging market made us much better at our jobs when conditions improved.

How did Foresite get started in 2014?

While my business partner Chad and I were at an investment sales firm, our clients kept asking if we did management and leasing. We had to refer that business out, but clients weren't happy with the referral partners. The idea behind Foresite was that I would handle leasing and management while Chad continued doing investment sales at the other firm and referred business over.

As we grew, people wanted to join Foresite as investment sales agents. They loved Chad but didn't like the aggressive culture at his firm. Eventually, we realized it would be easier to grow the team under one roof. After four years, Chad came over to join what was technically his own company, brought his investment sales team, and that's how we became a full-service firm.

So, just to back up for a second to when you started Foresite. This was just as you started making money in investment sales when Chad suggested starting your own company?

Yes, in 2014. The timing seemed terrible. I was finally making real money after three years of sacrifice. I had just had my son, my mom was sick and living with us, and my husband was traveling Monday through Thursday. I was dropping my son at daycare at 7 a.m. and picking him up at 6:30 p.m. Chad kept suggesting I start a property management and leasing company while he stayed in investment sales.

I told him I needed three things: childcare covered, office space, and not to do it alone. Then something remarkable happened. My son's daycare asked for help leasing a new location. After I helped them, they gifted me a year of free childcare. When Chad heard this, he talked to a client who offered me his son's vacant office free for a year. And it was right next to my son's daycare.

That was pretty obvious divine intervention. We started the company the next month.

Again, amazing. Could you walk us through your approach to growing the company, particularly your strategy for funding and hiring?

We grew naturally, without debt. For agents, commission structures made hiring easier, but property managers needed good salaries. Our first hire was a jack-of-all-trades person to handle what I felt was the absolute most crucial piece of running a brokerage firm, which was making sure you answered the phone all the time, so agents never missed calls while showing space.

That first salary was a point of contention at home. My husband would say, "You're paying someone else but not yourself." Every commission I earned went right back into the company because I was desperate to hire. I had this long-term goal of being able to pick up my son from school at 3:30 p.m. when he started kindergarten. Everything I did was focused on hiring in a way that would let me be there for those golden hours between school pickup and bedtime.

I was too afraid to take on debt. I wasn't sure I believed in the company or myself enough yet. It took a few years before I was bringing home a real income.

What was it like in those early days when you were doing management and leasing on your own?

It was really challenging. I wanted the company to look professional and large, which became a catch-22 because people assumed I had a team when I didn't have the revenue for one. I was doing everything. Accounting, maintenance, negotiating leases, showing space, marketing, and trying to grow the company. All while having a six-month-old. It was overwhelming and not mentally healthy, but we got through it.

The biggest challenge was that people didn't know it was just me. They had really high expectations, which was both a blessing and a curse. I had to rise to the occasion and set up systems and processes to prepare for growth. But there were times when my kid was sick late at night, and I still had to close the books and get things to the CPAs. It was a struggle.

I made some early mistakes taking on properties that weren't profitable. Just because a client says they'll sell their property if you lease up the vacancies, it doesn't mean it's worth your time. I was spinning my wheels on properties with unrealistic owner expectations. Without a mentor in third-party leasing, I had to learn the hard way about walking away from bad deals.

The turning point came when I heard about a developer planning a new retail project. I volunteered to lease it for free. The developer was skeptical. This was the kind of assignment usually given to major firms. He warned me that it would consume all my time and would only succeed if I could pre-lease enough space to get it built. But he accepted my offer.

It was incredibly challenging. The site was at an intersection that hadn't been built yet. He wanted rents 30 percent above market, and it was too close to existing retail to duplicate those tenants. I had to focus on local and regional tenants, selling them on a vision of what the intersection would become. But we succeeded. The project was 80 percent leased when the first tenant opened and eventually reached 100 percent occupancy at the target rents and in many ways that client was the mentor I needed to learn third-party leasing.

How did that success impact the company's growth?

It completely transformed our business. It aligned us with higher-quality properties and led to similar assignments. The developer actually insisted on paying me for all the leases, even though I'd agreed to do it for free. The commissions were enough to hire our first property manager and cover their salary for almost two years.

The relationship with that first developer continues today, though in a different form. He eventually needed a full-time in-house leasing agent, which I couldn't be while running the company. We parted ways amicably and still maintain a strong relationship. It's funny, he keeps saying each new development will be his last one, so I joke about buying him a shovel for the next "last" project.

Around 2018, things really accelerated when Chad joined full-time. He brought his investment sales team, which immediately gave us a strong presence in that sector. Then we made a couple key hires in property management and accounting. One was a former senior manager from a competitor who was looking for a better work environment. They brought their industry relationships, which made scaling much easier as they knew who to hire as we grew. Their connections helped us expand from managing six properties to nearly ninety within five years. We're now a team of thirty-seven people, with fifteen in property management alone.

That story of our early years has been really helpful during tough times. The company grew quickly from the outside, but it required constantly reinvesting everything I made while working long hours. Whenever I doubted myself, I'd remember how it started. It would have been like spiting God to not acknowledge how he perfectly lined everything up.

I think if I'd started with more capital, it would have been easier to quit when things got hard. But because everything aligned so perfectly, I felt called to do it. Those signs kept me going.

Before we dive into specifics, could you give us an overview of Foresite Commercial Real Estate and its different service areas?

We're a full-service brokerage firm with three separate departments. First is property management, where we manage properties for investors and allow them to be as hands-off as they'd like. Then we have the investment sales division, which focuses on listing income-producing properties. We tend to focus on retail, though we do some office properties as well. The third department is leasing, which encompasses both landlord representation and tenant rep. Every agent specializes in one of these areas, but we all work together and share information across platforms to benefit our clients.

Could you explain the difference between landlord representation and tenant representation?

On the tenant rep side, we're advocating for tenants in the market to get them the best spaces. We prepare pitch decks to present them in the best light to landlords, review listings, and negotiate deals. In today's tight market, we often try to find spaces before they come on the market by talking to landlords and property managers about potential availabilities. It's really challenging to find good spots for retailers right now, so being proactive is essential.

On the landlord representation side, we're working for property owners who need to fill vacant spaces in their retail centers, office buildings, or other commercial properties. We create marketing strategies for the properties, identify potential tenants that would be a good fit for the space and overall tenant mix, and then actively pursue those tenants. It involves showcasing the property's strengths, location benefits, and negotiating lease terms that maximize value for the owner.

The relationships usually develop through referrals from other clients. We might work with someone who has a coffee shop, and they'll refer their friend who owns another business. Or we'll work with a large franchisee who has multiple concepts, and we'll grow with them as their business expands.

How do you approach specialization within your team, particularly regarding landlord versus tenant representation?

They tend to focus on one or the other based on their personalities. We don't direct them, but you start to see which category fits them naturally. The landlord side is more process-oriented. You need to be consistent with marketing plans and reporting. The tenant rep side is more like the wild west; you're hunting deals and spending more time out of the office.

We actually require our tenant rep agents to do some landlord assignments, even if they've been in the business for fifteen to twenty years. They need to understand the landlord's constraints and how certain requests might impact building value. You don't really understand that until you put on the landlord hat. We encourage specialization but want them to understand both sides to be more effective.

Can you explain how property management works in terms of office hours versus field work?

It's much more organic than people might expect. Some firms are really strict about tracking hours, but we're not. You're being paid for your knowledge, not your time. While you're generally expected to be available between eight to five, you might get called on weekends for emergencies. Property managers typically work more than forty hours. It's not uncommon to see fifty or sixty-hour weeks in this industry.

Those companies that require detailed time tracking are actually a great source of recruiting for us. That kind of micromanagement creates tremendous stress on property management teams. While occasional time studies might make sense to evaluate project profitability, doing it consistently creates an unnecessary administrative burden on managers who already have countless responsibilities.

At our firm, we try to maintain better work-life balance, but there's still significant time investment between site visits and other responsibilities. A typical week might include regular property inspections, vendor meetings, tenant interactions, financial reporting, and handling unexpected maintenance issues. You have to be flexible because emergencies don't follow a schedule.

How do relationships work between competing firms?

We try to be extremely friendly with competitors. Coming from investment sales, where the mentality was that using outside brokers meant you weren't doing your job properly, I had to shift my mindset. Leasing is different. It's a team sport that requires collaboration. We even organize fun activities like paintball fights with other firms. Our clients win when we maintain good market relationships.

This collaborative approach is especially important in our market. San Antonio is relationship-driven, and burning bridges isn't an option. We often need to work with other firms to get deals done, particularly in leasing where one side might represent the landlord and another the tenant.

Could you walk us through how you turn around distressed properties? Maybe using that one severely under-occupied retail center as an example?

That was actually our first property management assignment. The owner was desperately seeking help because no other companies could increase the value enough. The main issue was that the anchor grocery store had failed and left, causing the national tenants to leave as well. Only struggling local tenants remained, bringing occupancy down to 30 percent.

The owner was underwater on the loan, which was coming due, and had no money for improvements or commissions. But the property had good fundamentals. It had a great location, freeway frontage with really good signage. I started approaching tenants from nearby centers, offering to match their current low rents if they'd move to our better-located property. We used very short-term leases since the ultimate goal was to sell.

Once we showed positive lease-up momentum, the bank extended the loan. The property started cash flowing, and eventually, the owner successfully sold the property.

Can you explain how leasing agents develop market reports and gather data?

For leasing agents, the reports focus on comparing properties that compete for the same tenants. We track asking rates, recent deals, vacancy rates, and tenant improvement allowances, then present it all in graphs. It's easier for leasing agents because we can get data from other brokers. You don't always have to go directly to owners.

We've developed sophisticated systems for tracking market activity and our own software for this purpose. Our research team monitors not just asking rates but also terms like tenant improvement allowances, lease lengths, and concessions. This helps us understand true market rates versus asking rates. We also track renovation and development activity that might impact property values or tenant decisions.

That background in property management has been invaluable throughout all of this. Starting in property management for a landlord gave me a lot insight into operations and what's realistic in terms of running an investment. When I moved into investment sales, I could immediately spot when someone's underwriting wasn't realistic. Things might look good on a spreadsheet but wouldn't work in reality. Then when I moved into landlord and tenant representation, I understood how lease terms impacted building value.

For example, I've seen properties where the rent roll looks great, but the operating expenses are unsustainable. Or situations where aggressive rental rate assumptions ignore market realities about tenant improvement costs or lease-up timelines. Having managed properties, I know exactly what questions to ask about maintenance history, capital expenditures, and tenant relations.

It's rare in our business for someone to spend significant time focused on each specialty. Usually, people are more like jacks of all trades. But spending five-plus years in each category gave me insight into how these different business models work. That's been incredibly helpful in growing the company and training our team.

Tell me about your approach to hiring. It seems you get both experienced people and fresh graduates.

Culture fit and integrity are paramount. I'm very direct about our values during interviews, almost intentionally intense about it. Some people opt out, which tells me we're doing something right. While we have over thirty-seven very different personalities, they all align with our core values.

I actually prefer mid-career hires over recent graduates because they already understand professional etiquette and communication. That's why I love hiring retired military personnel. They come with built-in discipline and strong work ethic. They just need to learn the industry specifics.

The transition can be challenging though. We had a retired Navy officer who had been a high-ranking official, used to commanding immediate respect. I had to be honest with him that in commercial real estate, he'd be starting from scratch. While we would respect his background, clients wouldn't know or care about his military accomplishments. It's been an adjustment, but he understood and was willing to build his reputation in a new industry.

When we're looking at candidates, we're really seeking people who align with our values of integrity and service. We've found that technical skills can be taught, but character and work ethic are fundamental. We've turned down experienced professionals who didn't fit our culture and taken chances on people with less experience who showed the right attitude and values.

You had a very specific vision for work-life balance when founding Foresite. How has that vision shaped both your personal schedule and company culture?

When I was starting Foresite, I told everyone I hired that I had a specific goal. I would say, "I want to create an environment you want to work in, and I want to create an environment where I can step away at 3:30 p.m. to pick up my kids from school." I shared that vision during interviews, that I was building a company large enough to have a team in place so I could take that block of time and then resume work after bedtime.

When my son started kindergarten early at age four instead of five, the timeline got accelerated. I wasn't sure if we were ready, but the team really rallied around it. They said, "This was your goal. You don't get to move the goalpost. You must leave." They held me accountable and made it happen. To this day, they still tell me to get out of here at 3:30 p.m.

How have you built a company culture that supports this kind of flexibility while maintaining high performance?

Actually, many people follow a similar schedule. We have a lot of young parents, which is why we have a kid's room. People will pick up their children, bring them back to the office for meetings if needed, then work again after bedtime. That's just how our schedules work in this season of life. Could they make more money with traditional hours? Probably. But that's not everyone's main goal.

We also have retired military members starting second careers who missed many milestones with their kids during service. They don't need to sacrifice that again. If we can be creative with scheduling, we'll do it. That's one of the perks of being self-employed.

While others post about their perfect 5 a.m. routines, my reality is much messier. Getting kids ready for school, searching for lost shoes, and juggling multiple priorities. But that's okay. You can build something meaningful without following someone else's blueprint for success.

Tell me about your training program. I understand it's something you're particularly passionate about.

It started during a really stressful period when I realized I couldn't personally train everyone anymore as we grew. I created what I called my "hit by the bus plan," documenting everything someone would need to know to operate in the business. This evolved into a formal learning management system that helped reduce turnover and reinforce our culture.

When COVID hit, we saw students who were losing their internships and needing credits to graduate. I impulsively offered our internal training program to them through LinkedIn. We expected maybe five or six students but ended up with two classes of twenty. Despite managing our business through COVID, homeschooling kids, and dealing with shuttered shopping centers, we ran this program from our closets over Zoom. It was wild, but we fell in love with it.

What really hooked us was seeing several graduates enter commercial real estate who otherwise wouldn't have. We realized we might be helping solve an industry problem by attracting young talent. Then our competitors started asking if they could send their people through the program. It felt like a great opportunity to help develop the next generation of talent. We're all going to be working together anyway.

Now we have a comprehensive ten-week program with two speakers weekly covering development, accounting, legal aspects, and more. Students complete a project that takes them from abstracting leases to defending property valuations. We pair them with mentors and build a strong foundation for their careers.

The program has grown beyond our expectations. We've expanded to multiple markets, and the online format allows us to reach students and professionals across the country. We're particularly proud of how it's helping diversify the industry by making commercial real estate more accessible to people who might not have traditional industry connections.

The success of your online training program raises an interesting question about the workplace environment. What's your approach to remote work for your regular team members?

For brokers, being in the office is crucial. You're not just learning technical skills, you're learning the soft skills from your mentor and staying connected to the market. For property management, I'm more flexible since we hire very experienced people. But even there, we emphasize office time when training junior staff because those spontaneous learning moments are invaluable.

How do you approach company growth and expansion?

Our investment sales team works nationwide, operating in over fifteen states, but our focus remains on Central Texas. We grow and expand at the rate of people. When we have a key hire in a particular area, that's where we tend to grow. It works better when growth happens naturally through the people we retain and recruit.

A great example is Alexandria, who joined straight out of college for investment sales. Chad noticed she had a unique talent for collecting and presenting market data. Now she's our head of research, producing reports that get quoted in newspapers. Similarly, our marketing person turned out to have exceptional video production skills, which transformed our training program. She created an incredibly professional virtual experience that allowed us to expand to multiple campuses. We'll be in San Antonio, Los Angeles, Austin, Houston, and Miami.

That's how we grow—finding unique talents in our people and building around them. It might seem backward, but it works and creates less stress. Everyone works in areas they're passionate about, and we help them execute their vision.

Some of our best growth has come from recognizing people's hidden talents and creating new roles around them. Like when we discovered one of our property managers had a gift for systems development. Instead of trying to fit them into a traditional role, we created a position that let them improve our operations across the company. This approach helps us retain great people while making the company stronger.

Let's talk about finding meaning in your work. How do you find purpose in commercial real estate, both as an industry professional and as a company leader?

I find the most meaning in being a firm owner because I love people and creating an environment where they can thrive. Though sometimes I've struggled with feeling like what I do isn't as meaningful as my parents' work in ministry, where they transformed people's lives and family trees.

I had a pivotal moment when I was about twelve, living in Chile. My dad needed to raise $20,000 for a bible school we were building. He wrote a letter to Hobby Lobby, and they just mailed him a check. No fanfare, no conditions. That was a lightbulb moment for me. I realized you could do meaningful work through business. That's when I started thinking about majoring in business.

Still, when I moved to the States, it was hard not to feel shallow, especially when I wasn't making enough to give back financially. Even now, when I can give back—though I don't love that term because it implies you took something—I sometimes struggle because it doesn't feel as important as my family's ministry work. But maybe it does matter in how we help people be happier where they work. Maybe my role is just to make people feel seen and heard.

What about the broader community impact of your work in commercial real estate?

I've experienced that impact more on the leasing side than investment sales. One of our new agents did thirty-four transactions last year. He was disappointed because he didn't make as much money as he'd hoped, but I told him to look at what he'd actually created. Thirty-four businesses, each with five to ten employees, each supporting families. That's like an economic development corporation bringing in thirty-four small businesses. Those businesses generate sales tax revenue that pays for schools, teachers, police, fire departments. It creates this ripple effect through the economy to improve people's lives.

It's easier to measure impact on the leasing side than investment sales, which can feel more detached. I think that's one of the reasons why I personally enjoy leasing, getting to know the stories and building relationships with store owners. Many become friends. You hear their struggles, watch them grow, and help them expand when they need more space.

I think real estate can be a platform for positive change in communities. When we help a local business owner find the right location or help a property owner improve their center, we're contributing to the neighborhood's vitality. Sometimes it's about saying no to the wrong tenants to maintain the right mix for the community's needs.

Looking back at your journey from starting in the industry at eighteen to where you are today, what stands out most to you?

My husband and I have been reflecting on that more this year. All these decisions that were hard at the time are finally adding up in a positive way. Sometimes it stings when people say, "You got really lucky." Yes, there was some luck, but there were also a lot of sacrifices. I remember getting teased in college for working so hard instead of having fun, but I was determined to finish. I'm very grateful for the wisdom God gave me to keep going.

Growing up overseas gave me a different perspective. When people say, "Look at all the luck in your life," I think everyone has blessings if they would just pay attention. Being born in this country already sets you apart from so many people who would do anything to be in your shoes. That mindset helped when I entered an industry surrounded by wealth and connections I didn't have. I could see God at work in different ways and knew it would be okay.

Do you think you'll ever know if you're making the right decisions, or is that just part of having faith? Making decisions and trusting they'll work out?

I was recently at a Christian Women's Conference where they discussed common fears. I realized my biggest fear isn't typical. It's the fear of not using opportunities well or choosing the wrong path when given options. I remember praying about this and feeling like the message was, "Haven't I used your mistakes before? Can't I use your wrong way?" It was almost like being told to relax, that it's going to be okay.

Even if I make the wrong choice, if I surrender my life to Him, He'll help figure it out. I tend to overanalyze constantly. I should have done this, I should have done that. But He's figured it out time and time again. What seemed like mistakes often turned into the right path somehow. Looking back now, we see all these seemingly "right" choices, but many were actually wrong choices that God shaped into something good.

When I see young people today working so hard to break into commercial real estate, I realize how I was just placed into it. There was definitely divine intervention in being exactly where I was supposed to be. Looking back at my career path, I see God's hand in it. All those closed doors, such as not getting hired at retail stores, were just guiding me toward the right door. That mindset helped when I entered an industry surrounded by wealth and connections I didn't have. I could see God at work in different ways and knew it would be okay.

Bethany found her way into commercial real estate through a temp agency's mix-up and turned that lucky accident into something special. In Foresite's earliest days, she did it all herself. Balancing books after midnight, chasing leads during daylight hours, and somehow giving clients the impression they were working with a seasoned firm instead of a one-woman operation running on determination. When tough times came, she passed on the easy path of unemployment checks, choosing instead to bet on herself in commission-only investment sales.

When making business decisions, she keeps a long-term framework in mind. She cuts through complexity with simple questions about lasting impact. It explains why her office has that kid-friendly room tucked away, why her team includes other parents with school pickup schedules, and why she's created training programs that open doors beyond her own company. When she discovered hidden talents, like the investment sales hire with an exceptional eye for data or the surprise filmmaker who elevated their training, she built new possibilities around these people rather than squeezing them into traditional roles.

Every afternoon at 3:30, Bethany walks out the door to pick up her children. That daily ritual is more than just about being a present parent, it's living proof of the business she purposefully designed. Those few afternoon hours represent the freedom she earned through years of strategic intensity. From walking through the wrong door at 18 to building a thriving brokerage today, her path shows what happens when purpose meets practical problem-solving. Bethany's approach teaches us that with enough grit and thoughtful planning, you can craft success that truly reflects what you value most.

Connect

- Websites:
    - foresitecre.com
    - cre-launch.com
- X: @bethanyjbabcock
- LinkedIn: Bethany Babcock

Kyle Matthews

Founder, Chairman, and Chief Executive Officer, Matthews Real Estate Investment Services

Nashville, TN

- Founded Matthews Real Estate Investment Services in 2015, growing it into the largest privately held brokerage platform in the U.S. with more than $66 billion in sales volume since its founding.
- Scaled the company from a startup to over 1,000 people across more than 25 offices nationwide, with a proprietary training system and technology platform.
- Maintained aggressive growth through market downturns, adding 200 agents and over five offices in 2023–2024 while competitors reduced headcount.
- Developed an innovative, tech-forward brokerage model while maintaining zero debt and complete independence.
- Hosts *The Matthews Mentality Podcast*, which can be found on YouTube, Apple Podcasts, and Spotify.

Kyle Matthews is the founder, chairman, and CEO of Matthews Real Estate Investment Services, one of the country's fastest-growing commercial real estate firms. Starting in 2015, he has built a brokerage that now employs over 1,000 people across more than twenty-five offices nationwide. I met with him at his office in Nashville and spent about two-and-a-half hours talking about everything from his years at USC to starting off in brokerage to creating a dominant brokerage firm, which is only getting stronger year after year.

In his younger years, he didn't have the discipline and work ethic that is so ingrained in him today. By his own admission, he was a "total slacker" who was more interested in video games and skateboarding than applying himself academically. His transformation began during his time playing football at the University of Southern California (USC), where he was part of the 2003 and 2004 National Championship teams under coach Pete Carroll. Those years instilled in him the discipline, resilience, and work ethic that would later define his approach to business.

At Matthews Real Estate, Kyle built a structured training system where brokers know exactly what's expected of them. His team has developed proprietary tech tools in-house, including Apollo, which automatically generates Broker Opinions of Value, while creating comprehensive resources tailored specifically to support his growing workforce.

The numbers reflect the effectiveness of his approach. In 2022, the firm completed 4,518 transactions totaling more than $14.25 billion in sales. A 56 percent increase from the previous year. During market downturns when many competitors contract, Kyle has continued expanding, opening new offices and hiring additional talent. This ability to expand during challenging economic cycles comes from Kyle's conservative financial management, building substantial cash reserves as a direct result of lessons learned during the Global Financial Crisis of 2008.

At the core of Kyle's philosophy is a relentless focus on fundamentals. He believes success in commercial real estate comes from consistent execution of basic activities over time. As he puts it, "It's simple, but not easy." His training program reflects this philosophy. It requires making

500 cold calls weekly, working weekends, and persisting through what he calls the "valley of despair" that causes most new brokers to quit within eighteen months. But for the rare few who don't quit, the payoff is substantial. Kyle says those who stick with it often earn six figures within two years and can break seven figures by year five, almost without fail.

Throughout our conversation, Kyle provides a candid look at what it takes to succeed in commercial real estate. He discusses everything from navigating the financial challenges of starting in the business to building a sustainable career, offering insights on both individual success and organizational growth. His perspective is shaped by his experiences as a former collegiate athlete and as the leader of a rapidly growing company.

Date of Interview: November 16, 2023

I wanted to start our conversation with something crucial for anyone considering commercial real estate brokerage. From your experience, both as a broker and now running one of the fastest-growing firms in the country, what's the reality of those first eighteen months for new agents?

Most of the industry today is still very primitive in their approach to entry-level positions. Typically, someone new gets hired not even by the company, but by an agent or team who tells their company, "Hey, I'm bringing this young guy on." The company gives the senior agent total control in creating the job description.

There's usually no real structure to the job. They might give you a loose description with a few bullet points, but it's intentionally unstructured because they don't want to commit to a training program. One day, they'll say, "Here's a list of people. Call them and see if you can get a meeting." That's brokerage activity, but it comes with almost no guidance in what to say or how to approach it. They're not looking to teach you brokerage skills or how to build relationships. They just view you as a lead source. Other days it's "Meet the buyer at the property and open the doors" or "Create a flyer" or even "Pick up my dry cleaning."

The best way I can describe it at most companies is that the inmates run the prison. The personalities that make a good agent are often the opposite of who would be a good manager of people. Most entry-level positions are what's called a "runner." You're basically a utility person for the senior broker in both professional and personal settings.

The real problem is what I call the "forever junior" structure. They bring you into the business and expect you to pay them for the rest of your life. Three to seven years in, after you've closed 100 deals, you're still paying this person 20 to 50 percent of every deal, even though you don't need their support anymore. When you try to renegotiate, they say no. Take it or leave. It's what I call a human pyramid scheme.

Someone did it to them, so they do it to you, expecting you'll do it to someone else one day.

So how should someone vet a team or firm before joining?

The best question you can ask when interviewing is: "How many people have you developed into established professionals in this business?" Ask for references. People who've gone on to achieve success, whether they still work there or not. Today's candidates expect to ask more questions than 20 to 30 years ago, and they should. You're signing up for 12 to 14-hour days with likely no immediate pay, working for someone who probably isn't a great manager and cares more about their own production than your development.

You've described the industry's traditional approach. How do new agents survive at Matthews compared to other firms?

Most people are on what we call "scholarship." Their parents provide room and board. That's just the reality. They go to their parents and have to sell them on why this short-term sacrifice is worth it. It's particularly challenging because most of these kids went to college, often with parental support, and now they're taking a job that doesn't initially pay.

I want to address this directly because a lot of people reading this, whether they're 21 or 41, are thinking about getting into real estate. I know some outliers who succeeded while working side jobs early on, but I argue strongly against that approach. If you take all that time spent bartending and apply it to brokerage instead, you'll be that much more successful.

Most people say, "I couldn't survive without income." That's where you need to have honest conversations with companies about getting consistent money to cover basic expenses. At Matthews, we have a draw program for exceptional cases. But we need to see your commitment first. Are you first in, last out every day? Are you hitting stretch goals? Is this the most important thing in your life?

Even then, we'll analyze expenses. Living in a Class A apartment alone? Switch to Class C with roommates. Going out for nice dinners? Switch to basic meals. You have to lean it up as much as possible. If you can demonstrate in interviews that you'll do anything within the coaching structure to be successful, you'll find someone to sponsor you.

You've emphasized the importance of structure. How does Matthews' training program guide new brokers from day one?

At Matthews, we're hiring mindset, not skill set. We'll teach them the skills. Within their first couple weeks, we have them interview 3 to 5 potential mentors across different product types. I call it the power of choice. See, every relationship will have tremendous tension, especially when money's on the line. If you're just assigned to someone, the default human response when things get hard is "Well, I didn't choose this." We eliminate that excuse.

We give them a comprehensive playbook. It's very structured. You get in at 6:00 a.m. and make 500 cold calls a week. Every meeting reduces your call goal by 25; every pitch by 50, but you never go below 300 calls. Work Saturdays and Sundays, though shorter hours. Live within a quarter mile of the office because we're not in the transportation business.

Anyone who sticks to that program—and almost no one does, maybe one in fifty—can be making a couple hundred thousand within two years. In a tougher market, or if the sales side doesn't come quite as naturally, it might take closer to three years to hit that $150,000 to $200,000 range. And usually within five or six years, they're making over a million dollars, almost without fail.

You've built a culture around pushing through those difficult early years. What have you learned about what makes people successful?

Everyone hits a wall when they realize this job is incredibly hard. If it wasn't, everyone would do it given the money you can make. We try to help with training and support. We're very aware of who's in what we call the "valley of despair." But ultimately, that decision to keep going comes down to the individual.

Most compensation structures come with different levels of authority. If you're on salary, you're their employee. Many agents view it as ownership. With a draw, they have less control since they're paying it back. Independent contractors have the most autonomy but often get the least support. That's why we've created a structured program that provides support while still maintaining entrepreneurial independence.

I tell them, "I can show you the way, walk alongside you, but I can't carry you." We've spent tremendous capital on personality assessments and tried to figure out who will make it, but there's no formula. I've had candidates with incredible hardship stories who quit in six months, and others who unexpectedly seemed soft become absolute warriors.

Everyone who starts here gets the book *Extreme Ownership* by Jocko Willink. The core message is that everything in your life, good and bad, is your fault. You can be victimized in a moment, but being a victim is a mindset you choose every day.

Here's what happens: We'll hire two people, Joe and Jack. Same day, same office, same product type, same senior mentor. Five years later, one's making a million dollars, the other quit after a year. It's proof that it's not the product. It's not the market. It's not your senior. It's just you. That's it. We give people agency over their life, but many never accept that responsibility. They quit and say, "It's not me. It's the market."

And what about those that do accept that responsibility?

One of my original juniors, until recently, was making $3 to $4 million a year, typically working 40 hours a week. About a year ago, he found out one of his 5-year-old twins had leukemia. Because of what he built in this business by working 90 to 100 hours a week early on, doing everything right, he's been able to step back and be there full-time for his son during treatment. Even in this terrible market, working maybe 10 hours a week, he's still making over a million dollars.

He tells me, "I want to be a spokesman for this industry. I am the example. No one should ever go through what I'm going through, but because of what I did when I got in the business, I've never once had to worry about money or my job while dealing with this." That's incredibly fulfilling to hear.

Given your success, I assumed you always had a strong work ethic. Was that the case?

Not one ounce. I was always kind and respectful, parents loved me, but I was just lazy. All I cared about were video games, skateboarding, and hanging out with my buddies. That's what makes this business amazing though. If you can develop the discipline and follow the program, it doesn't matter where you start. It matters where you finish.

Your approach to work changed dramatically during your time at USC. What drove that transformation?

My dad was a very disciplined person, and he tried to instill that in me as a kid, but it just didn't take. I had to figure it out for myself. He'd see my grades and say, "This kid is brilliant, but I can't figure out how to motivate him." Not one ounce of work ethic. My dad was a hell of a worker, but I was a total slacker. I just skated, went to the beach, got average grades. My dad would say, "This is insane. How do you get such bad grades?" He knew I was intelligent. I just never applied myself.

When I went to USC, there were some seminal moments where I had to make real decisions. Life isn't always about doing what we want; it's about doing what we need. For me, the change started with physical challenges. I'd never lifted weights or done strength conditioning before college. My first couple weeks there, I was the lowest guy on the totem pole. I was the scout team running back, full contact, multiple practices a day. These guys were absolute savages. The psychological pain was just as intense as the physical pain.

I realized I had to either quit or make serious changes. But quitting wasn't an option. That was one thing my dad had successfully instilled in me. When you have no options but one, the path becomes clear. I had to physically and mentally toughen up, get more disciplined in my approach to football, and that discipline spilled over into everything else.

How did that structured environment at USC influence your approach to both personal development and business?

That structure created the discipline. I couldn't not be disciplined. The program forced me to develop those habits.

Those early years at USC shaped everything. Our practices were incredibly intense. You're going full contact, multiple times a day, in brutal conditions. But it wasn't just the physical challenge. The mental aspect was even harder. You're constantly being tested, constantly having to prove yourself. Every day you had to show up ready to compete, no excuses.

What's interesting is that when I left USC, I thought it had been a waste of time. I was bitter because I didn't play as much as I thought I should have. I wasn't a starter. I just played special teams and backup duty.

I remember my senior night, I initially refused to participate in the tunnel ceremony because I felt I hadn't accomplished anything. Pete Carroll pulled me aside and said, "What the fuck are you doing? If you can't see what you've accomplished, you're the dumbest fucking guy." He made me run out that tunnel.

It wasn't until years later, when people asked how I was so hardcore in my approach to brokerage, that I realized it was USC. That experience was the best thing that ever happened to me. I'm actually just lucky that so many things aligned for me to be at that place, at that time, with that coach, in that program. Our greatest moments of growth often come attached to our greatest failures.

Those USC lessons seem to directly shape how Matthews operates today. Can you connect those dots?

Brokerage is really just about being disciplined over a long period. What made me successful was my willingness to do all the things nobody else wanted to do, for longer than anyone else was willing to do them. I didn't have some unique talent or hack. I just took a football player's mentality. Blocking and tackling fundamentals.

If someone was making 400 calls, I'd make 500. If someone got in at 7 a.m., I'd get in at 6. If they stayed until 8 p.m., I'd stay until 9. It was the most simple-minded approach, but it worked. That's how I teach brokers now. It's all about fundamentals and repetition.

In my first couple years, if I hit my 500-call goal by Friday at noon, I'd keep going and make 600, 650, sometimes 700. When you're making $300,000 to $400,000 four years in, you might stop at 500 and head to the beach. As the UFC fighter Khabib Nurmagomedov says, "It's hard to be hungry when your belly's full."

But then the Global Financial Crisis hit in 2008, and that fear of not surviving kicked everything up another level. Even the 2007 version of me, making $350,000 at twenty-six, was still a savage compared to others. But I definitely left some plays on the field. During the GFC, there was no more going to bars on Saturdays to watch football. It was work Monday through Sunday, but I didn't hate what I did.

Even with that intense drive and success, you've mentioned struggling with impostor syndrome. How did that affect you?

Even when I was doing north of eight figures a year in fees, I had impostor syndrome combined with Chicken Little syndrome. Impostor syndrome told me I wasn't really this good, and eventually they'd figure it out and stop hiring me. Chicken Little kept saying tomorrow the sky would fall.

This financial anxiety runs in the Matthews family. Even with all the professional athletes in my family who've made money, they're all good stewards of it. My dad played professional football for nineteen years, but we grew up middle class in a 2,000-square-foot house in Ohio with eight people. We could have lived much larger, but that wasn't our way.

That mindset of never taking success for granted, always preparing for the worst while working for the best. That came from my family. When you grow up watching professional athletes handle their money responsibly, it makes an impression. My dad could have bought a mansion, but he chose stability over flash. That stuck with me.

You made some strategic decisions about balancing work and family during the company's growth. Can you walk us through that thinking?

The work-life balance question is complex. We were taught growing up that "balance" often means mediocrity in everything rather than excellence in anything. Sometimes you have to make hard choices about where to focus your energy at different stages of life.

Around 2013 to 2014, with two young kids, my wife and I had to make a strategic decision. Either throttle down and become the dad who cooks breakfast and does school drop-offs, or go all in. We chose all in. I didn't see my son in the morning until he was eight. I was in the office at 5:45 a.m. every day, even as CEO making eight figures. If I'm doing that, what's anyone else's excuse?

On Saturdays, I'd bring them to the office, get snacks, put cartoons on the TV, give them a whiteboard to draw on, and work for four or five hours. Some people might judge that decision, but now I'm with my kids more than any other parent I know. I coach their sports teams, and I'm at every practice and game. Sometimes I'm on my phone or taking calls, but I'm there.

That kind of delayed gratification takes real discipline. How did you stay committed to that plan through the grind?

It was a crazy period. While my wife was doing the hard work of building our family, I was at the office every day at 5:45 a.m. building the company. And if I was there, everyone had to be there. That became the ethos of Matthews. Even in offices I've barely visited, they work harder than any competitors in their markets because that's just how we do it here.

It was a strategic decision that time with my kids at five was less important than time with them at 15. At 5, they're just roughhousing and kicking balls. At 15, you're developing human beings. I asked on Twitter recently: would you rather be the parent who's at every practice when your kid is five but none at fifteen, or vice versa? The answer is to be there at fifteen. Looking back, it was insanely well thought out and the right decision.

We recognized there was a chance this strategy might not work, but I knew there'd be some correlation between what you put in and what you get out. I saw this special window of opportunity with the market, my skills, and the team I was building. The plan was to get as much as we could while we could, then reassess in 4 or 5 years.

That's what we did in 2019. We looked up and made some changes, like deciding to move out of Los Angeles. But it all comes back to having the mental fortitude to execute over a long period. If you're a broker, you're founding a business. The business is you. People ask if I own a brokerage company. I tell them no, I own a venture capital company that invests in brokerage companies of one. We invest money, resources, coaching, guidance, and technology to accelerate growth of the individual businesses we're invested in.

How do you approach the entrepreneurial aspect at Matthews versus other companies?

At other companies, entrepreneurial basically means "figure it out yourself." We're different because we provide structured training, technology, and support systems. But even with all that support, our brokers are still 100 percent entrepreneurs. At the end of the day, it's them on that phone making calls. I can't lift the weight or make the calls for them.

When I started, I had to do everything. Underwriting, marketing, all of it. Today at Matthews, we provide comprehensive support, but we still make new brokers learn the fundamentals. For deals under $2.5 million, they do the basic underwriting because they need to understand it. On larger deals, analysts help, but the junior broker needs to learn how it works.

We focus on what we call RPAs, revenue-producing activities. There are really just four things: calling, meeting, pitching, and executing. The only nuance is that preparation for pitches and deal execution also counts as an RPA. If it's not in those buckets, it's probably not the best use of time.

What drives you to maintain that intensity even after achieving so much success?

I had a guy quit recently saying the market's too difficult. I asked him, "Is it going to be difficult forever? The worst market ever was the Global Financial Crisis. That was a 90 percent downturn for three years. We're only a year and a half into this one. What if it lasts four years but after that you have ten to fifteen years of a great bull market? You didn't tell me you ran out of money or hate the job. You're just quitting because it's hard."

Another guy who'd been here three to four years, making $500,000 last year, quit to "maybe be a developer, do a little of this and that." I told him, "Look, I like you, you're a hard worker, but you're making a dumb decision. I know how this movie ends if you stay here. You're making $3 to $5 million and punching your ticket to whatever life you want. I've never heard of someone becoming successful doing "a little bit of this and that."

I always say the train never stops moving. It's not the train's responsibility to stop and pick you up. It's your responsibility to find a way on the train. This is a pretty good train to be on. It moves fast and goes cool places, but if you stand on the tracks, it'll run right over you. And if you get off, you're never gonna get back on.

With all the training and support Matthews provides, how do you justify the value proposition to clients who question broker fees?

There's almost a stigma when owners see a $400,000 fee on a closing statement and get upset. My response is always, "Go do it then. You'll find out it's not that easy." Brokers sometimes get "overpaid" on deals because they got paid nothing on all the deals they worked on that didn't close.

The free market sorts this out. If brokerage was easy, everyone would do it, fees would get compressed, people would quit, and then fees would rise again as competition decreased. We're seeing this cycle right now. Three years ago, developers were saying they could sell directly, but now in a tough market, they're begging for our help and willing to pay full fees.

There's genuine value in marketing assets for sale, even if owners could technically do it themselves. It's about opportunity cost. If we save them 100 hours over six months, they can use that time finding their next deal or capital partner. We create value through sales skills, leveraging buyers against each other, and creating multiple bids.

But I'm convinced our biggest value is deal flow. We help owners recognize when properties no longer align with their goals, and we find them their next deal. It's very reciprocal. We often bring new deals to people who've sold through us. This business is ultimately about relationships and information. In real estate, unlike stocks, you actually get paid for knowing things others don't.

Your approach to training and culture is unique. How does that philosophy extend to Matthews' technology development?

For every successful technology we have here, we've had two failures and had to pivot. Our current automated program was the second try. The first attempt cost twice as much and was unusable. But you just keep going. I use my experience as a defensive back at USC to approach these challenges. In football, you have to have a short memory. When you mess up in the secondary, you're giving up a touchdown or committing pass interference, but you only have 35 seconds to think about it before the next play. How you feel about the previous play won't help you play the next one better. That's how we approach technology development. Learn from mistakes but move forward quickly.

We've built extensive resources for our brokers. Templates, automated tools, our knowledge base system with every document they might need. We've built technology like Apollo, an automated BOV creator for smaller deals. But the core focus remains on those revenue-producing activities while ensuring they understand the fundamentals.

How did you find the right tech people to build your team?

A lot of it was serendipity, honestly. Dave Harrington, who's now our president, came over to Matthews to launch our multifamily division. Before Matthews, he was at Berkadia where he met our current Chief Operating Officer, Duerk Brewer, who had built an incredible system there.

I was at this random conference in Orlando, which, in my opinion, is the type of thing that leads to success. I was willing to get on a plane, leave my family, step away from the company, and show up at these events. Dave and I were there, and he spots Duerk. They catch up, and six months later at another conference, I run into Duerk again. We were growing and needed someone specific for operations. Up to that point, myself and our CFO had been doing a bunch of the operations stuff, which for Matthews is like the marketing production platform and all of the support to the agents.

When I saw Duerk had a little frustration at his current role, I said, "Let's talk next week." He was skeptical but agreed to stop by our Orange County office while at Disneyland with his kids. He walks in and the office is absolutely electric—music playing, young guys in suits high-fiving, just incredible energy. He was like, "What is this place?" That's how we got him.

Through Duerk, we met Sean Clancy, one of their top tech guys who wanted to be CTO but couldn't at his current company. As Matthews grew and our capital position improved, instead of piecemealing technology initiatives that took twice the budget and two years to deliver, we brought in Sean as CTO. He then connected us with some amazing software developers he knew. Now we have a team of six engineers building everything for us. It all traces back to being willing to show up at that conference.

It seems building a company often boils down to finding the right operators and getting in position to meet them. Your particular skills clearly play a big role in pulling that off well.

One of our executives always tells people this story about my leadership style. He says, "Kyle's superpower as a CEO is finding someone who's much better than he is at something, hiring that person, and just letting them do their job." He says I give the longest leash he's ever had, almost to where he feels like he should check in more.

My philosophy is simple. If I hire the right person, I trust them. Maybe once a quarter I'll ask for an update on initiatives, but if I have to look over your shoulder, it's probably not the right hire. I got this from football. I played safety. I don't try to play linebacker or defensive end. There are people significantly better at those positions.

I'm built to message broadly, to aspirationally lead young men and women in building their businesses. I love taking chances and making tough decisions that would stress most people out. That's what makes a CEO. We find unique talent and empower them to operate at a level they've never experienced before, because most companies don't truly trust their people or want stars to shine too brightly.

How do you see technology impacting the future of brokerage?

We've seen some fee compression because of technology. If the average fee in 1985 was 5 percent, it might be 2.5 percent in 2025. But through technology, we can do twice the amount of deals. Forty years ago, creating a pitch book meant physically driving to properties, printing photos, manually creating everything. Now we can turn around a package in two hours using AI for underwriting and market analysis.

People worry about AI replacing brokers, but that's backwards. You won't be replaced by AI, you'll be replaced by a person leveraging AI. If our fees get compressed from 2.5 to 1.25 percent, we'll do four times the amount of deals. It's all about efficiency.

After building this unique approach to brokerage, how are you managing expansion while maintaining the Matthews culture?

We just announced D.C. two months ago. Got our first agent, Josh Ein, a top producer from Marcus & Millichap. We're taking twelve months to establish the office properly. Birmingham just opened up and Philadelphia will be coming online soon. We're looking at Detroit, Boston, Orlando, Portland, Seattle, lots of cities left to expand to. But it takes time, usually three to four years to get to thirty to forty people where an office really feels established.

The real challenge is maintaining culture during expansion. Each new office is a significant investment, not just in money but in cultural capital. You're essentially transplanting your DNA into a new market. We've focused on creating a phenomenally structured program that's consistent across all offices, with strong management oversight and a culture of accountability. We work our asses off and have fun doing it.

There's also a real cost to the company. Every desk has both soft costs, like our corporate overhead spread across all seats, and hard costs like computers, CoStar subscriptions, and CRM access to help brokers track leads and manage relationships. Beyond that, there's the cultural cost. As I say, the herd only runs as fast as the slowest buffalo. Sometimes you have to make tough decisions to keep the culture strong.

We have an informal policy, if you net more than $30,000 on a deal, you buy the office drinks Friday night. Over $100,000, you buy the whole night. Even had a Mormon guy close a $140,000 deal. He doesn't drink but still took everyone out. Cost him $3,200, but when you just made $140,000 in one check, you'll be fine.

Your USC experience taught you about resilience. How does that translate to leading Matthews through market cycles?

The GFC left me with permanent emotional scars. That experience drove my obsession with building massive cash reserves at Matthews. When this current market downturn hit, we were prepared. While other firms are laying people off and cutting support, we've opened five offices and hired 200 more agents in the last fifteen months. We're private, have no investors, no debt, and can make decisions that are good for us long-term without thinking quarter to quarter.

You've reimagined many aspects of the traditional brokerage model. How do you see the industry evolving from here?

The fundamentals of what makes a great broker haven't changed. It's still about relationships, market knowledge, and execution. What's changing is how we deliver value. Technology isn't replacing brokers; it's making the good ones better and exposing the ones who don't add real value.

We're in what I call the "talent acquisition business." Our job is to find people with the right mindset, give them the tools and training they need, and then get out of their way. The brokers who embrace technology while maintaining strong relationships are the ones who will thrive.

I use my football experience here too. The game keeps evolving, but the fundamentals of blocking and tackling never change. It's the same in brokerage. The tools change, but the core skills, those are constant.

What drives you to keep building and expanding Matthews?

I always tell people, "I've never made someone successful, I just put them in a position to be successful." The biggest reward I get now is what I call "phantom income," the compensation you can't measure, knowing you helped put someone in position to live the life they want. That's what brokerage offers. The opportunity to alleviate financial anxiety at a young age. Whether you start at 22 or 46, if you follow the program for ten years, you'll likely never have to worry about money again.

This is the best path because you make great money, meet tons of potential investors, and you're forced to analyze 300–400 deals a year. There's no quicker way to learn what makes a good deal. Sure, some people say they don't like sales or cold calling. But nobody likes cold calling! That's like saying, "I want to be in shape, but I don't like lifting weights." Nobody actually likes lifting weights, they like the results. It's about delayed gratification and doing the work that others won't do.

So if there's one thing to take away from this, it's the simplest message. Fundamentals. A lot of them over a long period of time, will put you in a position to do whatever you want.

As I wrapped up my conversation with Kyle, I found my mind racing: I was ready to abandon my current career, kiss my family goodbye, and show up at Matthews' doorstep ready to make cold calls at 6 a.m. That's the effect Kyle has on people. He has this way of laying out his vision, tough but somehow incredibly motivating, that makes you believe not just in his company but in your own untapped potential.

What sets Matthews Real Estate apart isn't just their growth but how intentionally they've built their training system. Kyle took what he learned on those USC championship teams and created something that cuts through the industry's typical sink-or-swim approach. Since 2015, when he opened that first office in El Segundo, the firm has continued growing to over twenty-five offices now and more than a thousand people strong.

The thing about Kyle's pitch? It leaves no room for confusion. Make your calls. Start early. Work weekends. Navigate what he calls the "valley of despair." It's brutal, but there's comfort in knowing exactly what it takes. His team has tracked and documented the entire journey, from rookie broker to seven-figure producer, with every step and milestone laid out. No wonder people sign up for his program despite knowing how hard it will be.

As business evolves and shiny new objects emerge, Kyle sticks to what he knows works. Do the work. Take ownership. Stick to the fundamentals. For those willing to put in the time, whether fresh out of college or midway through a career, the path forward couldn't be clearer.

Connect

- Website: matthews.com
- Podcast: thematthewsmentalitypodcast.com
- X: @kylematthewsceo
- Instagram: @kylematthewsceo
- LinkedIn: Kyle Matthews

Omar Morales

Director, Investment Sales, Berkadia

Miami, FL

- Rising star at Berkadia who has been involved in over $3.3 billion in multifamily and land transactions across South Florida, including a $355 million multifamily sale and a $130 million land deal.
- Leveraged social media to establish himself as a key information source for Miami's commercial real estate market, helping tech and venture capital professionals relocating to the area.
- Implemented a collaborative team leadership approach at Berkadia, emphasizing partnership with analysts to drive motivation and shared success.
- Laid the foundations of his success through an unpaid hedge fund apprenticeship, engaging in daily 6:00 a.m. market discussions with the fund's founder.
- Secured his entry into commercial real estate by persuading an investment firm to hire him without pay, which soon turned into a paid role due to his performance.

I met Omar Morales at his Brickell office, where he works with views that sweep across Miami's skyline and Biscayne Bay. At just 30 years old, the Berkadia director has carved out a place for himself in South Florida's commercial real estate scene, participating in over $3.3 billion in transactions while developing his distinctive approach to relationship-building in a city that refuses to stop reinventing itself.

Omar wasn't born in Miami. He arrived from Honduras at age 10, an experience that gave him a particular lens on opportunity in America, one that still colors his business philosophy today. His father worked as a residential broker, so real estate wasn't exactly foreign to him, but Omar's path to commercial property would first take a winding route through finance and insurance.

After graduating from college with an economics and finance degree, Omar landed an unpaid internship at a Miami hedge fund by leveraging an old high school connection. Early morning discussions with the fund's owner shaped his analytical approach to finance. By this time, he had decided to stay rooted in Miami rather than chase finance jobs in New York. He recognized the value of building lasting relationships in his home market.

Breaking into commercial real estate meant hundreds of cold emails and calls with response rates you could count on one hand. He finally got his foot in the door at a respected investment firm by proposing to work for free—a gamble that required both confidence and a willingness to sacrifice an immediate income. The firm started him on the payroll within weeks after seeing his potential. This pattern of trading immediate income for knowledge and experience became something of a signature throughout his career.

After we wrapped up the interview, Omar took me on a walk through Brickell's streets. He pointed to buildings and construction sites, casually discussing the history behind each property and explaining how the neighborhood had transformed. The tour revealed his granular understanding of Miami's evolution block by block.

Omar thinks about wealth differently than many of his peers. His immigrant background and family influence have given him a perspective that seems unusual for someone his age. Instead of pursuing the highest possible paydays through riskier deals, he's built a practice that balances steady income with personal freedom. He pours money back into his business through marketing and support staff while maintaining a lifestyle that reflects his careful consideration about what matters to him.

In our conversation, Omar discusses his transition from analyst to broker, his systematic approach to developing business relationships, and how his close experience with different career paths in commercial real estate has shaped his choices.

Date of Interview: February 24, 2024

I noticed on your LinkedIn you started at a hedge fund. What led you there?

That was honestly the luckiest break in my life that changed the trajectory of how everything unfolded. I'm the first in my family to graduate from high school and college. My parents are from Honduras, so when I graduated from high school, they were amazed. Then when I graduated from college, I thought, "We made it, we won." But that was just the beginning.

I didn't even know about the stock market until I was a freshman in college. I discovered you could buy shares of Google or Microsoft from your phone, and I was fascinated. That whole universe of investing, finance, and economics, I had no idea it existed.

So it sounds like college is where you first got interested in finance. What did you study?

I started with economics, then ended up doing both economics and finance. When I got to my upper-level economics classes, it started getting very theoretical. Both my parents are entrepreneurs, and I thought, "I don't know if I can help my parents in their small businesses with what I'm learning in economics." So I started taking finance classes, learning about bonds, debt, and yields. It made much more sense in terms of how the world works.

So how did you land the hedge fund opportunity?

It came through an incredible stroke of luck during my senior year of college. My prom date from high school went to Harvard, the only one in our class who did. She landed a summer internship at a hedge fund in Miami, which was rare. There weren't many hedge funds here back then, around 2014 or 2015. When she was finishing her internship, she mentioned they might need help with admin work and offered to introduce me.

I thought it was just going to be, "Hey, I'm here to help for free, when do I start?" But when I showed up, there were people who had flown in from New York and Boston for interviews. I was completely caught off guard.

How did you handle that situation?

During my last interview with one of the partners, I just laid it out: "Listen, I drove fifty minutes to get here. Everyone else is probably looking for a semester-long position. I don't need any money. I just need a lucky break. I will be here day and night. I'm not looking to put in just ten hours a week, I could be here eighty hours a week. What you guys do is fascinating, and it's a world I don't know anything about." I basically just sold him on my enthusiasm and dedication.

And to my surprise, they emailed me a few days later and said, "Hey, we'd love to have you." When I started, the owner of the hedge fund, Bill Strong, took a liking to me because I was showing up early every morning. At first, I started arriving at 8:00 a.m., even though my start time was 9:00 a.m., and he was already there. So the next day, I came at 7:30 a.m. He was still there first. I kept coming earlier until I was getting there at 6:00 a.m. I realized he had breakfast in the office every morning while reading newspapers, and he would call me in to chat. He'd ask, "Omar, what do you think we do here?" and I'd try to explain my understanding of efficient capital allocation. He taught me so much, and we had these morning discussions for about a year and a half.

Before moving on, let's talk about your earlier years a little bit. You mentioned your family came from Honduras. How old were you when you moved here?

I was 10, back in 2003. It was perfect timing because I had enough perspective from kindergarten through second grade to understand how tough an environment could be. Honduras is a very poor place. When I came to Miami, I was amazed. Everything was so clean and safe. People were healthy. There were yachts, buildings, and houses on the water. It was invigorating.

How did that background shape your approach to relationships and opportunities?

Even before getting into real estate, I was the type of person friends would call for advice. I developed this non-judgmental way of listening because I understood everyone has their own journey and perspective. I believe this has allowed me to relate to a lot of different types of people. They know they can call me for advice or thoughts because I'm not going to judge them for whatever situation they're in, or some mistake they made.

I also developed this concept I call your "luck surface area." You want to expand it by bumping into different people, places, and ideas. That's why I love being in Miami. When you're in a dynamic place, you have all these ideas and people bouncing around you, helping open your eyes to opportunities. It's about putting yourself in positions where good things can happen serendipitously.

How did your parents influence these perspectives?

What's interesting about my parents is they had me and my brother very young. They had him at 17 and me at 21. They were very honest in raising us, always saying "we don't know, we're figuring it out." They weren't these old souls telling us exactly what to do. So I grew up with the mentality that nobody has it all figured out, which made me comfortable asking questions and reaching out to people.

Your brother took a different path, right?

Yes, and it's interesting, we're polar opposites. His attitude is, "If I can make a $50,000 salary and that allows me to fish and spend time with my daughter, I'm happy." What changed my perspective about him was one day, when I was stressed out with work, I saw his Instagram story. It was him, his wife, and his 2-year-old daughter fishing on a lake at 11:00 a.m. on a Monday. Meanwhile, I'm dealing with this whirlwind of work.

I realized he's a winner. He is living exactly the life he wants to live. Who am I to impose my expectations on him? He's knocked it out of the park on a personal, marital, and family perspective, while I've done well in the professional and financial realm. We both succeeded, just in completely different ways.

What's your perspective on success and wealth, given all these influences?

I have uncles and aunts who stayed in Honduras. They're successful business owners there. They own the equivalent of Publix or Home Depot. They're the 1 percent in Honduras. But visiting them, I noticed they have the same exact problems as everyone else. Wealth doesn't solve everything. So I had this unique perspective of coming from a poor background but not being disillusioned with the idea that wealth solves all of life's problems. Instead, I focus on building relationships and creating opportunities through genuine connections with people.

Ok, so back to the hedge fund, how long were you there?

A year and a half, pretty much unpaid. I had the good fortune of being able to live with my parents thirty minutes away from Brickell, so I just took advantage of that.

I almost went to New York to do investment banking after college, the typical route. But I decided to stay in South Florida. I didn't buy into the narrative of "go somewhere to build your brand and name, then come back." I knew I wanted to be in South Florida long-term. It's where my parents live, it's home to me, and it's where I want to raise a family.

Fortunately, South Florida took off, and what I realized was that a lot of my friends who did the New York route were calling me four to five years into their career, asking who I could introduce them to. They were starting their reputation game over at 26 or 27, while I had built relationships here for six years.

So after a year and a half, basically unpaid at the hedge fund internship, I started to look elsewhere for paid opportunities. I landed a job at Aon as an insurance broker making $60,000 a year, which felt amazing after working for free. But I went from working with these multimillionaire hedge fund partners to sitting in a brown cubicle with assigned work. I lasted 4 months. I thought about staying for at least a year, people say you should, but I trusted my instincts. It's like Naval Ravikant says: if you're climbing a mountain and realize it's the wrong mountain, the first thing you should do is turn around. My parents supported me, saying, "You're young. If you don't like it, find something you'll like." That's when I started exploring other options.

What drew you toward commercial real estate at that point?

My father is actually a residential real estate broker. He works mainly with families in Honduras who buy luxury second homes in Miami. I got my real estate license my senior year of high school. My dad encouraged me to do it, saying it would help me someday. So I was fortunate to have made some money in college doing that.

I'd often go on weekend tours with him to apartment buildings. What I realized was I didn't like that residential real estate was very emotional. It was "Do you like the view?" rather than analyzing price per square foot and comps. I wanted to be more intellectually challenged.

Which is why you probably liked the hedge fund stuff, which makes sense. There's no emotion involved with that. It's like if you have emotion, it'll kill you.

Exactly. Residential is the opposite. So when I was at Aon feeling restless, my father would send me articles about commercial developments: "Did you see the big project they're building in Brickell?" These articles would mention developers, lenders, and brokers with quotes. I'd wonder, "Who are these people? What are they doing? How is this guy credited for this $2 billion project?"

So you started networking your way into the industry?

Right. I would look people up on LinkedIn and reach out. Strategically, I'd introduce myself as an equity research analyst at a hedge fund rather than saying I was at an insurance brokerage. That caught people's attention because it's not something common in Miami.

I very much see real estate and multifamily sales as a vessel to connect with people. It's about understanding their goals, their challenges, what keeps them up at night. I learned early on that being non-judgmental and really listening helps people open up. When you're genuinely curious about people and their stories, they sense that.

How many people did you reach out to when trying to break into commercial real estate?

Hundreds. My hit rate on responses was single digits for sure, one to five, maybe five to ten percent. But I never took it personally when people didn't respond. I understood that sometimes people are just busy. They might want to talk but get caught up in work and forget to reply. That's been a theme in my life I never take things personally, whether it's business or relationships.

A lot of people would give up after 20 or 30 rejections.

Where I got my big break was Lloyd Jones Capital, which bought multifamily properties. I reached out to the founder Chris Finley. No reply. I kept following up, still no reply. I reached out to the CFO. No reply. The director of acquisitions. No reply. The analysts. No reply. Finally, I reached out to Ryan, the intern, and he replied, saying, "Hey, I'm just an intern here, but happy to grab lunch."

I showed up to lunch with my resume in a manila folder. I knew he was an intern, so I needed to impress him enough to pass my resume to a decision-maker. We had lunch in Brickell, and he told me all about what they did. Super nice guy, military background, straight shooter. I said, "No pressure, but here's my resume if there are any opportunities." He passed it along, and I guess Chris Finley connected the dots like, "This kid's been reaching out forever."

So persistence paid off.

They gave me an interview but made it clear they weren't really looking for an analyst. During the second interview with the CFO, they mentioned that my salary expectations from Aon ($60,000) were way more than they paid first-year analysts. I could tell I wasn't going to get hired. As I was walking out, I noticed empty desks with monitors in their bullpen. I pointed and asked, "Who sits there?" They said nobody, and I said, "I'll work there for free."

The founder loved it. He asked what I meant, and I said I'd quit my job and be there in two weeks working for free if they'd have me. He took me up on the offer. I called my parents and told them I was going to be working for free again, but this was what I wanted to do. My dad was amazing about it, saying I'd been wanting this for months.

How did that work out?

Within a couple weeks, they saw I was working my ass off and started paying me a $45,000 salary. But since I had started expecting zero pay, that felt like gravy. Because I wasn't getting paid much, I knew the key was for me to learn as much as possible there. I was there 6:00 a.m. to 8:00 p.m. every day, not just doing assigned work but studying their previous deals. How did that deal get done? How did it sell five years later? Who was the lender? Who were the investment partners? What did the joint venture documents look like?

I probably learned in nine months what most people learn in two or three years. I was hooked from day one when they mentioned putting an offer on a $62-million complex. Coming from the insurance world where everything moved so slowly, this was exciting. These people were making money, investing other people's money, compounding it.

What made you eventually transition from the principal side to the broker side?

Working at Lloyd Jones helped me realize something important about the principal side. When you work for a company like that, they tell you, "Your location is Florida, you're buying multifamily value-add assets." Your job is to build relationships with brokers who sell those assets. So I started meeting these brokers, and I initially thought they'd be sleazy car salesmen. But when I met them, I realized they were actually super smart, very plugged in, and talked to all these funds.

What I realized was, on the principal side, you're looking at a very narrow slice, like only value-add multifamily in Jacksonville. But when I talked to brokers, they'd say, "Not only am I working on that value-add deal we discussed, but I'm also working on a piece of land in South Beach and a new construction deal in Brickell." That was fascinating to me. As a broker, you get exposure to the strategies of every major player. The Lloyd Jones Capitals, the Jorge Perezes, the Steve Rosses. They're basically telling you their playbook, saying, "This is what we're looking for. Help us find it."

How did you choose which brokerage firm to join?

I mapped out all the top brokers in South Florida and analyzed their transaction volumes and team sizes. The biggest team at the time was Cushman and Wakefield. They did about $4 billion in a single year, but they were a twenty-five-person team. I thought, there's probably a lot of politics there, a lot of heads to feed. I wanted to be on a team that did the most deals with the fewest people. I didn't want to be told, "Omar, go work on this other shitty deal." I wanted there to be so many deals and so few people that we're just trying to run as fast as possible.

That narrowed it down to HFF (which later got acquired by JLL) and Walker & Dunlop. HFF was where everybody wanted to be. They were doing all the coolest deals with a lean team. But it was like the Blackstone of Miami, really tough to get into. Walker & Dunlop had two producers and needed an analyst. When I met with them, they loved my attitude and energy. Even though HFF had more volume, I chose Walker & Dunlop because they had a ton of deals to work on and they had just lost their analyst, so I felt there was more opportunity there. At HFF, there were six other people just like me who were all Type A and charismatic, two to three years older than me, and had more tenure.

How long were you at Walker & Dunlop?

Almost three years, from early 2017 to late 2019.

And you were an analyst the whole time?

Yeah, analyst to senior analyst. It was a very prudent decision to go with them. We were overflowing with deals, and it got to the point when they started trusting me very early on. Where they're like, "Hey, Omar, I can't make it to this meeting. Can you go for me instead of me canceling it? I can't go to this tour. This guy's flying down from New York. Can you go?" And I'm like, yes, yes, yes, yes. And they were some of the smaller clients, but for me, I'm like, for sure.

So now I'm having these amazing reps very early on in my brokerage career, where I'm sitting in front of important people and being like, "How can I help you? This is what we've sold. This is what we've done." Then, my partners at the time were getting a positive reception from the clients about me. "Hey, don't worry about it. Omar showed up. He's great by the way. We love him." And they're like, oh, great. So they started giving me more rope. And from that, the momentum builds. Whereas at HFF, there was more of a pecking order just by the nature of having more people there.

What prompted the move to Berkadia?

There's a really interesting dynamic in commercial real estate brokerage where firms actively "buy talent" rather than develop it from scratch.

What happens is these larger shops want to have a presence across different markets. They'll reach out to successful teams and essentially recruit them with significant incentives.

In my case, there was a producer from another firm who was recruited by Berkadia to build out their South Florida multifamily team. He needed to assemble a team, and he remembered me from previous interactions back from when I was originally trying to make connections in the business. Unlike some firms that try to poach entire teams, which often leads to cold feet, this was an opportunity to build something from the ground up at Berkadia.

So Berkadia was looking to establish a stronger presence in South Florida?

Exactly. They had other business lines here but needed to grow their multifamily investment sales team. What's interesting about Berkadia as a company is that it's a joint venture between Berkshire Hathaway and Jefferies Financial Group. It's not as well-known as CBRE or JLL because we don't do leasing or property management, which are very people-intensive. We focus specifically on investment sales and finance, which allows us to generate significant revenue with a much smaller team.

And I had a great opportunity to join. Greater resources, better platform for building a personal brand, and a chance to be part of building something from the beginning rather than just joining an established team. So in 2019, I made the move to Berkadia along with others, and we've been building our presence in the South Florida market ever since.

Can you talk more about Berkadia's business model? I understand there are different components.

Berkadia has three verticals. First, there's investment sales, which is what I do, selling buildings, like a real estate agent selling houses but at an institutional scale. Second is mortgage banking. Financing, acquisition loans, refinances, construction loans. Everything bank-related, including Fannie Mae and Freddie Mac.

The third vertical is actually the reason why we're a Berkshire Hathaway company. Loan servicing. Warren Buffett doesn't own bad businesses. We service about $400 billion worth of loans, which means we ensure loans are current, properties are checking boxes, and we handle tax and insurance escrows. The servicing business provides steady revenue that becomes even more valuable when interest rates rise.

When interest rates shot up and the market got dislocated, traditional brokerage shops had terrible years because nobody knew what things were worth, so deals weren't getting done. But Berkadia thrived because of our servicing business. While most brokers are having one of their slowest years ever, the company is doing great and actively hiring talent while others are cutting back.

That's fascinating. How does this model benefit you as a broker?

It creates amazing synergies. If I sell a $100 million building to a client, they often need financing. I can introduce them to our mortgage banking team, who helps secure the loan and provides long-term servicing, all within Berkadia. That integrated approach adds real value for the client, and it also strengthens internal partnerships across the company.

Berkadia offers meaningful economic incentives that encourage brokers to keep everything in-house, which promotes collaboration rather than competition between teams. That model also allows the firm to offer more favorable splits, 60 percent versus the typical 50/50, because the business is supported by stable, long-term servicing revenue, not just brokerage commissions.

That's really interesting. Do you also handle land deals for developers?

Yes, and it's another example of how the business model creates synergies. We sell land specifically for multifamily development. Think about it, if we sell a piece of land to a developer like Mill Creek Residential, they might need a land loan. Our financing team can help with that. Then they need a construction loan, we can help with that too. When the building is complete and stabilized, we're well-positioned to handle the sale. It's about building lasting relationships and being a trusted partner from start to finish.

Many brokers eventually start investing in their own deals. Is that something you're interested in?

I think about this a lot, especially when respected people in the industry ask me why I'm still brokering. Here's how I see it: Let's say a broker makes $500,000 a year with no risk, no capital raising, and it comes in manageable increments. Some years might be $300,000, some years $700,000, but it's relatively consistent.

I've seen clients buy buildings for $110 million, then have to sell for $90 million when interest rates shot up, losing their own capital and their investors' money. I've also seen the opposite, someone buying for $65 million and selling for $125 million six years later. In either scenario, the broker makes their commission without taking on the risk.

I don't aspire to have a private jet and a 200-foot yacht. I want freedom and financial security. The fact that clients might make $50 million on a trade doesn't change the fact that as a broker, you might make $300,000 with no risk. They're signing personal guarantees, dealing with potential disasters. I don't want that stress.

When you see the potential upside in development projects, does that ever tempt you to reconsider your approach?

Developers can make a lot of money, but they're taking enormous risks. For a $30 million project with a $20 million construction loan, you need to pledge 10 percent in liquid assets, $2 million of personal guarantee. Then what happens? They build successfully and want to do an $80 million project. Now it's an $8 million pledge. Then a $200 million project requires a $25 million guarantee.

Look at someone like Stephen Ross doing Hudson Yards for $4 billion. The personal guarantees must have been astronomical. When I see developers succeed, I think, "Good for you, you deserve every penny." Meanwhile, I'm making my steady income with minimal stress, just strolling along.

Have your views on wealth and success evolved over time?

My dad made me realize that I had my head down and made me appreciate how well I was doing. When I was doing well but still living with a roommate, he sat me down and did the math. He asked, "How much does a Porsche cost? What about a one-bedroom apartment with a den in the best building? How much is it to travel every year?" We added it all up, and the "millionaire lifestyle" I imagined came to about $8,000 a month, and that helped put things in perspective.

He wasn't telling me to spend all my money, but he wanted me to understand my position. I'm not materialistic. I've had offers where I could make more money, but they involved more risk and stress. I'm happy with my path. When I do eventually invest in real estate, it will be with my own capital. I don't want to be raising money and dealing with investor pressure. I've seen how that can weigh on people.

What's interesting about my dad's perspective is that it made me realize I was so focused on saving and compound growth that I wasn't recognizing how good things already were. It's not about working harder endlessly. There is such a thing as having enough. Especially in Miami, where things are getting more expensive, it's important to have that perspective.

You've mentioned you think a lot about business branding. How does that influence your approach to real estate?

What I love about brokering is that it's amazing for brand building. Berkadia as a company incentivizes you to make a name for yourself and get recognized in social circles. They're very supportive of personal brand development. They're even giving me a panel to talk about social media at our national production meeting. The whole company understands that building individual brands helps build the business.

Great segue. Let's talk about your rise in social media. When did you start taking it seriously for business?

It really took off because of COVID. I'd been on Twitter since high school, but had stopped using it. When I started talking about real estate on Twitter in 2017, it was like, this is interesting. I was just posting articles and having conversations with random people who'd reply. Then 2020 hit, and people started flocking to Miami. And now, people are looking for information about Miami.

What's interesting is that the tech world and crypto community were much more Twitter-centric than the New York real estate crowd. I was the only one talking about multifamily and what was happening in Brickell and South Beach on Twitter. Everyone else was doing it on Instagram and LinkedIn. So when people from Silicon Valley and the crypto world started looking at Miami, I became a source of information.

How did that impact your business?

The influx of people to Miami during COVID was incredible. Keith Rabois from Founders Fund is credited with bringing many people here. He bought a place on Star Island and started championing Miami on Twitter. A lot of the tech and VC world were on Twitter, and I was already there talking about the market. When Mayor Francis Suarez would retweet my posts about Miami stats, I'd wake up to hundreds of new followers. It just kept compounding from there.

I started taking content creation more seriously during that period. For six to nine months during COVID, there weren't many deals happening, and since I only get paid when I close a deal, I had more time on my hands. I focused on creating more sophisticated content about the market. I'd share detailed statistics and analysis about what was happening in Miami, and key figures in the tech world would amplify it. That really helped establish my position as a market expert.

You mentioned reinvesting in yourself. That reminds me, you recently did something else with your money that was meaningful to you. Can you tell me about what you did for your grandmother recently?

My grandmother from my mom's side was born with dirt on her feet. Literally living in a location without floors, very village-type background. She married someone who was reasonably wealthy in Honduras, which changed the trajectory of our entire family lineage. But more than that, she's probably the most important person in my life because of how she carried herself. So poised, helpful, communal, and charismatic.

She even took my father in when he was going through a tough time as a teenager. His parents had a rough divorce. He was kind of a troubled rebel kid with money in Honduras, but my grandmother took him in, made him part of all the family celebrations. That's actually how my parents met. My father was friends with my mother, and my grandmother basically adopted him into the family.

So recently, I flew her first class to Miami. When they sat her in first class, she kept saying, "No, no, this can't be mine." When I picked her up, she was crying. She had never experienced anything like it. Now she jokes, "Are you not sending me first class anymore?" She's so funny, she says she's only coming back to Miami in first class.

How are you reinvesting in your business now?

I met Bob Knakal, who told me he was spending about 20 times more on marketing than any other broker I knew. That blew my mind. Most brokers I know barely invest in marketing at all. Since then, I've started investing much more in videographers, editors, and a social media team.

What's interesting is that I haven't really changed my lifestyle since I was 24. I drive the same car, live in the same apartment. But now I spend more on growing my business than on living expenses. Sometimes I get heart palpitations about it, but I know it's the right investment.

Can you walk me through what a typical day looks like for you?

Whether the market is hot or cold, my day is exactly the same. I wake up very early. It used to be 4:30, 5:00 in the morning, now it's like 5:30 in the morning. If I wake up at 6:00 a.m., it's like, I'm up late. But it's typically 5:30 a.m. I wake up, I go straight to the gym, I work out till, call it 6:30, I'm back at my place and sort of getting ready at like 7:00 a.m. While I'm working out or while I'm getting ready, I'm replying to emails and texts from the night before. I'm a big believer in momentum. If you're up early and work out, you just have a better day. When you're having difficult conversations or dealing with arduous tasks, you've already won the day by getting a great workout in.

I try to spend as little time as possible in the office because I believe business happens outside. Someone gives you their listing because they've had lunch with you, played tennis with you, gotten to know you. If that person only knows you as a voice on the phone, you probably won't get the business.

So you're constantly meeting people?

Yesterday is a perfect example. I had a coffee meeting, then a breakfast meeting. Then there was one of the best local real estate events of the year from noon to six, followed by a reception. I had scheduled a dinner afterward with 6 industry leaders who I knew would be at the event. They all know of each other, but they don't typically have reasons to talk day-to-day. Even though Blackstone's local guy knows KKR's local guy, they're not calling each other to grab lunch. So I connect them, help deepen their relationships.

The key is that I have support staff handling the desk work. If I'm in a meeting and someone asks for sales comparables, I call our analysts as soon as I get in the car. While I'm driving, they're already working on it. This allows me to focus on relationships while staying current on market information.

That's interesting. Do you find it challenging to keep up with market knowledge now that you're not doing the analyst work yourself?

It's actually turned into a collaborative process. Our analysts might spend two hours researching comparables, and when they send them to me, I might notice something missing: "Wait, didn't this guy buy something in Pompano? That one's not there." They'll confirm and add it. I tell them that by doing this research, they're building their own knowledge base that will help them impress people at events or meetings.

I actually delegate a lot, sometimes too much. I have to be reminded when I should be the one on certain calls. But I want my days to be as client-facing as possible. Whether the market is hot or cold, I'm working just as hard. The only difference is that in 2021 and 2022 it was much more lucrative, while 2023 and 2024 are tougher. But the work ethic stays the same.

Correct me if I'm wrong, but it seems like the skills that make someone a great analyst don't necessarily translate to being a great producer.

Exactly right. Morgan Housel wrote something in his blog that really resonated with me: the skills that make someone rich aren't the skills that keep someone wealthy. To become rich, you need to take big risks, go all in, make big bets, bet on yourself, go for it. To stay wealthy, you need to be conservative, diversify, invest in what you know, be much less risk-oriented, and more about cash flow.

What got you here isn't going to be what gets you to the next level. When I was an analyst, I focused on being hyper-responsive and studying everything I could. But I knew that to become a producer, I needed to start building relationships. That's also why I'm investing in social media. I believe the audience I'm building now will give me leverage for whatever I do next.

The next transition, which is even tougher, is going from successful broker to successful leader. Some brokers go from everyone knowing them individually and making $1 to $2 million a year to building a team of fifteen people doing $20 million in fees, where they're making $6 to $8 million as the team leader. But that requires a completely different skill set. You can't just be focused on clients anymore. You need to take care of the people who enable you to do your job.

So after progressing from an analyst to a broker, the next level is becoming a successful leader of brokers. Can you discuss that role some more?

The brokers that make the most money are the ones that become leaders and build an organization working for them. But to do that, you need to be a very good leader, which is very different from being a very good broker. In my market, the guys making $6 to $10 million aren't just good brokers, they're great leaders. They have four brokers crushing it for them. Say one broker is making a million dollars a year and is happy, but the leader is making six because they've built such a strong team.

Can you give an example of what great leadership looks like in this industry?

Mitch Sinberg, who runs Florida for Berkadia, is probably the most successful broker in the state. He's a phenomenal leader. Everyone in this office loves Mitch. He walks in and he's like, "What's up, man? What's going on?" During COVID when everyone was on Zoom, he'd always crack jokes and keep the energy light. Everyone would love it.

Compare that to brokers who rule with an iron fist. They might be very successful, but they're going to struggle to reach that next level because eventually, the people they're ruling over will say, "I don't need someone yelling and screaming at me anymore. I'd rather do this on my own." Whereas with Mitch, you're thinking, "I'll do whatever you want. You're making money, I'm making money, let's all make money."

How do you think about developing your own leadership style?

I hear "take care of your people and your people will take care of you." I want David and Walter, our analysts, to be invigorated and fired up to help the team bring in and close deals. I treat them as partners versus ruling with an iron fist. I don't want my power and leverage to be the reason why somebody works with me. I want them to want to work with me.

You seem to think deeply about motivation and success. What shapes your philosophy?

I've had a very spiritual journey throughout my career, trying to figure out why I'm doing what I'm doing. There's this concept that everything you do in life is either love-focused or fear-focused. You want to find out what you're doing out of fear, and what you're doing out of love, and do as many things as possible out of love.

When I come into this office, whether it's 7:00 a.m. or 2:00 p.m., I'm like, "Good morning, everyone! How's it going? What are you working on?" I'm bringing loving energy. I'm never walking in here stressed out saying "I'm behind on this deal," even though I could be. I come in with positive energy, and I feel like people are invigorated by it.

That's an interesting perspective. How does it apply to career decisions?

Again, this goes back to that saying by Naval Ravikant that really resonated with me: if you're climbing a mountain and you realize it's the wrong mountain to be climbing, the first thing you should do is turn around. I see people who don't like their job but convince themselves to stay because "In four years, I'm going to get a bonus" or "That's going to help me get somewhere else."

They don't even like the mountain they're on, yet they talk themselves into staying there for another four years. If you know you're on the wrong mountain, stop wasting time. Go find another one.

What mountain are you climbing?

I know that becoming a millionaire and having a house on the water isn't going to solve my problems. That's not the mountain I'm climbing. The mountain I'm climbing is finding the life I want to live for myself. For me, brokering where I'm not taking huge risks, meeting lots of people, helping people, being in a city I love. I'm pretty happy here. I don't think AI or a global workforce is going to be better at selling Miami than I am.

Sam Altman talks about how when you finally achieve a milestone you've been striving toward for so long, it's actually very likely that you'll have an existential crisis. You think, "Now what?" That's why it's so important to understand your real motivations and what actually brings you fulfillment.

That's a great perspective on success.

The great thing about commercial real estate is there are so many different avenues you can take. You can be a coder, a data scientist, a content creator, a general contractor. You can be someone who's in jeans and a dirty shirt all day if that's what suits you. The key is knowing yourself and finding where you can truly excel.

I think that's what my journey has really been about, finding alignment between who I am and what I do. It's not necessarily just about what you're good at or what you're passionate about. It's about finding where your skills and personality can create the most value. When you're climbing the right mountain, you know it. The work energizes you rather than depletes you. For me, I love connecting people, building relationships, and helping others succeed in this market. That's the mountain worth climbing, and I'm fortunate to have found it. I literally found the best gig for me.

Omar found his way into commercial real estate through a series of deliberate trade-offs. He consistently chose to learn over earning to form the foundation of his career. Starting as an unpaid analyst at a hedge fund, he then cold-called his way into commercial real estate, each time prioritizing experience over immediate income. These calculated gambles have paid off. He's now a recognized voice in Miami's multi-family market, with billions in transactions behind him.

His clear-eyed vision of success separates Omar from many of his peers. "I don't aspire to have a private jet and a 200-foot yacht. I want freedom and financial security," he told me during our conversation. This isn't empty philosophy. It's woven into how he structures both his business operations and personal life. His family background instilled a practical approach to wealth that favors sustainability over flashiness.

Each professional leap—from Lloyd Jones Capital to Walker & Dunlop to Berkadia—came after a thorough analysis of team culture, compensation structures, and growth trajectories. The switch from principal work to brokerage wasn't just some impulsive career move, but a calculated assessment of risk-reward dynamics and recognizing his natural strengths. When COVID prompted people to move to Miami in unprecedented numbers, Omar's established social media presence positioned him perfectly when newcomers sought market insights.

As his earnings grew, his spending habits stayed largely unchanged. Rather than upgrading his lifestyle, he reinvested in his business, bringing on support staff and expanding his marketing footprint.

These days, Omar thinks about the gap between individual brokerage success and true leadership that builds something lasting. He approaches client relationships and team development through a simple lens: decisions ultimately stem from either love or fear. For anyone in commercial real estate, or really any field, Omar's path shows the power of understanding industry economics from the inside out, building strategic relationships that compound over time, and aligning career decisions with personal values.

Connect

- Website: miamimultifamily.kit.com/opportunities
- X: @OmarMora1es
- Instagram: @OmarMora1es
- LinkedIn: Omar Morales

Beth Azor

Founder and Owner, Azor Advisory Services

Southeast Florida

- Owns and operates a portfolio of retail centers valued at $80 million across Southeast Florida.
- Led Terranova Corporation as President for six years after rising from leasing agent, helping the company grow from 11 to over 40 employees.
- Created retail leasing training programs that have educated thousands of professionals nationwide, authoring two influential books while establishing one of the industry's only comprehensive curricula for shopping center leasing.
- Revitalized a struggling Cleveland mall at age 63 in a city she'd never visited, signing 49 leases in under three years using her own training techniques.
- Founded multiple women-focused investment initiatives, including the CRE Women's Investment Summit and WIRE, with a mission to increase women's participation in commercial real estate investing.

Beth Azor didn't plan on becoming "The Canvassing Queen." The title found her after decades of pounding pavement and knocking on doors, literally and figuratively, throughout her commercial real estate career. As founder of Azor Advisory Services, she now oversees four shopping centers worth $80 million in Southeast Florida while training industry professionals nationwide on the techniques that built her reputation.

Beth found her way into commercial real estate through a chance encounter. During a conversation with a woman who explained what retail leasing involved, she saw an opportunity that clicked immediately. After stints in residential real estate and fundraising, Beth joined Terranova in the late '80s as a leasing agent, taking a massive pay cut to $18,000 annually to learn the business from the ground up. The gamble paid off. By her third year, she'd broken six figures while managing eighteen shopping centers. Weekends at the office became her norm, knowing her bosses would notice her there. "It's not who you know," she'd later tell her mentees, "it's who knows you."

Beth climbed to the presidency of Terranova before stepping away to prioritize family, a pivot that led to launching her own firm. She transitioned from being a limited partner on seven deals to calling her own shots as a general partner. Her first solo venture was an outparcel Terranova had passed over, and in just two and a half years, she made herself and her investors a return of 299 percent.

Teaching comes naturally to Beth. She's authored two books—*Don't Say No for the Prospect* and *The Retail Leasing Playbook*—and maintains a YouTube channel packed with strategies she's tested herself. Her most impressive case study? At 63, she tackled a struggling Cleveland mall in a city where she had zero connections, signing forty-nine leases in thirty months. Proving her methodology could work anywhere, with or without an established network.

A Florida State alumna, Beth serves as a Foundation Trustee and established the FSU Real Estate Foundation. But her most passionate mission targets a stubborn industry statistic that she shared with me during our interview: women make up just 3 percent of commercial real estate investors, with only half investing independently. Beth aims to boost that 1.5 percent of solo women investors to 10 percent before she turns 70.

In a relationship-driven field, Beth creates connection points everywhere by organizing targeted networking groups for women, young professionals, and newcomers while sharing market insights across social media. With all the personal success she has found in commercial real estate, it's clear she's most proud of her work helping others be successful too.

Date of Interview: October 3, 2023

First of all, Beth, thank you for doing this. You've done quite a lot in the industry, particularly in retail, through your work at Terranova, your education efforts, and owning your own shopping centers. What is your main focus today?

My main focus is my portfolio, which is four centers valued at about $80 million, and my mission to get women to invest. I read a stat that only 3 percent of commercial real estate investors are women, and of that 3 percent, half are spouses or inherited family money. So only 1.5 percent are women who, like me, built their commercial real estate portfolios on their own. As a single mom who didn't inherit wealth but now owns four shopping centers worth $80 million, I find that statistic deplorable. I'm 63 and I have a mission to get that to 10 percent by the time I turn 70.

I created a conference where I interview successful women investors. We usually have eight to nine women on stage for fireside chats. I ask them how they got involved, about their first deal, whether they lost or made money. So the 200 to 300 women in the audience can see there are women doing it. It's just not widely touted.

Speaking of conferences, you just finished one in Wyoming?

That's called WIRE, Women in Real Estate. It was our eleventh year, and it's basically a boondoggle. Years ago, I wanted to travel, learn while traveling, and grow relationships. I sent an email to women in the industry asking if they wanted to go to a spa weekend to rejuvenate and learn about retail. The spa only had eleven rooms, and I sold it out in three minutes. I thought, "There's something here."

I got the idea from some guys in Miami who would go on ski trips. Every morning they'd have a couple hours' discussion about the market over coffee. We do the same. One morning we have a three-hour market session. The rest of the time is focused on relationship building. We've had mergers come out of it, deals, referrals, women investing together. This year we had forty-four women, ranging from 31 to 71 years old.

What are their roles?

We have lawyers, CEOs of big companies, CFOs of public companies, leasing agents, accountants, insurance brokers. So something to do with commercial real estate. It's such a huge ecosystem with so many different roles and paths you can take.

Before we discuss your commercial real estate career, I'd like to understand your early influences. I understand you started working at a remarkably young age at just 11 years old?

Yes, I wanted to make money! I had a checking account at 11. I still have the register with my first blue jeans purchase. My mom was big on teaching us to earn, save, and spend money responsibly. We had a tavern in Milwaukee, and I would sort the recycling bottles in the basement. The companies paid 5 cents per bottle.

My parents eventually transitioned into residential real estate, and when I was fourteen, we moved to Florida. They'd often have me talk to families considering moving from other states. I was the salesperson for how great Florida was, and I wasn't lying! I loved it. Also, moving to a much smaller school made a big difference. After coming from a freshman class of eight hundred in Milwaukee, I felt like I could really make an impact, and that stuck with me.

Your parents exposed you to both residential real estate and running a business. Did those early experiences influence your approach to building relationships in commercial real estate?

I owe everything to my parents. My mom was a workaholic, and my dad was a dreamer. I got the best of both. But I was actually better in small groups than large ones. Throughout my career, I've always created opportunities for people to network in small groups. Even at Florida

State, though it was huge, I became an RA of my dorm to impact that community. I've always liked making an impact and accomplishing things.

I think you also started working in real estate during college, but you decided to join a sorority too. Am I remembering that right?

During college, I got my real estate license at eighteen. If you're part of a real estate family, that's just what you do. I'd work summers doing real estate, sitting open houses for my parents or at condo developments. I'd sometimes waitress at night, but I was making commission checks during the school year.

The sorority decision was interesting. My parents said they'd pay for either the sorority or studying abroad. I thought, "I can always travel, but I'll never be able to be in a sorority again." Being in the sorority taught me incredible leadership skills. I was running Greek Week for the entire campus at twenty-one, dealing with the president of the university. We raised over $100,000 for Muscular Dystrophy and were invited to the Jerry Lewis telethon.

After graduating, you started working as a chapter consultant for the sorority?

Yes, but technically I hadn't finished my degree. My last semester, I was running Greek Week for the whole campus—28 fraternities and 26 sororities. After the event, I got mono and had three incompletes. I was supposed to finish them over summer, but I got this opportunity to travel the country as a chapter consultant.

Looking back at your decision to take the chapter consultant role instead of finishing your degree, how important is it for young people to weigh those kinds of decisions. Looking at the experience you'll gain versus what you might miss out on?

Making a decision, even if it turns out to be wrong, is crucial. Too many people get stuck in analysis paralysis. When that opportunity came up, I applied while I still thought I was going to get my degree. They picked ten people out of hundreds. I knew this was an opportunity I'd never get again. They'd only hire recent graduates. The training was incredible. Two weeks in Atlanta, 12-hour days covering everything from budgeting to public speaking to professional image. It was the best training I'd ever had, and I was only 21 years old.

I could always go back and finish those three incompletes. I just had to read three books and write three papers. But I'd never have another chance to visit fifty sororities in fifty cities and states at fifty campuses. The training and experience were worth so much more than rushing to finish those credits. I was right. I did eventually finish my degree, but that consulting experience was irreplaceable. The training covered everything from budgeting, to accounting, suicide prevention, recruitment, alumni relations. I didn't finish those three incompletes until many years later.

So after traveling the country as a consultant, how did you find your way into real estate?

I followed a boy to Miami and met with a sorority sister who worked for Norwegian Caribbean cruise lines. She looked at my resume and said I should be in special events. The Heart Association was looking for a special events coordinator, so I interviewed and got the job. The salary was $11,000, which is about $30,000 in today's money. I knew I couldn't live on that, so I did residential real estate on weekends.

After two years, my Heart Association salary doubled to $23,000, and I was making good money between both jobs. Then my executive director called me into her office and said, "We love you, but your ambition exceeds us. I don't make much more than you're making now as Executive Director. You should probably go do real estate full-time and just volunteer for us."

So I left and took a job with a residential developer. I was basically sitting in a trailer five days a week reading People Magazine, waiting for people to walk in and look at model homes. I wanted to be more proactive and do marketing events, but the developer said, "We're building luxury homes. Just wait until people walk in the door."

One Mother's Day weekend, we needed extra help because it would be busy with model home tours. This woman came in who worked for my boss's son in retail development. I was complaining about how much I hated sitting in the trailer, and she said I should try commercial real estate. I said, "Gross, that's selling land, that's more boring than this!" That's what I thought commercial real estate was, probably because I heard my dad say that or something.

And that's when she said no, there was this thing called leasing and retail. My boss builds shopping centers and does deals with supermarkets, and our job as leasing agents are to fill in the vacancies around the supermarket. And mostly they're the mom and pops, entrepreneurs, and when you lease a space to them, you're literally helping them achieve their American dream. She said once you lease to them, you're invited to every wedding, bar mitzvah, communion. You become part of their family. I was sold. I said, "Where do I go to find out how to do that?"

That woman could have kept quiet, she actually told me later, "Don't tell anyone I told you about this, my boss's father will kill me." But she didn't stay quiet, and it changed my life. I always say the thing between you and your next job, between you and your next check, is a person. So make sure you're meeting lots of people. Whether it's leaving the house to get coffee, going to an event, or sitting next to someone on an airplane. You never know.

This brings us to a major turning point at Terranova. How did you end up there?

When I got the tip about commercial real estate from the woman at the residential developer, she suggested I call Terranova, a company that trains leasing agents. When I called and asked who does the training, they said Donna Abood. I recognized the name and mentioned I went to Florida State, and they said, "Oh, she's a Seminole!" Then Donna picked up the phone and recognized me from our sorority. She immediately said, "You're hired!" Just like that, I was brought into the company. They had 11 people at the time.

You've mentioned that when you walked in, it clicked immediately. What was it about the company?

First, I took a huge pay cut to work there. I went from making about $35,000 to $45,000 between my two jobs to starting at $18,000. But when I walked into that 800-square-foot office, I got goosebumps. I felt like I had found my place. Day one. I knew I didn't even know what it was. I didn't know anything about the business. There was something about it that I just went, oh my god, this is what I'm going to do for the rest of my life.

They started me in office leasing, which wasn't what I wanted. I wanted the retail side, helping entrepreneurs achieve their American Dream. Three months in, we got a shopping center assignment in Boynton Beach. It was an hour drive each day, but I said I'd do it because that's what I'd signed up for. There weren't cell phones then, so I just listened to motivational tapes on the drive.

Within two years, I had 18 shopping centers to lease in Palm Beach County. By year two, I was making $63,000, and by year three, I broke $100,000. I was working incredibly hard. My friends who worked at banks would criticize me for working weekends while they were out partying. But I was happy when I finally started out-earning them.

The key was that I'd go into the office on weekends when the bosses were there. It's not who you know, it's who knows you. I'd be there three Saturdays a month, doing paperwork, and the boss would buy pizza for whoever was around. As we grew to twenty-five people, they got to know me as that young leasing agent who was always there. That's why I got more properties faster than my peers.

How did you learn the business?

Donna trained us to canvass for office buildings, but when I got the shopping center assignment, she couldn't help, she was an office person.

So I shifted to working directly with Stephen, the boss, which was great. He had some shopping center experience, but we were really learning together. That's how I built my reputation and eventually became known for always pushing rents and helping improve the whole market.

You've mentioned listening to motivational tapes during your commutes, and I believe I've heard you mention they were mostly Tom Hopkins in your early years, is that right? Was he your main influence on your sales training?

Yes, he was significant. Stephen took the whole company to one of his seminars, and I bought his tapes and books on my own. I couldn't really afford them. I was making $18,000 and had to put them on my credit card. But I still use things today that I learned from those cassettes. It was the first of many self-improvement investments I've made over my 39-year career, and I'm still learning.

Would you recommend that same approach of continuous learning and self-investment to young people starting in the industry today?

Absolutely. A lot of people think, "Okay, I graduated from college, I'm good. I just need to learn my field." Then they're in it for five years and think they know everything. But we can always learn, and if we stop learning, we coast, and coasting in a wagon goes downhill. You can learn from podcasts, books, conferences, masterminds, or your peers. Learning is part of life. If you're not learning, you're dying.

You mentioned you had some memorable deals in those early years. Can you share one?

We had this hospital deal for an 18,000-square-foot second floor space. In retail, you don't typically build second floors unless you're in downtown Miami with 2 million people. It was a greedy developer's mistake. They told me not to worry about that space and focus on the ground floor. Then Bethesda Hospital Systems called, looking for suburban space for MRIs and physical therapy.

The negotiations went on forever. My bosses and owners kept calling, "Is it done? Is it done?" They kept coming back with more requirements or saying they needed board approval. One day, I just called the guy and asked, "What would it take for us to get this done in the next couple weeks?" I was thinking maybe we'd need to drop the rent a dollar or five dollars.

He said if we could drop the rent from $9.75 to $9.35 (per square foot) and give them another $25,000 in tenant improvement dollars, they'd sign next week. It was such a no-brainer. I said I'd check with my boss, though I knew we'd do it. We called back, said yes, and signed two weeks later. It was a huge deal for me. 18,000 square feet was huge. My first couple of years in the business, I was on the front page of the Boynton newspaper.

But the most important thing was that nobody told me to ask that question. I don't know how it came to me, but I'll never forget it: "What would it take to get this done?" It became a great lesson, and I've used it throughout my career.

That was such a great instinct. Did you end up learning other techniques from people like Tom Hopkins, or was this something you developed through experience?

Both. I learned from Tom Hopkins, from Donna, and especially from Stephen, but mostly by doing. In 1990, we had a property that had lost tons of square footage. The previous year, the developer had given full build-outs, no guarantees, and a year of free rent. When tenants had to start paying, 50 percent moved out—200,000 square feet. They fired that partner and brought me in because I had a reputation as the rock-star leasing agent who could fix it.

For six months, I couldn't lease anything. I'd go in crying to Stephen every day, saying I couldn't do it anymore. I had binders and binders of prospects. I was canvassing 80 to 100 people a day, with no results.

Stephen just kept saying, "You're doing the right thing, keep doing it." After six months, we did our first deal. Then in the next six months, I signed 50,000 square feet of leases. That's when I learned about compounding effort and the importance of persistence. It was my first time making $100,000 in a year.

I would get to the office around 8:00 a.m., leave at 10:00 a.m. when stores opened, canvass until 4:00 p.m., then come back and do cold calls. You had to get the reps in. That experience taught me more than anything else could have.

By this point, you had established yourself as a successful leasing agent at Terranova. What led to the discussion about you potentially taking on the role of president, and what were your initial thoughts about this career shift?

By that time I had been promoted to an executive position, but it wasn't something I wanted anymore. Stephen was pushing me to be president, but I actually wanted to have a baby. I'd been married eleven years with no baby, and the doctor said I was under too much stress and pressure. So I actually quit the executive position and went back to being a leasing agent for a year. I gave up all my responsibilities, took two days off a week to decorate my new house, and tried to reduce stress. No baby came, and I got bored.

Then Stephen was offered a bunch of money to buy gas stations around the country. The only way they'd do the deal was if he stepped down from Terranova, which meant he needed a president. He came to me and my husband and said, "Can you come be president? You only have to do it for two years, and at the end, you'll have a great bonus." I thought I could do anything for two years, and since it looked like we weren't going to have kids, I agreed. Six months into the job, I found out I was pregnant. I ended up staying president for six years.

Why did you ultimately decide to step down?

I was the last mom at a Halloween party when my son was four. He kept asking, "Mom, you're gonna come to the party, right?" I promised I would. I left on time, but when you're president, you have a bunch of employees following you down the elevator, talking to you at your car. When I finally got there, he was at the window looking for me. There was no one left except him and the teacher. I missed the whole party. "Mom, you promised." It was heartbreaking.

I had a live-in nanny. I'd rush home, and she'd be shaking her head. He'd been sleeping for hours. Others I've known have had terrible relationships with their kids, and I said, "That is not going to be me." I loved my job, I loved him, I loved the people, but my son had to be number one.

So you made the difficult decision to leave Terranova for your family. What was your next move?

I became a T-ball coach and went back to college. My mom had passed away in August 2003, and on her deathbed, she asked me to finish my degree. So I quit in February 2004, became the room mom for kindergarten, and started investigating how to get my Florida State diploma. I was a huge FSU alum. I'd donated money, was involved in everything, but no one knew I didn't have my degree. I got it in 2005, so I started in '78 and finished in '05. Probably the longest-running student.

About six to nine months into semi-retirement, I knew I wanted to buy properties on my own. I'd been an LP with Stephen on seven deals, so I thought I could GP* my own deals. Then I got a call from a public company in Detroit asking if I'd train their new leasing agents. That created this whole training business I never envisioned.

I actually interviewed with companies, thinking I'd be a director of leasing working 30 hours a week. But no one wanted part-time. It was all or nothing. If that was the case, I might as well have stayed at Terranova.

---

* **LP** (Limited Partner) and **GP** (General Partner): In real estate, LPs invest capital with limited control and liability. GPs manage the deal, make decisions, and take on more responsibility and risk.

I never wanted my own thing, but things happen. Your kids come first, and you do things out of necessity.

After focusing on family for a while, you eventually got back into deals. I understand your first independent one was quite successful?

Yes, it was an outparcel that Terranova had passed on for being too small. Six months after I left, I saw it was still available. I bought it, raised money, and we made 299 percent on our money in two and a half years.

But getting there wasn't simple. First, the appraisal didn't match. The bank said they couldn't finance it because the appraiser didn't do enough due diligence. I had to start all over, raising about $600,000 for a $1.2 million deal.

Then came the Walgreens complication. I was literally three months into the deal when I woke up in a cold sweat realizing Publix probably had a pharmacy exclusive. I called my partner and discovered the lease indeed had that restriction. So I had to call Walgreens and tell them we couldn't do the deal. They were furious, having already spent legal fees.

But I wasn't giving up. I called Publix and asked if we could pay for a waiver. They said yes. I negotiated with Walgreens and we each agreed to pay an amount to Publix to get the waiver. Then I discovered we needed approvals from nine other property owners.

My attorney said, "Just give it up. You'll never get those approvals." But that was like waving a red flag at me. I ended up getting seven approvals for free and negotiating reasonable terms for the other two.

In the middle of doing the deal, the developer for the Walgreens tells us they wanted to buy the property instead of doing a ground lease. We were planning to hold this forever, but for a ridiculously good price, we'd sell. So we negotiated a great price and made 299 percent on our money.

Then, right before closing, the title work showed that a utility company had a transformer improperly located on the property. I literally sat at their office with cupcakes for two days until a utility guy came in and I convinced them to move it.

I learned so much from that deal. Being a GP is completely different from being an LP. You're signing the debt, finding the debt, raising money, all things I'd never done before. It was night and day going from LP to GP. In my ego and confidence, I thought I'd done it seven times, no problem. But it was very different.

This experience taught me that persistence and creative problem-solving are key in commercial real estate. Every obstacle is just another opportunity to find a solution.

Did your experience pitching to pension funds help with raising money?

Actually, being a rockstar leasing agent helped more. Everyone knew I was good at leasing, so if they were investing in something that needed to be leased, they trusted me. My second deal was $22 million with Blackrock as my partner. I put in $125,000 with a partner matching that, Blackrock put in $6 million, and we assumed $16 million in debt. They did it because they'd been my client at Terranova, they knew my leasing capabilities.

You've mentioned that understanding tenant mix is crucial for shopping center success. Could you walk us through this concept, particularly regarding strategic placement like elbow spaces and caps?

Most tenants want visibility and signage to bring people in. In a U-shaped shopping center, the two corners are called elbows. You have impulse tenants versus destination tenants. An impulse tenant might be ice cream. You're driving by and think, "Let's get ice cream." They need to be in impulse spaces. The elbows are for destination tenants like daycares. People will bypass fifty daycares to go to their daughter's daycare.

This is called tenant mix, and understanding it is crucial. As a new leasing agent, if a daycare calls and you have an end cap space available, you might be excited just to lease the space. But if you put the daycare in the end cap, when an ice cream place calls, they won't go in the elbow, while the daycare could have. You end up running out of good spaces. I'd say 90 percent of vacancy in shopping centers across the United States is in the elbows.

Are you surprised how often these mistakes happen?

No, because there's a lack of training. Most people fall into this business by accident. I'm one of the only trainers in the country for retail real estate. There are trainers for office leasing and investment sales, but no one teaches shopping center leasing. There's one woman now starting an internship program with about fifty kids, which is great, but I've been the only trainer for thirty years.

Let's talk about development. You've mentioned you'd never want to do it again?

I'm actually in the middle of a second one, and I almost did a third even though I've sworn it off three times. I keep seeing opportunities. I just lost a deal with an empty Wells Fargo. Everyone wanted to be there, but you can't fight the city. They were going to charge half a million dollars for traffic and water impact fees. It's basically raising taxes without legislation. Then there's the 18 months for them to approve the use change, and my land use attorney wasn't even sure they'd approve it after that.

Development has so many moving pieces. It's just easier to take a shopping center and lease space. When you buy an existing center and fill vacancies, the city's not much involved. But with development, you're not cash flowing. You buy an empty bank, there's no cash for three years while you're funding all expenses.

Did that give you a new perspective on developers?

Absolutely. It's incredibly risky. You're signing on everything. I think development in South Florida is dead for the next three to five years unless you already have a shovel in the ground. You can't get loans, the cities are awful, construction costs are double, nothing makes sense. Which is actually great for those of us who own shopping centers, because that means our rents will go up.

Do you get involved with city politics or planning meetings?

Only when I need them, like when I have an application. I've never wanted to sit on any boards. Politics isn't my thing. I have no patience for it.

Let's talk about one of your most unique current projects, the Cleveland mall. This seems quite different from your typical focus. What attracted you to this opportunity, and how did it come about?

They called and said, "We want you to lease out this mall." I said, "Mall in Cleveland? I don't do malls. I don't know anything about malls." Then they mentioned Dan Gilbert owns it. He owns the Cleveland Cavaliers. Initially, they only wanted me for six months to fill up a bunch of vacancies. That was to help revitalize the mall prior to the NBA All-Star weekend. They'd heard me on Clubhouse where I was matching landlords and tenants during COVID.

They flew me up to see the mall. It was beautiful. They just wanted five or six tenants in the food court. I ended up doing 26 deals in six months, and they asked me to stay. It's been two and a half years now. I love it.

Do you often do leasing out of state?

I get offered to, but I never take it. Cleveland was unique. They put me under contract, pay me a monthly fee, plus I spend three to four days a month there. I've met with over 3000 Cleveland business tenants. They call me the mayor.

So you canvassed Cleveland like you would anywhere else?

Yes, and this story shows that even at 63, I could go somewhere where no one knew me and make it work. People in my training classes would say, "Of course you're successful in South Florida, you've been there 30 years, everyone knows you." But I went to Cleveland where I knew nobody, doing one-year and two-year deals where tenant rep brokers weren't interested, zero sign calls, and I had to knock on doors like I'd been teaching for 30 years. I've signed 49 leases.

Originally, I started going after the best operators in each category. The best nail salon, the best liquor store, the best pizza place. But they were upscale businesses, and they'd say, "You couldn't pay me a million dollars to go downtown." Then the Cavs' DJ posted on Instagram asking if people would want to open a business in Tower City. Of the 300 comments, 200 were "hell no" and 100 were "yes." I went through every "yes" and met those people.

I realized African American businesses would be our target because they rarely get opportunities. We offered $1,000 a month including utilities, which was unheard of. Of the forty-nine leases I've signed, forty-five are Black-owned businesses.

Building trust took time. I had to keep showing up. I just signed a deal with someone I'd visited twenty times. He has three stores in another mall, and I kept saying, "Just do a holiday pop-up." Finally, he agreed to try it for $500. Then I found out he hadn't had air conditioning in his other stores for six months. Now he's moving all three stores to my mall.

What's your approach to pop-ups?

It's about getting their attention. I tell them, "If you have staff and merchandise, you can do a pop-up. I'm only charging $500 for November-December, and I'm spending half a million on Christmas events. What do you have to lose?" During COVID, staffing was impossible, but now that's changed.

You have to keep following up. I had a bridal salon where I'd dropped off flyers, emailed, DM'd. Nothing. Then one day, on my twelfth attempt, I ran into the owner. She said, "Oh my God, my lease is up in October, I'd love to talk!" She hadn't gotten the flyers, and thought my DMs were scams. If I'd given up after six months, I would have missed that deal.

She never said no, she just hadn't connected. That was a valuable lesson. Now that pop-up is a two-year lease. You have to get their attention, then you can talk to them.

Your success with the Cleveland project shows how retail real estate continues to evolve. Having experienced multiple economic cycles throughout your career—the dot-com bust, GFC, COVID, and now what's happening with credit markets—how does the current market environment compare to previous challenges you've faced?

This one is the strangest I've experienced. Tenant sales are everything to me. They're my early warning system. Usually, I know problems are coming when I see sales dropping and rent delinquencies following. We have none of that right now. For the last few years, I've been telling people we're not having a recession, I've seen no signs of it. My tenant sales have never been stronger.

That tells me the consumer is still healthy. Yes, if people have to start paying their student debt again or can't refinance their mortgages because of rates, that could change. But right now, in my area of South Florida, tenant sales are incredibly strong. The Wall Street Journal just wrote about consumers still spending. I could have told you that. When you have 100 tenants giving you sales data, you have a good pulse on what's happening.

The strange part is I can't do deals right now. I want to expand and help my women friends invest, but it's impossible. The cities are charging huge impact fees, construction costs have doubled, and interest rates are high. Nothing makes sense.

I think there's going to be brokerage mergers and layoffs. I'm hearing numbers like 80 percent down in investment sale transactions. I have friends in development I've been warning for a year or two about their jobs being at risk. A year ago, they said, "No, we're good," but now they're saying, "Oh crap, I'm going to be out of work."

What's happening with tenants in this market?

Right now, landlords have the strength. Tenants are doing things I've never seen in my career. National tenants are doing annual increases, which is unheard of. Typically, they do no bumps for five years. They say they'll pay 10 percent in the fifth year, which means 2 percent annually. The average local tenant will pay 5 percent annually. But nationals are credit tenants who draw traffic and spend on marketing, so there's usually give and take.

But there's no supply now, they can't move anywhere else. Tenants are calling me asking about spaces coming up in 2028. I tell them if I had anything, I wouldn't be negotiating for 2028 now. It's a totally different market.

You mentioned you get insights from tenant sales data. Is that why it's part of your deals?

I won't do a deal without it. I want to know if they're hurting so I can prepare for potential vacancy. I tell tenants, "Your business might be worth a million dollars, but this is a $30 million shopping center. You're a cog in this wheel, and I need intelligence on all the parts."

Local tenants might underreport. If some store says they're doing $1.2 million, they might actually be doing $1.8 million. That's fine. Some nationals like Starbucks won't give sales. But tenants with kick-out clauses have to provide sales because we need to know if they're hitting their targets.

When you get financing or sell an asset, retail companies are assigned cap rates based on the security of their rent payment. Is Starbucks' rent payment more secure than the local coffee shop? Yes, by several cap rate points. But I've been able to convince bankers to lower cap rates on local tenants by showing their occupancy costs.*

Speaking of tenant sales data, this reminds me of a great story you told about a hobby store during COVID. Could you share that experience and how it illustrates the importance of understanding your market?

I love this story. During COVID in Florida, I saw an opportunity. With supply chain issues, Amazon backed up, and Toys R Us closed, I knew parents were going to overpay and overbuy for Christmas. They'd had a year of no birthday parties, no graduation parties. All these parents are feeling guilt. And the last-minute shoppers wouldn't be able to rely on Amazon.

I decided I needed a pop-up toy store in my little strip center. Pop-ups aren't really a thing in strip centers. They're more for malls and lifestyle centers. But I don't care. I said I needed a pop-up. I visited all twelve toy stores in South Florida, DM'ing them: "Would you consider a pop-up, free rent October-November-December, in my strip center in Davie, Florida across from Nova University?"

Most said they didn't have enough staff, but I found a hobby store. They didn't even have an Instagram page, so I had to use their website contact form, which I never do. About a week later, someone called, skeptical: "What's the catch?" I told them, "No catch. I'd love it if you come, do great, and sign a lease, but if you don't, it's no problem." I explained my prediction for Christmas retail.

They came to see the space around 7 p.m. one night after closing their store. The wife was pregnant, and they absolutely weren't trusting me. I

* **Occupancy Costs:** Total rent, taxes, insurance, and CAM fees paid by a tenant, often expressed as a percentage of sales in retail.

told them to call Brett, my Canes Wear tenant who had started at 1,100 square feet and was now in 4,500. After Brett vouched for me, they signed up.

They'd actually just had a fire at one of their two locations and were looking for another spot. It was just kismet. They moved in October 15th, did $80,000 in two weeks. Then $130,000 in November, $280,000 in December. They signed a five-year lease and now they're doing over a million dollars in my shopping center.

The location was perfect. Davie has high income people, high disposable income, and we're on a street with 75,000 cars. We're by a hospital and university, so we have good daytime population and suburban population. Plus, 300,000 people moved here from New York and California who think our housing prices are a bargain. They're coming in shelling out money.

They've now closed their Weston location because mine was doing so much better. Why have two stores when one was doing $300,000 and mine was doing a million? They love me, I love them, and now they're my walking billboard. When I'm showing space to prospects who are hesitant, I have them talk to Leo, the owner. Because if I say it, it's just a sales pitch. You need someone else to say it.

That's such a great example of a brick-and-mortar not only surviving but thriving. It really pushes back on the idea that retail is dying. What's your take on the e-commerce versus brick-and-mortar debate?

Everyone thinks retail is dead and everything's online. When I speak to audiences and ask what percentage of retail is online, they yell out "80 percent!" or "60 percent!" The reality? It's 16.4 percent. Even at the height of "retail is dead," the prediction was 30 percent. Now we're seeing all these direct-to-consumer brands opening stores—Warby Parker, Bose, Wayfair. They've realized it's cheaper to open stores than pay for online customer acquisition.

COVID actually helped brick-and-mortar. People realized they want physical interaction. Online retailers aren't making money with shipping and returns. I'm comfortable if 30 percent goes online. That leaves 70 percent for brick-and-mortar. But I don't think it'll get there.

When I first started, we'd have three or four shoe stores to choose from. Now it's just DSW. Payless is gone. All these stores went out of business because of Amazon. The number one use in demand now in South Florida is restaurants, but the city restricts how many you can have in a center because of parking concerns.

You've talked about your passion for teaching others in the industry. How has your training business adapted to current market conditions?

It's actually slow right now because there's no vacancy. No one needs to learn how to fill vacancy when occupancies are through the roof.

The calls are just coming in left and right from tenants. It's the weirdest time. We have a healthy consumer, more tenant demand than ever, but we can't build or do deals.

For people with cash, there will be opportunities when refinancing gets tough. Some owners have variable-rate loans, so their rates are already going up. They're not distributing to their partners. Others have balloon notes where they had 3 percent loans and now face 8 percent. They're not going to walk away, but those deals will be available for people with cash.

My parents paid an 18 percent mortgage, so at some point, we'll adjust to 7 percent. I believe we'll adjust. I think we've been in an anomaly for many years. But we're not there yet. The rents are going to have to go up. Even when I had a Mexican restaurant willing to pay $100 per square foot, the deal didn't work. Maybe at $150 it could have worked, if I had certainty from the city.

You've built a reputation not just as a successful real estate professional but as someone who actively builds communities within

the industry. Could you share your philosophy on creating and nurturing professional groups?

I create all kinds of events. Women's events, young people events, FSU events, sons of friends events. I just believe in bringing people together. Recently, there were three women in our industry who are big foodies and always posting about restaurants. I kept saying, "You guys need to do a supper club," but they ignored me. So I started posting about "the next supper club," and suddenly people were interested. Now we've had thirteen supper clubs, and it's fabulous. We limit it to ten to fifteen people, everyone contributes, and we try great new restaurants in Miami.

There was also this young woman who was new in the business and going to ICSC* Orlando. She called asking what I was doing Monday night, and I had to tell her I had a client dinner planned for weeks. She said everyone she called was busy with client dinners. But instead of giving up, she thought, "I bet there are other newbies having this problem." She called me back a week later saying, "I'm having dinner with thirty-two people!" She had called every new person she knew and told them to call other newbies. She found a place with a private room and made gift bags. Now those thirty-two people know her because she coordinated it. She solved a problem for them all.

What advice do you have for people trying to break into the industry and get real-world exposure early on?

I tell students to say, "Can I shadow you or someone on your team for a couple hours?" Not a week, not a day. A couple hours. That takes the pressure off the person you're asking. Google everyone who went to your school who's in real estate. If you Google 50 people, you'll get five shadows over Christmas break.

Then have a second page to your resume. If you're a sophomore and you do five shadows every Christmas break, five every spring break, plus

---

* **ICSC**: A global trade organization for the retail real estate industry.

summer internships where you get Friday afternoons off to shadow. Now you have 30 shadows on your resume. When I'm interviewing five people and this kid has shadowed in self-storage, multifamily, retail, office, across multiple cities, I'm going to want to talk to them!

But I tell 100 students this a year and maybe one does it. Usually they call me saying, "I graduated three months ago and haven't found a job yet. What's your advice?" I say take two months to shadow. They say, "No, no, I need a job." This IS how you get a job. I just did ten mock interviews where I asked what asset class they wanted to go into, and they said "commercial." They didn't even know what asset class meant. They'd learn this and much more with shadowing.

What about the sons' group you mentioned?

One day I realized I kept meeting sons of people in the industry. I had an intern count how many sons we knew. It was forty-seven. I invited them to lunch, and thirty showed up. I told them, "You guys have something unique in common. Your dads are all in the business. This could really help you." I hosted the lunch and said someone needed to take it over. Two of them did it for about six months. They did poker thing, a fishing thing, but it died off.

Recently, I had two new interns, one was a son, and I told them about what we'd done years ago. They loved it and started it up again. Now they're including daughters too, since more young women are coming into the business. They have people all around the country. Every time I meet a son or daughter in the business, I tell them about it. They mostly have Zoom meetings, but they did an event at ICSC in Orlando and Vegas.

How do you handle competitors working together?

I was just in Wyoming with an attorney and a residential realtor. They were shocked when I asked if they ever have lunches with competitors. The attorney said, "Never." I explained that our women's retreat started with four direct competitors twenty years ago. When we're competing for the same account, we don't talk about it. But there are 40 other things we can discuss.

Both of them looked at me like I was crazy until I pointed out they were sitting in a room full of competing tenant rep brokers and landlords. The level of competition in the room was intense, but you put that aside and be discreet. There's so much we can learn from each other. I told them to think about it. Why couldn't four or five women from competing law firms have lunch? They could talk about being a mom and working, continuing education, the partnership process. There's so much to discuss beyond competitive deals.

I believe in sharing. You have to put competition aside sometimes to grow.

You've built such strong networks both in person and online. How has social media changed the way you approach business and relationships in commercial real estate?

Social media is absolutely essential now. Eight years ago, I wasn't on any platform, not even Facebook. An intern introduced me to Facebook prospecting, and now it's a huge part of my business. I started realizing I could impact people with my training advice through social media without them hiring me.

The key thing in our business is "it's not who you know, it's who knows you." Even college students can use it effectively. There's an FSU student who connects with industry leaders like Bob Knakal through social media. I had a young professional ask me what he could post when he couldn't talk about deals. I said, "What's your passion?" He liked reading books, so I suggested he post book reviews from a newbie leasing agent's perspective. He called it "Tuesdays with Tim" and built 20,000 followers.

It takes hard work to be consistent and creativity to stand out. A lot of people are insecure about putting things out there. They worry what people will say. I don't care. I'll talk to friends and say, "You could do a post about this, this, and this" just from a 30-minute conversation. But it takes a different mindset.

How did you end up on Twitter?

Strip Mall Guy influenced that. One day my phone started blowing up with Twitter followers, and my son asked what was happening. This anonymous account had said, "We need more Beths on here." I DM'd him asking who he was and why he wanted me on Twitter. He said we were of the same brain. We'd both been investing in strip malls since the '90s. We eventually met at ICSC in New York.

He kept pushing me to join Twitter. I finally did, and my first post about a bridal salon deal in Cleveland got one hundred eighty-five thousand views. I started getting consulting gigs and made more money in three months on Twitter than in eight years on LinkedIn. Now I primarily post on Twitter and have someone repost that content to other platforms.

What's your approach to mentoring?

I don't do formal mentoring, but I'm happy to jump on calls. I tell people I can do 20 to 30 minutes on Saturday mornings at 7:30 to 8:00 a.m. Most people respond by saying they can't do 7:30. Can we do Monday at 10? I say no, I'm working then. I reserve Saturday mornings for people to "pick my brain."

And as I mentioned before, I tell students to shadow professionals.

You've shared so many insights about your journey and the industry. What final advice would you give to people wanting to get into commercial real estate?

For young people interested in commercial real estate, I tell them to watch my free YouTube videos first. Then I ask if they're analytical or sales-oriented, because our industry breaks down into those two aspects. You're either an underwriter/analyst or you're in sales/leasing. Right now, if you want to get into commercial real estate sales, you've got to be ready to knock on a lot of doors. In my early career, I did eighty a day.

There are a lot of different areas, but you have to shadow and narrow down what fits you. Cities, large companies, small companies. Shadowing is the best way to figure out if it's something you like. Like I tell students, take advantage of Christmas break, spring break, summer internships. Build up those experiences and relationships. The opportunities are there, but you have to put in the work to find them.

Beth's career has made her an expert in retail shopping centers, but her role defies easy categorization. Known as "The Canvassing Queen," she has leased millions of square feet, developed shopping centers, built a portfolio of four centers worth $80 million as a general partner, and created training programs that have shaped countless real estate careers.

Her playbook offers actionable advice for anyone in commercial real estate: track tenant sales data as your economic compass; embrace tenacious follow-up—she's visited some prospects twenty times before landing a deal; and never hesitate to ask directly, "What would it take to get this done?" When she stepped down as Terranova's president to focus on family, it was a mindful recalibration that eventually led to greater independence.

Talk to Beth about brick-and-mortar retail, and she'll quickly challenge popular narratives with hard data. "Everyone thinks retail is dead and everything's online," she told me. "When I speak to audiences and ask what percentage of retail is online, they yell out '80 percent!' or '60 percent!' The reality? It's 16.4 percent. Even at the height of 'retail is dead,' the prediction was 30 percent." Her leasing approach goes beyond filling vacancies. She evaluates whether businesses are impulse-driven or destination-based, analyzes co-tenancy requirements, maps demographic needs, and scrutinizes space configurations. This meticulous matching process has maintained high occupancy rates even in locations others had written off.

One figure Beth cites drives much of her work: independent women represent just 1.5 percent of commercial real estate investors. Through her conferences, she showcases successful women in the industry, creating opportunities for newcomers to build concrete connections. Her mission is to grow that figure to 10 percent before she turns 70.

Beth keeps building connections. From Cleveland mall tenants, to industry supper clubs, to the networking programs she leads. Her approach hasn't wavered: match the right tenants to the right spaces, follow up until you get an answer, and cultivate relationships that matter. These fundamentals transformed her from a new leasing agent making $18,000 at Terranova into an established industry leader with an $80 million portfolio and a legacy of professionals she's guided along the way.

Connect

- Website: bethazor.com
- X: @Bethazor1
- YouTube: youtube.com/@bazor1005
- LinkedIn: Beth Azor

Part Two
Private Equity Investors

Look behind major real estate deals and you'll find these market strategists. They pool capital from institutional investors and wealthy individuals to reshape property portfolios. Their work goes beyond simple acquisitions to transform assets through careful planning and execution. Their firms become active players in their chosen markets. They identify underperforming properties that others miss, implement operational improvements to boost performance, and time their exits to maximize returns.

Their work spans every property type, from office towers to industrial parks. The investors in the coming chapters navigate a challenging balancing act by generating strong returns through financial structuring while managing market volatility. They combine data analysis with relationship-building, constantly evaluating risks against opportunities as markets cycle through growth and contraction phases.

Chris Powers

Founder and Executive Chairman, Fort Capital

Fort Worth, TX

- Founded Fort Capital, a private equity real estate firm specializing in Class B industrial properties, now managing over $1.2 billion in assets across Texas and the Southeast.
- Together with his team, created the Fort Operating System, a proprietary AI software that streamlines property management, improving efficiency and tenant retention.
- Assembled and transformed Fort Worth's River District through 80 different property acquisitions totaling 90 acres, creating a thriving area with over 2,000 multifamily units and commercial spaces.
- Built a substantial real estate portfolio beginning at age 17, acquiring 12 properties around Texas Christian University as a college student and executing a multi-million-dollar land deal by age 23.
- Hosts *The Fort Podcast*, a widely respected show with over 2 million downloads that offers candid, strategy-rich conversations with top executives and entrepreneurs across real estate and business.

Chris Powers makes you believe anything is possible. It's not just his clear thinking or business savvy that strikes you. It's how he carries himself. Humble. Down-to-earth. Genuinely encouraging.

As founder and chairman of Fort Capital, Chris has built a private equity real estate firm in Fort Worth that's redefined how industrial properties are managed across the Sunbelt. With over $1.2 billion in assets, Fort Capital acquires Class B industrial properties and transforms them through systems that few competitors can match.

Chris stumbled into real estate during his freshman year at Texas Christian University (TCU). He'd started college early at 17 and found himself surrounded by wealthier peers. After reading about a fellow student investing in rentals, Chris tracked him down. The meeting changed everything. The student explained how to buy properties with minimal down payment using what were then called NINJA loans—no income, no job, no asset verification required. By sophomore year, Chris had twelve properties around campus and over $100,000 in the bank.

Then 2008 hit. While his student rentals stayed stable, Chris watched the broader market implode. That collapse shaped his approach to risk, instilling a vigilance that still drives his daily decisions.

After several successful development projects, including helping shape Fort Worth's River District, Chris partnered with Jason Baxter in 2014. By 2016, they faced a critical decision: continue doing one-off deals or build something more intentional and scalable. As Chris puts it, committing to a clear focus is among the hardest things to do in business.

That commitment led to the Fort Operating System, a proprietary framework with AI at its core, designed to make property management incredibly efficient through automation and standardized processes. The system allows a lean team to manage an expanding portfolio while keeping tenants happy.

In 2021, Chris stepped back from the CEO role, recognizing that Jason's operational strengths complemented his own visionary tendencies. He stayed involved as Chairman, and the handoff became a catalyst, unleashing new growth and profitability.

Visit Chris at Fort Capital's offices and you'll learn about both the man and his philosophy. His workspace tells the story: professional Zoom setup and standing desk on one side, his kids' artwork proudly displayed on the other. That same balance shows up in the book collection he shares annually with friends, colleagues, and investors. From day one of this project, Chris has been one of its strongest champions, giving time and energy freely, embodying the mentorship philosophy you'll hear throughout our conversation.

In this interview, Chris talks about his journey from college entrepreneur to industry leader, the turning points that shaped Fort Capital's evolution, and where he sees both the company and the market heading next.

Date of Interview: November 3, 2023

Fort Capital invests in industrial real estate throughout Texas and has expanded to the Southeast. How are things looking for the company's future right now?

They're good. A lot of people get into this business to do deals. And doing deals is great, but what makes a deal great is being able to operate it really well. What tends to happen is as companies get larger, and they're not focused on operations, they're still doing deals, but now they're operating each deal with a little bit less quality than they were. Then if you get two, three, four, and you're not looking through the lens of how to maintain the best operations at every price at every property, no matter how large you are, you start taking your eye off the ball.

The second part is we've been living in basically a free money interest rate environment for the last ten or fifteen years. I think everyone got used to it, but now the wool has been pulled back again. Sam Zell said something last year, I got to see him speak about three months before he died, and he just said, look, when you're in a zero-interest rate environment, you don't have to operate as well. You can get away with a lot of mistakes because money is free. It doesn't cost anything. But we're heading back into a world where money isn't free. It's now getting expensive. And that inherently is correlated with you better be operating really, really well.

And so one of the things I'm really proud about our company is we started beating this drum in 2016, we said this mission statement: We want to be the best real estate operator in the world. What does that mean? We want to operate our assets really well. We want to operate our company really well. You could say, "Well, what is operating?" It's managing your assets, it's managing your revenue, it's managing your costs, it's managing your overhead. Not just at the property level, but at the company level.

You started when you were 17 years old, back around 2004. So you went through a cycle where you were getting these free NINJA loans*. And then you went through the GFC. Do you think your experience starting in the early 2000s and then going through the GFC made you consider the possibility of another downturn more?

One thousand percent. To be fair, when '08 hit, I owned twelve properties around TCU. All student rentals at a thriving Texas university. I didn't actually feel the pain in my portfolio. I'll tell you the one thing I remember the most, which was the point that I knew something was off. And you have to remember, this was '08, social media wasn't really a big thing yet. People weren't staring at their iPhones all day and you weren't being blasted by media. I walked into my finance class one day, and my professor was crying hysterically. A grown man in his sixties, he had virtually lost 70 percent of his net worth. I think this was the day Lehman failed. And that's when I knew something was off and that's what made me get kind of more interested in what was going on.

Now, what I would tell you is, by luck, I had gotten a line of credit that was tied to all my properties. All I really did was buy foreclosed properties. And everything was a foreclosure. I don't have the scars of having a portfolio that was dragging me down, but I do have the scars of two to three years where we were buying residential houses for 30,000 bucks which had sold for $125,000 the year before. I mean, that seems crazy to people, but it was happening.

I would tell you, I still have this thought every day I wake up, that today could be the day that something happens. And so I think we make investment decisions like that. Because, again, I'm playing a multi-generational game. I'm playing 'til I'm 90. But yeah, I think those two or three years coming out of the GFC were some of the—nobody's really asked me that before. But yeah, I would tell you I err on the side of conservative to the point where I've missed out on a lot of this bull run.

---

* **NINJA Loan** (No Income, No Job, and No Assets): Mortgages issued to borrowers with little or no verified financial qualifications, often associated with higher risk.

Let's go back to the beginning. How did you get started in business?

I was motivated. I entered college having already had entrepreneurial opportunities throughout high school. Mowing lawns, washing cars, and a couple other things. I was very money driven back then.

So you were one of those kids in high school that was working and hustling.

For sure. I was making bucks. Then I got to TCU, which is a private university with a lot of wealthy children and a lot of wealthy people. And I was not wealthy. So a lot of my motivation was I needed money to do things with people at school. I was at a place where people were flying private home for Thanksgiving, so it quickly became very obvious to me.

I had seen enough to know if I was going to hang out with these people that I'm surrounding myself with, I need to figure out a way to make money. Thank God I picked up a newspaper one day. This guy, who's still a great friend of mine, Alex, had just won entrepreneur of the year. This is back in '04 and he was buying rental houses.

Did you know him already?

No. He had been on the TCU football team. He had gotten his scholarship kicked, and he was going to have to leave, and he figured out how to start buying rental houses with NINJA loans. He was buying lots of houses. I took him to lunch and asked, "How are you doing this?" He said, "This is how you're going to do it. Owning a rental house is not complicated. You got to find a good location and buy it. You have expenses, and you have to rent the place. The houses need to have three bedrooms and two baths so you can get $1500 a month in rent, 500 bucks a bedroom. And you can do all this without putting any money down." Basically, that's it.

Were you like, no way?

It wasn't really a "no way" thing. I didn't have anything to compare it against, so I just didn't know. He told me, "You're gonna go to Countrywide Home Loans, tell them that you're going to make 100 grand this year." It was no stated income at the time, which is what caused the collapse. They'd say, "Well, how are you going to make your 100 grand?" And I would say, "Because I'm gonna buy these houses, and I'm gonna flip 'em." They'd be like, "Oh, ok." And boom, you're off to the races.

You didn't need a sponsor or a co-signer?

No. Nothing. 3 percent down, 6 percent cash back at closing. It was a home equity loan so that you could do repairs, which needed to be done, but basically, you left closing with cash in your pocket.

That's incredible.

Now the crazy part is then you would go get it leased. So you'd buy a house for like $110,000, get it leased, take it back to the bank, and then it was worth $150,000. You could re-fi and pull that cash out. And that's when the light bulb went off.

By the end of sophomore year, I had over $100,000 of cash in the bank. I was still so naive. I thought I was making money. All I was really doing was just borrowing more as I was taking on more debt.

But now you have cash flow.

For sure. And then I got good at it. I figured out how to turn a living room into another bedroom and get another 600 bucks a month. I eventually started a property management and leasing company. But there was never this mission to become a real estate guy long-term. I truly believed I was going to get into investment banking on Wall Street.

Did you know about private equity real estate at this point?

What you're going to know by the end of this interview is my life is characterized by great people that wanted to help me succeed. Unequivocally across the board. I'm not self-made. I'm made by people that cared a lot about me. Now I had to do the work, and I had to figure it out, but at every point in my life I can almost tie back to somebody that helped me.

I'm from El Paso, Texas. So another guy, Meyer Marcus, was the largest real estate owner in town at the time. And his son, Ben, was my best friend. Their family owned everything in town, everything you drove by. I interned for him throughout high school. And so I never really heard of private equity until later on in college, but I did know there was this world where you could buy a lot of real estate and own it and do really well.

When did you decide you're not going into investment banking? When did that idea change?

At the time, we had a leasing business. We were the top company that leased properties to students.

But here's the crazy part. I still thought I'd go into investment banking. I started interviewing for jobs. But then it dawned on me where I was like, what am I gonna do with all this stuff? I had 12 houses. I was like, okay, I gotta figure something out.

So during the aftermath of the financial crisis, I went into partnership with Meyer Marcus who had been my mentor that owned all the stuff in El Paso. We were buying stuff that had been $120,000, for $30,000. We'd repaint it, fix it up, and list them for $89,900. That was the flavor of the day: buying foreclosures. And they were everywhere. I mean, everything was a foreclosure.

While I was flipping houses, I met a guy who's still a good friend of mine. He was buying lots, scraping them and building houses. I was making at most 20 grand on a flip. He was making $70,000 to $80,000 on a new build. I was like okay, I gotta stop doing this. I gotta start building.

And this is another common thread of how I've had partners in my life. I said, "Why don't you just move into my office? We won't partner. Let's just office together for a few months and talk and share ideas." And sure enough, about six months in we said let's partner. Then about six months in this piece of land came around. At the time, I never would have known to develop it had I not already been in the building mindset. Great location right by the business school. It was in foreclosure from a developer that had tried developing it in '08.

How did you find out about this?

By being in the dirt. Being in the trenches. This is leasing hundreds of houses. This is trying to buy hundreds of houses. This is talking to people and being immersed in real estate. I spent three or four hours every day of my life during college getting to know this tiny neighborhood around TCU. Nobody knew TCU better than I did. So you asked how did you find the land? I drove by it every day. For years. I knew there was a development that was supposed to be going on. I knew the economy had crashed and somebody had told me the seller was in a bind and needed to get out of it. I remember them saying you could probably buy this and build 16 townhomes to rent to students.

I remember thinking there's no way in hell we're gonna get this. At the time this was my biggest deal. It's a $4.5 million deal. But to me that might as well have been $100 million. The seller was a very wealthy guy and was trying to get it off his balance sheet. I called him and set up a meeting. He took me seriously, and we made a deal.

Now I had to go raise $975,000 and get a $3 million loan. So what'd I do? This goes back to my whole life has been predicated by being around the right people. By this point I had graduated from college. People knew I had success in real estate. I passed the hat around to a bunch of friends and family and raised $975,000. Then Alex comes back into the story, the guy who taught me how to buy houses. He helped me get a $3 million loan and get that deal over the goal line. This is four years after he had taught me to buy my first house.

That's incredible, and I wanted to circle back to that. Had you not looked at the newspaper that day back in college and read

about what Alex was doing, do you think you would have ended up in real estate?

That's a good question. I would just say I think the real part of the story that matters is if you really look at your life, and the things that really changed it, they're not planned out. In hindsight, it's all these little moments that shaped us that aren't the ones you think are going to shape you. So would I have not gotten into real estate? I don't really know. But it was one of the most serendipitous moments in my life. I remember just happening to look out and reading the cover and it was just a light-bulb moment.

Okay, back to that development project, was this the official beginning of Fort Capital?

This was still called Powers and Curtis. I think it was from 2009 to 2012. In that time, I think we built something like 10 homes together, and we built a few more duplexes around TCU. And then in 2012 my dad died. My partner was from a big oil family, out of north Texas, the panhandle. I think there was a pull for him to go back into the family business. It was a big year for me. It was very traumatic. It was basically like if we're gonna go get into a bunch more development deals, we're committing to like another three or four years together. We really liked each other but it was just the right time to split up.

But there's one other deal in there that I think should be talked about. It was the first time we made a million dollars each.

We were 23. And this is a crazy story. It was probably the most prolific mixed-use development that's happened in Fort Worth. Big old Class B industrial park that was totally transformed into thousands of apartments and retail and nightlife and all this stuff. We were building homes in this neighborhood. We had our deals going on at TCU. The paper was starting to show up every day that there was this new area, West 7th. And so I started driving around the neighborhood to get to know it.

I saw how the new apartments were going and saw how it was going to shake out. I went up to the city and saw how they were thinking about zoning, and I got to see their future maps of how they saw it developing over 20 years. And I went to this area that was clearly going to get developed, but it was on the edge at the time.

Where were you seeing these maps, in the city zoning office?

Yeah. Your city offers you, like, free gold. I tell people this all the time, if you're a nerd, go sit at the zoning commission just once a month. It's in a public setting. You can sit in the back, and you get to listen to developers or city people or whoever is trying to change zoning, and you get to hear their pitch while they're doing it. So a developer could be like we want multifamily and here's our project. Okay, what would you do? So right now, it's just vacant land. But if you're sitting in that room and you go oh, they're gonna zone it multifamily. He's going to build all these apartments, what might you do? Go start looking at every piece of land around there.

You and your team would go to these?

It was me and my partner or somebody from our team sitting there. It was your chance once a month to find out where the city's going or to find out why somebody wasn't getting zoning. Why things weren't going to happen.

Those years were so great, because not only was I going to zone the stuff I owned, but I was sitting there for three hours just listening and picking up on all this stuff. If somebody tells me they're serious about being a developer, and they tell me they've never gone and sat in the zoning committee, I'm like, either you don't know or you're not that serious. It's better than college.

So anyway, I was gonna buy this one-acre site and I was talking to the broker, Bruce. He said, "Before you decide, you should go talk to the old man." There was this older gentleman that had assembled twenty-six single-family homes over the past fifty years. And it was made up of about eight acres. His name was Jim.

"You should go talk to Jim about what he's gonna do with his land." He's like, "Here's this little one acre you're trying to buy, and here's Jim. Go figure out what he plans on doing with his stuff. It'll help inform what you're going to do here."

I called Jim up and he said to meet him at the Starbucks at Target the next day. I said okay. So I met him the next day. And I'm going thinking all I'm doing is hearing what he's doing with his land so I can go buy this site next to his.

And he shows up and basically gives me a full sales pitch of why I should buy his land. It was an assemblage with twenty-six rental houses that were all rented. He laid out this map and he showed me everything and he goes, "You should buy this. You shouldn't buy that."

So a totally different agenda. Were you ready to even entertain something like that?

We had our deals going on at TCU which were big, but I just thought, man, to buy a $3 million piece of land and then develop it, that's going to be like a $50 million deal. It's just a big deal. So I was like, we're not capable of that.

So I left the meeting, thanked him, and about four days went by. I don't know why I will never forget this moment. I was driving back from Dallas and there's Six Flags and for some reason right as I was driving by Six Flags, it all clicked.

It was like oh, no, you should buy Jim's site.

So I called him immediately and said, "Jim, I think you're right, I think I need to buy your site. Let's work out a deal."

All the houses on the land were rented and cash flowing, so it was basically going to be a covered land play*. I didn't even know what a covered

---

* **Covered Land Play**: A real estate investment strategy in which an investor buys property with income-generating improvements (like a building) while planning to redevelop the land later for a higher-value use.

land play was at the time. I just knew it was really good land. Development was heading straight toward it.

We bought it for $11 a foot to the dirt. And we're thinking in five years, we're gonna sell it for $23 a foot. Everybody's gonna double their money and it's almost like a guarantee because there were other sites already selling for twenty and thirty bucks a foot. We just had to wait.

We bought it, and about ninety days later, one of the largest multifamily developers in the country called us and said, "We want to buy your site."

My partner, Andrew Curtis, asked, "What do you think we should tell them we want for it, should we even tell them twenty-three bucks a foot?" We were thinking we were gonna get that in five years.

He called some people and goes, "Let's tell him 50 bucks a foot." And I was like, are you kidding me? We'll be making millions of dollars. There's no way they would go for that.

That must have felt like a moonshot.

And this is where I probably learned about negotiating. We told them fifty bucks a foot. We signed for $48 a foot.

So we bought for eleven, and ninety days later we're under contract for forty-eight. So bought for $3 million and are now under contract for $12.5 million in ninety days. I would say that was the biggest education in my career.

It took eighteen months to entitle that land. We had to get it rezoned, replanted, there was a big sewer line that ran through it that we had to get rerouted. It was a full block of houses. And then there was like another half block of houses with a public street going through it. We had to get rid of a public street.

Anyway, it took eighteen months to get everything ready. And I learned everything you could about development. I mean everything that could go wrong with a site we learned about it.

So the contingency was you had to get this entitled? Was there a time limit?

Correct, it was contingent on getting the land entitled. We thought we could do it in nine months, but we had to keep extending the contract. I've never been involved in a deal where so many things had to happen. It's one of those things where I probably would have never bought the site to begin with if I knew that we were going to have to go through all that. That was the first time I had sleepless nights.

But the payoff though, you must have been like, this is happening.

Once you see the numbers you can't unsee it. It was going to be life changing. On many multiples. All I could think about was if I get that money then I can go buy way more real estate. It was never like I'm gonna go buy a car, a house. I was like, I'm just gonna keep growing.

Another amazing thing about that deal was, I met an amazing guy, Laird, who was the buyer at Greystar. We became great friends. When I signed the contract with him to buy it, I told him, "I will sell you this land, but I've never worked for anyone before, so my one caveat is you have to teach me how you're going to buy this land." And so he was like an open book. He would say this is how we're thinking about it. He was letting me go to meetings. I'd get to see how they were planning it.

They're the buyers and he's letting you come in as a seller to all the meetings?

Yeah, and again, another guy that really helped me out. Funny story. The whole time we were under contract he'd ask, "What did you buy the land for before us?" I'd say, "I can't tell you, but here's the deal. At closing, we're gonna go to lunch, and I'll write on a piece of paper what we paid, and I'll slide it across the table." So we finally got to closing, went to lunch and I wrote it on a piece of paper. He was like, "Damn!"

I went on to sell another four sites to them. It ended up being repeat business. We learned, oh wow, big institutional capital needs land to build these big projects but they can't take the entitlement risk. They can't buy sites that aren't fully ready to go, shovel-ready. So they're willing to pay others to take that risk. And that's one way in this industry you can make big multiples on your money.

Interesting. And what a cool movie moment.

Yeah. I couldn't believe it. I remember selling it thinking those idiots aren't going to make any money, there's not a single penny left in this deal to be made. They ended up building that project and making like thirty million more dollars on top of it. But it did three things for me. It helped me make some money, gave me an education that I could have never gotten anywhere else, and it gave me a new lens to look at the world. I could think bigger. That's when I gave myself permission to start thinking much, much bigger.

Were you married at this point?

No, I met my wife in 2012. A week before my dad's bicycle accident. So my dad was in a bicycle accident riding bikes, like Lance Armstrong rides, not like motorcycles. He was with his friends. He took off from the pack, got into a terrible accident, and was airlifted. He basically lost oxygen to his brain for three minutes in the helicopter on the way to the hospital. And for forty-five days, his brain never regained function, but we just kept feeling like you would see brainwaves. Like every now and again, you'd see a blip and they basically kept him alive for forty-five days on machines until the end. My wife met my family at my dad's funeral. That's where she met my family for the first time. We had just started dating. That's part of what brought us really close. I don't know if I would have kept dating someone like she did.

Wow, what a testament to your wife, I don't know if I would have been able to do that either. Speaking of your dad, and his influence on you back in your childhood, do you think you were just

built a certain way where you wanted to mow lawns and be like that, or do you think it was the way your parents raised you that made you like that?

I did not want to do that stuff at first. It was out of necessity. I had to do it if I wanted money. It just wasn't available. And another crazy thing about my dad's story is that he was a partner at a law firm and decided at age thirty-seven he wanted to be a doctor. It was eight years later, when I was around fourteen, when he became a full-time doctor. That's after eight years of making no money. I mean anybody that's ever watched somebody become a doctor, it's brutal. And when you get out you got all these loans and everything so it's not like you're immediately out you're just living the high life, it's a grind.

Was that inspiring for you guys?

For sure. I think it's a big part of my life today. My dad did not care a lick about money. And I think that's one of the most admirable things about him. To me, money was always about freedom. It wasn't about fancy things. I don't drive a fancy car. I have no gold watch on. There's nothing super fancy and I've always treated money like it was what gave me freedom.

There's one thing about my dad. There were thousands of people at his funeral. This doctor from El Paso. There were screens in the parking lot. He was an incredible guy. Everywhere he went he was adored and liked. The medical students and residents loved him. He was like their dad. He was their classmate, but he was like their dad. And yeah, he worked really, really hard.

What an honor to have thousands of people at his funeral. I think that's what we all kind of hope to have that kind of impact.

I'm trying to say this without crying, because I think it's important.

At his funeral, the only thing I really remember from that day, it was a very emotional day. Call it serendipity. Or just a moment in life. It was one of those things you don't see coming.

He had been in the ICU for forty-five days before he passed away. So it's just an exhausting month and then we thought he would make it, and he didn't.

It was at the end when they're doing the condolences, after the services. The family kind of stands there and people walk by in a line and tell you they're sorry.

This one man came up. He was a little Mexican man. Probably in his seventies. And he said, "I'm the janitor at your dad's hospital." And I said, "Nice to meet you."

And he said he'd worked in hospitals for like forty or fifty years. He said nobody has ever cared about him more than my dad. He knew about his kids. He knew all sorts of things about him, he just cared about him. And he said it's easy in this world to not pay attention to people that are janitors. He said every day he felt important.

As I think more about my life and where I'll go with my life, that is something I'll never shake, that conversation.

Thank you for sharing that, what an experience to have gone through. And it was after that, and after the biggest deal of your life, you and your partner moved on to other things.

Yeah, so anyway, Powers and Curtis, we split up. I stay in the office. I don't really have a strategy at that point, other than I now have a million bucks in the bank. I'm twenty-four years old. I went through a transition year. It was good because from eighteen to twenty-four I had been on this mission. We had done a lot. Now I had some money in the bank and also had a lot of knowledge. During that year I just bought some land, flipped it, and just did little deals.

I renamed the company from Powers and Curtis originally to Rum Stick Capital, which was to pay respect to my dad because he grew up on this little peninsula in Rhode Island called Rum Stick Point. I thought this is how I'm gonna repay my dad. I'm gonna build this company and everybody's gonna ask. And the funny part was—I'm big into branding and marketing—people were like, is this a liquor company? Do you sell rum? And I was like, ah, shoot, this is never gonna work. So I turned it into Fort Capital after about six months. I had about a year off and then went and found another area of town.

I went and I raised $15 million at the end of 2013, early 2014, to basically go do what I had done with Greystar, which had taught me about buying in the path of growth, buying on entitled land. And I basically did this new area of town that nobody was touching. I went and bought ninety acres of land through eighty different property acquisitions, buying houses, land, commercial buildings, and assembled it all in about nine months.

I went back and I hired two guys, and talk about being in the streets. We were going door to door knocking on doors every day and every night for nine months and assembled all this land. It's now called the River District which is a thriving area of Fort Worth. It has over two thousand multifamily units, hundreds of townhomes, office buildings, and commercial. I don't ever talk about that publicly. It was a big deal for me and my career. There will just be an area of the city when my kids go to and be like, "That's dad's mixed-use deal."

When you started Fort Capital, you were by yourself, but not for long. Eventually, you partnered with Jason Baxter, who would later become CEO, so it was mainly just the two of you. Is that right? And what led you two to make the decision to focus on industrial?

I had assembled the River District. I raised $15 million to start assembling this land solo, but there was also that year gap where I was buying and flipping land. A lot of that land I was flipping was to Jason when he worked at David Weekley homes, which is the second largest privately held home builder in the country. They are an amazingly run company, they have thousands of employees. He started at the bottom and worked his way from a project manager, to sales, to a manager, to a market leader. But in doing that you go to David Weekley University, you're learning management and you're learning leadership and you're learning how to build budgets. You're learning how to run a company.

But he was really good at doing deals and he could understand if I was selling him an acre of land, he knew how much we can pay, how many units we can get on it. And so to back up a second. In 2014 he left to start doing his own deals, but him and I would also do some deals together. What did we do? Moved into an office together. He stayed in the office for like a year and was building some of his own projects. He was developing some townhomes. We were doing some deals together.

And then it just became clear near the end of that first year. I was like, why don't we just partner. We started building townhomes together all over other parts of the city. We were doing all kinds of deals. We had no strategy other than to make money. We kind of knew how to develop infill urban land and residential on a smaller scale.

And that's when at the end of 2015 it started becoming apparent. We were working really, really hard. We had so many plates spinning. We probably had seven or eight people. We didn't have culture. We didn't have processes. It was just like everybody showing up and fending for themselves every day. And so the second part you asked me why we got into industrial was, one, we needed to raise more capital on a focused strategy. Two, it's really hard to retain and hire good people when you're running kind of an indiscriminate deal shop.

They don't know what they're gonna step into every day.

Correct, so it's just war every day. And like, I enjoyed it because that's my nature, I love being at war. But most people don't. Jason was the one that recognized we needed to turn this into a real business. I think that's important. Most people in our industry never make the commitment to build a real company. They're just a bunch of guys or girls doing deals. There's nothing wrong with that. But if you want to build an enterprise that can do deals while you're asleep, there has to be a conscious decision to do that. In 2016, we read *Good to Great*. It talked about a few concepts centered around the idea of the flywheel. It talked about staying in your lane and focusing on something, and you just get better at those things every day. Then it takes less effort to move the company forward. At the time in our company, it took max effort to move the company up the field, and I just remember thinking, this can't last forever.

Anyway, I think this is where the story takes a huge pivot. When we decided to go all in on Class B industrial.

So part of it was due to the desire to turn Fort Capital into a real business, but were you also hearing this from investors?

Investors were telling us we're not going to give you big checks unless you're focused on one thing. At the time we were trying to raise $5 million for a townhome deal, and the investors were like, look, we want to give money to the guys that are trying to build townhomes every day. We don't know if you're gonna wake up tomorrow thinking about townhomes, land, student housing, or multifamily. And that conversation came up enough to where the light bulb goes off.

One, we're never going to be able to raise copious amounts of capital unless we're focused. Two, Jason knew that to really build a great company that we could grow and scale we had to be more focused. Three, we didn't want to be a development business. We wanted to buy existing assets and have recurring cash flow. And then the fourth thing was, well, what were we going to pick. That's probably where I spent the majority of my time and Jason spent the majority of his time designing the company to be able to do great things.

What are some of the things you did to become a great operator?

When you have all these buildings, you ask, "What's the property manager's job like? What should they do really, really well?" They should know all their tenants, they should collect rent on time, they should walk the property once a week, they should be able to talk with the leasing managers three times a week. And you can kind of go down the checklist of all these things. And so while none of them are complicated, and everybody kind of knows you need to do them, at scale, they're happening at rapid speed, it becomes about efficiency.

We've built software that does a ton of the thinking for doing those things. They're kind of checklists and tasks that you do over and over, but we automate it, so the person doesn't have to do it. It makes it so easy for them to understand what to do and staying on top of them. Nobody's ever waking up wondering what they need to do today.

That's the Fort Operating System that you talked about?

That's the Fort Operating System, and we don't need as many people to accomplish the same amount of work because of how efficient we've gotten. It's just like any operationally efficient company, they get a lot more done with less. And the other part of that is going back to focus. At least for the last eight years, we've only focused primarily on one asset type. And so we're constantly compounding knowledge that's really for one asset type.

We've built a culture where it's literally upon everybody and how they're rewarded and how they're incentivized to constantly be seeking out any kind of edge that we can get. The majority of the days are just these tiny little incremental improvements that compound over time.

When you were transitioning to industrial, was there a learning curve or did your past experience make you feel comfortable? Did your investors feel comfortable giving you the money because of your past experience?

That's a good question. Not the first few deals probably. But these were the same guys that had been with me since the beginning and they were like, Chris will be successful. And the truth is the first few deals weren't that big.

What made you choose Class B industrial anyways? Was there another light bulb moment?

It wasn't like that driving-past-Six-Flags moment, or a "I'll never forget that" kind of moment. But I just remember this period of a couple months where it was just becoming glaringly obvious. And to this day I'm still more convicted in it than I've ever been. I know way more about it now. But the big thing was, if you really sit back, was that they're not going to build any more of this. In fact, like what I just told you about West 7th, they tore down around 2 million square feet of industrial to build all these apartments. It's depleting one percent to two percent a year. Even with apartments, you might say well, you can't build more Class B apartments. No, but you can go build way more Class A that become Class B. You can't even do that with what we're doing.

Like apartments, can't you build Class A, and then the older Class A becomes Class B?

But that doesn't happen in industrial. You literally cannot rebuild the stuff that we're buying. It was all built thirty years ago and if you look at the new supply over the last twenty years; it's like 2 to 3 percent of the total market. So there was that. Then if you get real simple, you can ask if there's going to be more demand for this or less demand. You could talk about e-commerce, but also, if you look around downtown or out these windows, how many service businesses are required to make sure these trees are cut, the roofs are clean, the windows are washed, the streets are good, the landscaping is good.

They need garages, they need places to park their trucks and do maintenance.

For sure. Where are all those companies going to be? Now think about it even more. Imagine tomorrow that there's a two-acre piece of land right across the street. Imagine you go build a high rise there. Now you need even more services for downtown but there's no new buildings. The companies need to grow. It's a real problem. As the cities become more urbanized, there's more density and more things to fix and build and clean and wash. But there's not more of these buildings being built to have more landscaping companies work out of. And then with population growth on top of that, and the markets that we're in, it makes a lot of sense.

You guys are buying and managing what a lot of people might consider a boring asset, but in the everyday ways a city works, and society works, you need these blue-collar businesses.

I'd say the backbone of America operates in our buildings.

Right. Do you feel like you hit so many sweet spots with this asset class as a great investment, but it's also providing this service in the world that makes you feel good to be a part of?

You know, you pick up a newspaper or magazine or whatever, and everybody wants to talk about the big companies. Those people don't run the world. Who runs the world? They're the people that clean, that fix toilets when they're broken, that build houses. That actually build stuff. And vastly the majority of those people are in our buildings. So that does feel really good. I think what also feels really good, and maybe this has nothing to do with industrial, but it just feels good about the company we're building is that we treat our team really well.

It sounds like focus was the driver for all things.

Yeah, committing to focus. If you put something in all bold and underline in this book, maybe it's this:

> **<u>Committing to focus is easily said, but it's the hardest thing to do. And the more successful you get, the harder it becomes.</u>**

Because on one hand, you can start believing that because you're good at one thing, you can be good at anything, but two, the world really sees successful people and they think of them the same way as like, oh, you're successful, we'll give you this idea to do. It's funny. Once we became successful in industrial, most people wouldn't say hey, you should do more industrial, they'd say you should start doing multifamily now. When I see most problems when I'm talking to friends or I'm just looking at businesses that once were great that are not great anymore, it goes back to the book, is at some point they lose focus. Most business problems are from a lack of truly focusing.

For us, focusing meant only looking at Class B industrial real estate in Texas. And that was all we were going to do. We had this pivotal leadership retreat where Jason and I, along with our key team members, mapped out our strategy and the future of the business. And when we came out of that retreat, we said, we'll finish every other deal that we have, that's already in the pipeline that we're committed to. But any new deal that walks in, if it's not Class B industrial, we're not doing it.

And so that was the first thing. We decided to focus.

Is there another decision you can look back on that you could say was a pivotal moment for propelling Fort Capital forward?

I think the flywheel is one of the most under-discussed and underrated concepts in all of business. And when you talk about bad businesses, there's one thing they have in common, they don't have a flywheel, but more importantly, they don't even know what their flywheel would be if they had one. They're just fighting every day. And that's what you see with a lot of small businesses. Small businesses don't stay small on purpose. There's the quote, "every process is perfectly designed for the results that it's getting." That's very true.

From there, we knew every goal or big initiative had to align to one spoke of the flywheel. That was an immensely pivotal moment, when we understood what our flywheel was, and we started directing all of our goals towards it.

The second is we were on EOS, which is the Entrepreneur Operating System. There's a book, *Traction*, a lot of companies use it. We started using the OKR (Objectives and Key Results) method as a way to align our goals or our objectives to the flywheel.

Third, we started using the Culture Index, which is a way to assess the traits of your people when they're coming to work for you. So I don't really care what their skills are, what they're capable of doing. I want to know their temperament. You'd never put an accountant personality in a business development role. We decided we were going to be religious about only hiring people that have the same temperament that match the role.

Once you guys committed to focus, you got the flywheel going along with the processes and procedures in place, was it like a hockey stick growth for you guys?

Once we had the clarity of focus, but the clarity to kind of know what drove our business forward and what to work on, things really started to lift off. The second thing is, it takes a little bit of time for your people to adapt. Once they all did, and they started compounding on their knowledge, things really started to take off.

Another big part of things taking off, and I'm not scared to admit it, was when I made the decision, roughly four years ago, to not be the CEO anymore and let Jason run it day to day. I mean, you could just look at the trajectory and the growth of the company and the profitability since that took place. It's infinitely better than when I was there. And so that was a really key moment.

We also learned to give people time and runway to build within the team and the culture.

What makes you guys stand out as a successful real estate operating company? What makes you guys profitable?

At the end of the day, all this stuff that we've talked about is for naught if you don't have a great track record of creating returns for investors, so I never want to lose sight of that. We've talked a lot about the operations side. But all of that's leading up to doing all this work and creating a team and a culture that can deliver returns to investors. So the number one thing people want to see when you're raising money from them, especially for the first time, is to show them how you've done on other deals and show them the performance of your current portfolio. The second is people obviously wonder, well, how are you doing it? And that's where we get into a lot of the operations.

Have you guys seen incremental increases in your returns to investors as you become more operationally efficient and sophisticated?

We have. Our track record of full-cycle deals* is exceptional. Our ongoing portfolio continues to perform really well. On top of just performing, another thing that matters is the investor experience. Again, none of this matters if you can't produce returns. But we have an investor relations team that people can call into and get information from quickly. We report quarterly on the dot. It's never a day late, with consistent reporting across all the assets that people come to expect. We use Juniper Square software, which makes it easy for them to log in and see us present deals. It's very systematic. And we have built this incredible process for forecasting cash needs.

What are the key, fundamental things you do that produce returns on any given asset? Is it a combination of your basis† and value add?

Great question. So there's two things that are forever, diamonds and your basis. It starts with the buy and that's an obvious thing. But when you buy what we buy, you could have two different groups buy it and have two totally different outcomes.

A lot of tenants in this asset class have generally not been treated great. One way that we actually generate returns is we said, well, we're going to be the best at treating the customers in our specific asset class great. And so what you get is retention. A lot of these tenants have lost trust in their

---

* **Full-Cycle Deal**: An investment spanning purchase to sale, including all stages and returns.

† **Basis**: A property's original cost, adjusted for improvements or depreciation.

landlords in this asset class. And so retention causes less turnover, it causes less CAPEX* spend, it causes less leasing commissions. So that's one way to enhance returns is treating tenants better. But again, it's just not easy to do at scale.

Second, we buy properties with vacancy. We like buying something that's 20 to 30 percent vacant. We believe we can lease it up better than the person before us could. Sometimes that's just putting a better leasing team on it and marketing the property better. Sometimes, a lot of long-term owners look at every dollar they have to put back into the property as a dollar lost. And so they'll see tenants move out.

Third is operational efficiency and economies of scale. We can do CAPEX at a cheaper cost than some of our competitors because our contractors are always full of work, and we have more bargaining power. A lot of it is also mark to market. In multifamily you're mark to marketing every year. Industrial leases are three, five, seven years, so you're only changing the rent every so often. Also, we're converting gross leases to triple net leases, which creates value for cash management. Later, when you go to sell these properties, buyers will pay you more and banks like it when leases are on triple net leases.

It's all of this in combination. Not every deal is the exact same. You're creating a building that more people want to lease because now it's functioning better. Everyone's a little bit different. But all of those combined create definite ways to create value. And again, none of them are rocket science groundbreaking ideas, but they work.

What's your ideal hold time for these properties?

Right now, the way we're structured, we can hold anything as long as we want. We just say that we sell when we think we've created the most value.

---

* **CAPEX** (Capital Expenditure): Funds spent on acquiring, upgrading, or maintaining physical assets like buildings or equipment in a property.

Fort Capital is now at about $1.2 billion assets under management (AUM), you're still growing and you're going into other markets. Do you see yourself continuing what you're doing but at a scale where you're in all the major markets throughout the United States?

Yeah, I think the future of Fort will be continuing to grow. Maybe not the entire United States, but for now the Sunbelt has plenty of great markets to be in. Continuing doing what we're doing I think we're getting to a point where we could add a new asset type and have a fully dedicated team that works on that independently, but with the same tools as the team that's focused on industrial.

And then I think the thing that excites me a lot about the business and our software is, as you grow, there's all these tangential revenue streams. They say the best business to start is to go down your P&L, find your largest expense line item, and start a business doing that.

Again, we think of ourselves a lot like software where you're starting to build tools that are already part of your ecosystem. They're already things you're paying for. And you're just saying, can we do it better? Can Fort make a meaningful lift on that? And if you look at the world that way, it excites me.

The last thing we'll touch on is I think there will come a day where we start buying other people's platforms. If we really want to get great at industrial in Atlanta, maybe we go buy the best platform that's doing industrial in Atlanta and grow that way. Those are all kind of part of a 10-year roadmap.

What are your recommendations for young people looking for mentors or more information about the industry?

Finding a mentor starts with having the confidence to go talk to somebody. I think a lot of it is fear-driven. You have to have the courage to ask them questions. I don't remember a time in my life where it didn't seem obvious to me that if I wanted to know something, I should just go ask somebody that's already done it. I thought that everybody thought that was the way to do things. And it turns out, a lot of people never do that. It turns out a lot of people never do that because they're scared. It's the fear of looking like an idiot.

The encouragement I give is most people that have been successful in something, whether it's business, marriage, friendships, they want to teach other people about it. They usually have a giving spirit about it. Very few people I've ever met who are super successful just want to keep it all to themselves. That's one of the beauties of success. You get to share it with other people.

The other thing I would say, and maybe this helps somebody, there are things like YouTube and podcasts now. And while you might not have that person directly in your life that you can call, you now have access to some of the most brilliant minds in the world. I can promise anybody, if they spent a year reading your book, or listening to my podcasts or David Senra's *Founders* podcast, and that's the only content you let into your brain, it would change who you are.

You've built quite a following on social media yourself. How has the internet changed the way people can build relationships and find mentors?

Anybody who grew up in this generation has been given a gift that you just didn't used to have. If you are willing to go and put your thoughts, your ideas, and the things that you value out there, you attract people that are interested in what you're interested in. Whether it's Twitter, my podcast, Reddit, whatever. And on the contrary, you repel people that are not interested in what you're interested in. And here's the truth. You don't need 10 million followers to build a new life. You could have 1000 or 100 of the right followers and change your life.

I remember when I hit 100 followers on Twitter, I was like, "Damn, this is awesome." When I got to 1000, I was like, "Oh my gosh!" But the truth is, I've felt as valuable at 1000 as I now do at 100,000. Because with 100,000, there's a lot of people that may not align with me, they're just following because it's a big account. But my life changed at 1000 followers. I met Moses, and Keith, and Nick*. Now we've been friends for five years. We've traveled together. Our kids have met. It's crazy, I see my "internet friends" more often than I see people who live a mile away. I don't even call them "internet friends" anymore, they're just my friends.

Through this one event I hosted, only four people came from Fort Worth. The other fifty-one were people I've met over the last five years online. In most arcs of life, you're meeting fewer people the older you get. My arc is totally different. I'm meeting more friends and more interesting people at a pace that can honestly get exhausting. I'm here with you right now, and we'll become friends. We'll be attached for a long time because of this book, and it just would have never happened without the internet. Again, it takes a little courage to put yourself out there, but you can radically change your life.

Chris turned college rental properties into a $1.2 billion industrial real estate firm by recognizing when to narrow his focus. What began as opportunistic deals around TCU became something entirely different when he and Jason Baxter made the defining call to specialize exclusively in Class B industrial properties.

That decision changed everything. Instead of chasing any deal that popped up, they created a framework to filter out the noise and built systems to optimize what they already knew worked. Fort Capital stopped being just another deal shop. They evolved into an operational powerhouse.

Chris looks past individual transactions and sees the systems that connect them. His team finds great assets that are underperforming and they implement their operational framework that unlocks the value within them. By converting gross leases to triple nets, implementing

* **Moses Kagan** is also featured in this book. Keith and Nick are other well-known voices in the real estate Twitter community.

responsive property management, and treating tenants like valued customers, Fort Capital creates returns that others miss. Their flywheel approach ensures every initiative feeds back into their core strategy, whether they're moving into new Sunbelt markets or considering platform acquisitions.

Money, to Chris, was never about status. Following his father's example, he sees wealth as a tool for freedom. Nothing more, nothing less.

His advice for finding mentors cuts through the complexity that stops most people from asking: "Most people that have been successful in something want to teach other people about it." This straightforward approach mirrors how he's built his business. Identifying what works, systematizing it, then executing with discipline. By doing a few things exceptionally well rather than many things adequately, Chris has created a company that stands out in industrial real estate while staying true to the values that guided him from the start.

Connect

- Website: fort-companies.com
- Podcast: thefortpod.com
- X: @fortworthchris
- LinkedIn: Chris Powers

Moses Kagan

Co-Founder and Partner, Adaptive Realty

Los Angeles, CA

- Built Adaptive Realty into more than a $200 million real estate portfolio specializing in completely renovated, long-term hold multifamily properties in Los Angeles.
- Implemented a practical investment strategy in the LA market by recognizing properties' untapped potential, transforming outdated spaces, and focusing on long-term value creation rather than short-term gains.
- Leveraged content marketing through his blog and Twitter presence to attract more than $50 million in capital and establish himself as a thought leader in the real estate investing community.
- Co-founded Reconvene with his wife, creating a small-scale real estate conference designed to foster meaningful relationships and collaborative learning.
- Launched ReSeed Partners in 2023, selecting an initial cohort of eight entrepreneurs from more than 2,000 applicants to replicate his business model nationally, creating a scalable platform for institutional capital deployment.

Adaptive Realty's headquarters sit in a nondescript Echo Park strip mall, with nothing suggesting there's a $200 million apartment portfolio being managed from one of its storefronts, causing me to walk right by it not once, but twice. Fortunately, the classic stereotypical L.A. weather didn't disappoint. I was glad to be back. The last time I was in California fifteen years ago, Moses Kagan had no portfolio, just a 16-unit building he and his brother purchased while others were getting crushed by the market.

Moses got into real estate a bit unexpectedly. As a kid, he went to Albany Academy, which led to Phillips Andover, then Princeton, and then the London School of Economics. That pedigree landed him a job in M&A banking in London, where he excelled but felt increasingly out of place. He then made his way to southern California and took a crack at tech entrepreneurship. As that business began showing it wouldn't last long, he started looking elsewhere. When the markets crashed in 2008, Moses found himself buying a Los Angeles apartment building, knowing almost nothing about property management or renovation. But he knew there was an opportunity there.

The early years were rough. After watching transaction costs eat away his profits when selling his first small portfolio, Moses decided that selling wasn't necessarily the right move. From then on, his strategy would be to buy and hold forever. This became the core of Adaptive Realty's investment approach, drawing multigenerational investors who wanted lasting value, just like him. After a painful early lesson from city inspectors, he began to insist on pristine, by-the-book permits for their extremely thorough renovations. Initially, it put him at a disadvantage, but it produced better buildings and steadier returns over time.

Moses decided early on that he didn't want to grow his business through cold-calling. Searching for another way, he ended up reading a marketing book that resonated with him and how he wanted to interact with the world. So instead of making phone calls, he began writing online. He started with *Kagan's Blog*, where he was candid about both triumphs and failures in the L.A. real estate market. Later, he took his writing to Twitter and started sharing his market insights there, which attracted even more attention. This eventually led to Reconvene, the boutique real estate conference known for its intimate atmosphere, and ReSeed Partners, which now mentors and funds emerging operators nationwide.

In our conversation, Moses recounts his times from counting cash for tenant buyouts to building a portfolio worth hundreds of millions. He talks about early setbacks that might have derailed a less determined person, his never-ending learning process, and how choosing the harder, more principled path forged relationships that endured. The following pages will dig into what he believes is needed to create a successful career in real estate, or as Moses explains, "The ideal real estate career is one where you come up with a differentiated view and then you go out and explain to the world how your view is different."

Date of Interview: October 19, 2023

Since you guys just finished Reconvene not too long ago, I figured we'd start there. How'd it go?

Went great. We had three hundred people. We leaned into making the event more interactive than it has been in the past, with fewer main stage talks and more interaction between and among the guests. And I thought that was great.

So based on the past experiences, you felt this is what people are more receptive to?

One of the crazy things about Reconvene is you literally could walk into the crowd, randomly point at someone, bring them up on stage and it would be a very interesting hour talk about their business. We realized that it's a waste of talent having all of them sit there quietly listening to other people talk. We're going to lean more into that in future years.

Now this was year three of Reconvene. Have you decided to put a cap on how many people can attend since it's such a curated event?

Yeah, I think we've decided to keep it capped at three hundred going forward. I've been to so many real estate conferences that are the opposite of that where everyone's got a suit and tie and doing the five minutes of small talk, the business cards and all that bullshit. It's just like, that's not how you create relationships. So the whole point of Reconvene is to put people together in a number of different contexts over a three-day period such that hopefully you have meaningful conversations with a number of people two or three times. It's just a complete re-imagining of what one of these real estate conferences can be. And the larger you get, the lower the chance that you have multiple interactions. The less intimate it is, the worse it gets.

Was Reconvene born out of your dissatisfaction with the standard conventions?

Yeah. The most egregious example of which was I went to a real estate private equity conference and paid, I think, $20,000 to speak on an emerging managers' panel, and literally got zero out of it.

Then I had the experience of going to Capital Camp. I'd never seen anything like that before. I don't think there is anything like it. We've copied it shamelessly. I'm friends with Brent (Brent Beshore, one of the owners). Their team has been very kind in terms of giving, helping with ideas, whatever. They've been nothing but wonderful.

For young people coming into the industry, do you find any value in going out and shaking hands at some of these bigger CRE conferences?

I don't think so. I think the last thing you want to be is another faceless guy wearing a suit, you know, shaking hands just like everyone else. I mean, you can see the way I look, for example, as a reaction to that. When I go to a real estate conference, which happens pretty rarely now, I literally look different from everyone there. Part of it is a conscious effort to signal in every way that I do not think about real estate the way that other people think about it, and that the way we do business is different than the way other people do business.

So I think as a young person, their efforts are much better directed at building a social media presence and letting people know how they think and to spend a lot of time talking one on one with a smaller number of smart mentor-type people. The ideal real estate career, in my opinion, is one where you come up with a differentiated view and then you go out and explain to the world how your view is different. And then what happens is people come to you, instead of you having to go be some faceless person who's trying to make an impression in five minutes, shaking hands.

My blog, which was really my first attempt to do this, came out of the decision that I didn't want to be cold calling, which is the other thing that people do when they're young. It was like, look, I want to attract the kind of people who want to do business with me. I want to repel everyone else. So let me just go say how I think about the world, and it turns out that works. I was on a panel with Brent Beshore recently, and he describes social media like a scaled conversation, where you could have a conversation with many, many people at once and over a length of time.

Let's go back to what it was like for you in your younger years. One of the things that struck me about you is when I heard you say you made a decision when you were around 15 years old to purposely be friends with people who are smarter than you. People that you respect, that you can learn from, and who are on the right track in life. What made you make that decision?

I went to this all-boys military day school in upstate New York called the Albany Academy for Boys. I was there from fourth grade through ninth grade, and it was a pretty anti-intellectual environment. There were a lot of great things about it, and the older I get, the more I appreciate it. But at the time, it felt pretty terrible. I was really nerdy, really into books and into school and it was not the kind of place that valued that. It was the kind of place where you got stuffed in lockers and hazed and that kind of stuff.

I saw a sign for CTY (Center for Talented Youth), where seventh and eighth graders could take the SATs, like, the real SATs, and if you did well enough in either math or verbal or both, you could go to CTY. It's a program where you go and take one college class in three weeks. You're basically in a classroom for six or seven hours a day and there's homework. My math score was abysmal, but my English score was really good.

It was the first time I'd been in a school environment where all the other kids were smart, and some of them were a lot smarter than me. Then through a girlfriend who went to Andover, I learned about this completely different school environment. No parents, great teachers, no uniforms, no marching. And I was like, that sounds amazing.

And it's a very good school too, right?

Yeah, the best. So I basically went on a campaign to force my parents to send me there. I was accepted and got a partial scholarship, but it was still a stretch for my parents financially. My father was a college professor, and my mom was a mid-level New York State bureaucrat. On the side, they were buying tiny little apartment buildings in Troy, New York. So they had two units here, four units there. My dad did the leasing and dealt with maintenance issues. And my mom did the bookkeeping.

So it was a full family effort.

Yeah. My brother and I were involved too. When there was a snow day, we'd have to go shovel snow. Despite being in a low-end rental market, there was RPI (Rensselaer Polytechnic Institute) where he taught, so there were professors and graduate students who needed rentals, and he would make nice ones. We were not rich, so it was a big sacrifice for them to send me to private school.

So back to Andover, I ended up meeting my best friends through the wrestling team. I've tried to think back about what it was that allowed me to sublimate my own ego and get comfortable with the idea of being the dumbest person in the room. I don't know what it is. I think my entire life I've just been attracted to smart people, and part of what was so great about Andover was being around people who were much smarter than me. I had the experience of being humbled, but also found I was exceptional in subjects like history and politics. So I learned I could win if I picked out the exact area that I wanted to be in. I just wanted to hang out with smart kids, and slowly, this group sort of coalesced. Very ambitious and talented people that have gone on to do incredible things.

After Andover, you went to Princeton. Were you also happy with that decision the way you were with Andover?

Yeah, it was amazing, but I should say this about Princeton: I do not think that I took full advantage of my experience there. I very stupidly thought of Princeton as the end of the race as opposed to the beginning of the race. I thought of Princeton as something that I got for working hard at high school, so now I could fuck off. Smoke all the weed and do all the drinking I didn't do in high school.

I also thought of myself as an outsider so I constructed walls around myself and sort of pre-selected who I would be willing to be friends with because of how I perceived myself. And it was all bullshit. The reality is, everyone was reinventing themselves. I limited my experience there, but it wasn't because other people were limiting it. It was me limiting it.

What I tell disadvantaged kids going to elite schools now is that they got in because the schools thought they should be there. Act like it's your school. All the opportunities at the school are open to you. Be open to those and go join clubs, go sit down with new people at dining rooms, go to the professors' office hours, go take full advantage of this amazing opportunity in a way that I didn't.

After Princeton, what did you end up doing?

I became aware of these programs at the London School of Economics (LSE) where you can go get a one-year master's degree. So I applied, got in, and spent what I thought was going to be one year in London, studying history of international relations at LSE. The idea was I was gonna go to London and then I would go take the LSAT there. But I did not study for the LSAT the way I should have and therefore I got a score that was substandard from my perspective. Having gone to Andover, Princeton, and LSE, I wasn't going to go to some crappy law school.

The other thing, at the time, I was living with another one of my best friends from Andover, Max, who was working for a guy who was on his way to becoming a billionaire. And the way that he was doing that was rolling up classified advertising newspapers, primarily in Europe.

It's similar to other businesses where you find these little niche things that have moats in their little area and print cash. They don't have huge growth opportunities because their markets are small, but if you roll them up with other similar businesses, they're cash machines, and if you roll them up, they're enormous, amazing businesses. And you can lever up because the cash flow generation is so consistent. So you're buying this consistent cash flow generator with a huge moat with leverage, and you just keep buying them and keep accumulating and keep re-levering. And that's the story of so many business successes, and by the way, that's what we're doing with Los Angeles apartment buildings, which also are small things that have a moat. It's the same thing.

Anyway, Max was working for this guy, and he was doing these deals, and he would do an LOI* to buy one of these businesses, and then he would call the partner at some Boston law firm, and be like, look, we're gonna need a sale and purchase agreement by Monday morning. And it didn't matter if this partner at the law firm had plans with his family to go to his lake house or whatever, he was going to have to grind out Max's SPA. So I sort of had this moment where I was like, you know, I much prefer to be Max than to be that lawyer getting that phone call.

And so Max got me a job with this tiny boutique M&A (Mergers and Acquisitions) firm that was helping them do these deals. They had never hired anyone without any training before. But they were like a) this kid went to Princeton, so he's smart, and b) Max, who is a close subordinate of our biggest customer, this is his best friend from high school. We should probably give him a job.

How long did you end up there for?

I was there for a couple years.

You've stated, admittedly, that you didn't feel like you were very good at it.

Correct.

---

* **LOI** (Letter of Intent): A non-binding document outlining the key terms of a potential real estate deal, often used to start negotiations.

Do you think the people you worked with would agree with that?

Yes. But let me be a little bit more specific. The job of a low-ranking finance person at that time was primarily to do a bunch of financial modeling.

And you never took accounting or financial modeling classes.

Exactly. And it was a small boutique firm, so there was no training course. So I sucked. I think this is a very good lesson for young people. I had got through college with good grades without working particularly hard because of my facility with writing primarily. I was able to write papers quickly, but I wouldn't proofread it, and it would have a bunch of typos because I wrote it in two hours. And to be honest, the difference between an "A" and an "A-" didn't really matter to me.

It turns out that when you go into the real world, you're doing PowerPoint presentations where multiple hundred-million-pound deals rely on those presentations, and therefore, people's bonuses and how they're going to feed their families depend on those presentations. If you don't proofread them, people get really angry and justifiably so. I combined a total lack of financial modeling and accounting experience with a kind of a lackadaisical approach to quality control in the documents that I was creating. And that is a horrific combination.

However, I had some, let's call it compensating skills that were unusual. If people like you, see that you're smart and honest, they want to work with you. My mother had always emphasized to me that's where the power was.

So I'm sitting there in this bank, and I'm like, clearly incompetent at the stuff I'm supposed to be doing. On the other hand, I was interested in these little internet companies I was reading about. I saw opportunities in these little companies that aren't being called on because of the recent dot-com bust. And I recognized that the senior guys in the firm are only graded on whether they can bring business in or not.

So I'm like, let me write to these little internet companies and see if I can get a meeting. I basically convinced one of the MDs (managing directors) to come along with me on these meetings. And so from his perspective, it was great because the only thing that he was being judged on was if he can bring in business, and he's got this junior who's bringing in business.

It got to the point where I would help bring in business but then I was so incompetent at doing the junior part that they would assign the junior work to someone else who was good at it, but I would get to go to the meeting with the CEO of a company, which is very weird. Effectively I leveraged myself into a senior position.

So that might be your first instance of understanding that you were good at recognizing a good asset.

Yeah. But what was amazing about it was I got to go to meetings. So I'm 24 years old, sitting there in a meeting with the CEO and founder of a 150-million-pound company, talking to these guys, and they were treating me like I knew what I was talking about. Which is an amazing experience when you're that young. And it was like, these guys are smart, but they're not that smart. They're not like some superhuman class of beings that I could never be. It was like, oh, actually, I could do this.

And then the next realization was, I'm sitting here in this office at three in the morning, and I'm like, I went to Princeton, and my colleague had gone to Harvard, and another person in the office had gone to Cambridge, and we're all there at three in the morning. And it's like, these guys who went to some no-name college, if they even went to college, we're about to sell their company for 150 million pounds. And they're gonna get generationally wealthy. And we're the idiots sitting here at our desk at three in the morning. So I was like, okay, I gotta get on the principal side. I gotta own stuff, not just be a middleman.

So it was this realization that helped you leave this boutique M&A firm, and you moved from London back to the States?

I spent another year there. At the time I had started dating a woman who became my first wife.

Because of the tech stuff, were you thinking this is the business to be in?

Yeah, I thought I wanted to, but in retrospect, I didn't know anything. My capital base was all in the States where my network was, so I knew I was going to have to move back.

My brother and I started what turned out to be a very stupid idea in Los Angeles. My best friend, the one who staked me in real estate later, first staked me with this tech company and he lost $700,000 of his money over a couple years. The business was providing technology services to actors and casting directors.

So how did you guys fall into real estate? Was it around the same time you guys are starting this tech company?

Yep, it was pre-crash 2007. Everyone had the real estate bug. My parents said they'd help. My great grandfather had owned some buildings in New York and when he died, the family still owned this one building. The family sold it and some of the money from that went to my mom and would eventually be used for the first building we would buy.

So for months we were looking for duplexes when my brother found this building on the MLS*. This guy had bought a derelict 16-unit building, had done a gut renovation, levered himself to the gills, and run out of money. He was buried under debt, and we were able to step in, make a deal, and buy it at a price that was very good for the time.

Did you guys know what you were doing at this point?

Well, it was like good old fashioned immigrant stuff. What do you think

---

* **MLS** (Multiple Listing Service): A shared database used by real estate brokers to list properties and access listings from other brokers.

the rents are? What do you think the expenses are? Okay, we know what the property taxes are. Okay, it looks like it makes sense. We saw that we could get some cash flow. So we buy it, and now we had to fill it up really quickly.

Did you guys know how to get tenants, screen them, do all the paperwork, and all that kind of stuff?

The bank made us hire a management company, because they were like, you guys don't know what you're doing. They started marketing it and on the second unit they're gonna fill, they call us up and say, "Listen, we have this tenant, she's willing to pay the rent, but she's an illegal immigrant, doesn't have documents, but she seems good." We're like, you know what? We're nice liberal guys. No problem. So we rent to her. She turned out to have a boyfriend who was a pimp who started running hookers out of the apartment.

So my brother and I go into their studio apartment and this guy is sitting there, and she's sitting there, and I'm thinking this guy is pretty scary. But my brother's a pretty big dude and not afraid and he tells the guy, you gotta move out of here. At first, he stuck around living in the basement and on the roof for a while until, fortunately, he eventually left. He was arrested like six months or a year later trying to climb into her window from the neighbor's property, and the cops came and arrested him. So that was the last we heard of him. That was our introduction to landlording.

I bet that's the first of many stories you have.

I've got a million of those. I won't go down that road. So anyways, we filled that building up.

And it was cash flowing like you guys expected?

Yeah, and then we had a meeting that got us thinking about doing it again. It was with the head of the management company who the bank forced us to hire. He was also a broker, and he was fishing to sell us another building. I'll never forget this meeting. He asked us, "You guys think you did a good deal, right?" And we're like, yeah, LA is a rent stabilized market, and we bought this vacant, renovated building, and were able to put new tenants in at market rents. So he says, "Well, yeah, you paid a price for the building that reflected the market rents. What I like to do is go buy piece of shit buildings and harass the tenants until they move out. And then I renovate the apartments and raise the rents." And I'm looking at him like, you are a disgusting human being.

But the value-add part made sense.

Yeah. I was like, there's so much value that's being created. Why don't you just pay these people to move out instead of harassing them? Just pay them. So shortly thereafter, it's now 2008, that same guy comes back to us, and he says, "Listen, I've got this client, he's a syndicator." So now the wheels have really come off the market and you don't know who's swimming naked until the tide goes out. And this guy was naked, he had cross collateralized different buildings, and he had people up his ass to get their money back. It was a disaster.

So this broker-property manager comes to us, and he's got another 16-unit building in Silverlake. The guy will sell for $1.45 million. I look at the numbers and I'm like, no way, $1.25 million. It was so ridiculously cheap. It was like we can't screw this up with sixteen apartments in Los Angeles for $1.25 million. But I didn't have the money. And I also didn't expect him to say yes, because I low-balled them. But the guy was like, "Sure, done."

But I don't have the money. So I go to my friend who had invested in our tech company, whose money I was in the process of losing, and I'm like, here are the numbers. We've done this, we already own one building and now we kind of know what we're doing. And he agreed to do it. And the reason he agreed to do it was because, I don't know if you remember at that time, banks were going out of business.

Kind of similar to what's going on now.

Yeah, but even scarier. His trading business was minting cash. He was doing high frequency currency trading. His problem was, what do you do with the money? Because you didn't know if you put it in some large financial institution there was a reasonable chance that the thing would literally go out of business.

So now I come to him and I'm like, I'd like to buy apartment buildings —hard assets—in Los Angeles. He's like, look, as long as you don't use leverage, how can I really lose money? He needed a place to park money. He trusted us and from his perspective, this was a pretty safe way to do it.

Now you guys all of a sudden have two apartment buildings under your belt.

Yeah. And we immediately get to work testing this thesis that you could pay people to move out. We were paying people cash. I still have videos of people counting out $100 bills because we didn't want people to say they never got the money. We'd sign a buyout agreement and give them ten or fifteen grand of cash, and people are just taking the cash and moving down the street. We didn't buy out all the tenants at the same time. We bought like two out and started renovations. And then maybe we bought another one out. So it took a long time. We made so many mistakes with the renovations too. We overpaid and underpaid, just a bunch of dumb stuff. But it worked.

Now we have these really distinctive apartments in Silverlake, they're not in the best part of Silverlake, but they're really nice and we start getting these insane rents for them. That gave my friend confidence in us. So when we brought him deal two, he was like, okay, these guys know what they're doing. We didn't have to wait to go full cycle on the first deal. And then boom, boom, boom, over the course of the next couple of years, we ended up buying deals two through twelve, all with his money.

We effectively had unlimited money to do whatever. There's no one looking over your shoulder, there's no bank telling us what to do and this allowed us to make all kinds of stupid mistakes. It was painful and stressful and all that stuff, but it was like going to graduate school for two or three years. All you have to do is create value and you can't use leverage.

Are you guys surviving off your salaries from the tech company at this point?

There was a little bit of salary from the tech company, but not much. This was one of the insane things that we did. He refused to allow us to take fees, but we were like, we can't live. So he let us borrow from the real estate entity. So we're living at this point by borrowing cash at the pref rate which was eight. So I lived for three years of my life basically on debt, which was terrifying.

How stressful!

So stressful. When we ultimately exited the portfolio, because I had basically borrowed so much against it, I didn't make any money. I made a little bit, but it was awful.

Wow. So you had this debt to pay back and if things didn't work out, you're in the hole, a ton. Were you married at this time?

Yeah, I was married. It put stress on my relationship with my wife—we'd eventually divorce. We were broke. We started to have kids. My first son was born in 2011. Also, I was in business with my brother, so that put enormous stress on that relationship.

Stresses me out just thinking about it. So you guys are buying all these buildings at the bottom of the market, which turned out being the best possible time to buy them. And you guys ended up selling them?

We didn't want to. We had renovated all those buildings and finished by 2012. The banks had been so burned by the GFC that even by 2012, if you wanted to get a cash out refi, they were limiting you to something like sixty-five percent LTC*. In other words, they would not loan on the new stabilized rent roll. It didn't matter. They were basically ignoring the value creation.

If we had waited another year, after which the banks started loaning at sixty-five percent LTV†, refinanced, returned his capital and just let the properties cash flow a little bit, we would have paid down the pref and we would have owned half of the upside of the portfolio. It took me until 2017 or 2018 to make as much money as I would have made just by holding that original portfolio. It was incredibly painful.

Was it this experience that led to your long-term strategy?

Yeah, the motivation came from that sales process and a few other things. Remember I said we made a bunch of mistakes? In the beginning, we were renovating buildings without permits because our contractor assured us it would be fine. The city caught us in 2012 on about six buildings simultaneously. They could tell it was us because all the buildings were renovated similarly. They threw the book at us with violations, and we've never skipped permits since. It was a terrible way to operate.

The problem was, when we went to sell these now-perfectly renovated, permitted buildings, they were selling for the same price as properties with superficial renovations. What I call lipstick bullshit. They looked pretty good but had no permits, original plumbing, original wiring. The market wasn't appreciating our permitted work. We've been at a persistent disadvantage in the Los Angeles apartment market for over a decade because we operate impeccably with permits while many others don't.

You're instantly at a disadvantage.

---

* **LTC** (Loan-to-Cost): The ratio of the loan amount to total project cost (acquisition and construction).

† **LTV** (Loan-to-Value): Compares the loan amount to the appraised value of the property.

Exactly. Plus, when we sold the buildings, seeing the escrow closing statement was eye-opening. You see the price you're selling at, then all these deductions start piling up: five percent brokerage commission, two percent city and county transfer tax, plus title and escrow fees. You vaporize seven to eight percent of the gross purchase price on day one. Then you file taxes and lose another huge chunk to state and federal. It was just like, whoa, this is really stupid. There's no way that's the right strategy.

We also sold this beautiful 8-unit building in Silverlake. A perfect jewel box in a great location. We busted our backs doing the renovation work, sold it through this brutal process, and the buyer flipped it less than a year later for a $500,000 profit, more than we made from all our work. We felt like complete morons. That's when we realized the easy money comes from just owning properties as rents and values appreciate over time.

So you guys end up selling the other properties. What was the plan from there?

My friend tells me we're going to have to sell the properties and gives me about a year's notice. We started slowly unwinding the portfolio to not overwhelm the market. The tech company had stopped paying my salary, and I knew I'd be off the draw from the LLC loans since we were selling everything. I was thirty-two, married with one kid, and my income was disappearing. I couldn't return to banking and didn't know what I'd do. It was a scary time.

And by this point you probably see all your school friends doing okay.

Oh, my friends were crushing it while I was broke. They were already rich. But I had gotten a broker's license as part of this business, and my brother and I decided to separate our business to preserve our relationship. During the portfolio sale period, I started my blog because I wanted to attract investors, and I wanted to attract brokerage and property management clients.

One thing I'll say, just to circle back, the downside of having one amazing capital provider is that you build up all the muscles for sourcing deals and getting them, but you do not build up a commensurately strong fundraising muscle.

That was the beginning of Adaptive Realty. I started brokering immediately, helping friends buy homes and condos. I helped a couple from Princeton buy a house in Echo Park, then helped a friend of my brother buy a condo. It wasn't great for my ego. Here I am at thirty-two, no money, driving around to open houses on Saturdays in my mom's old car, trying to earn $10,000 commissions.

But what starts to happen is that I kept noticing these junky buildings that looked like amazing deals to me. I'd be like, "This is way too cheap for Silverlake. You should buy this. We'll relocate some tenants, fix up the building, and look at these potential yields." But these clients would say, "That sounds awesome, dude, but what the fuck do I know about construction?"

So I brought in Jon, our former employee who had been overseeing our construction projects and told them Jon would consult. He'd oversee the renovation while I handled the brokerage. Rapidly it became clear we should just do it as a partnership and split the brokerage and construction management fees.

During the sale of one of our original portfolio properties, there was a guy who offered on the building, one of the losing bidders. Later on, that guy joined the mailing list on my blog. So I Google him and realize, oh, this guy is serious. I reached out and ended up having lunch with him and a colleague. He turned out to be a very successful developer of creative office buildings trying to get into multifamily.

He hired us to manage one project in Echo Park, which we still manage today. He had raised a high eight figures fund to do creative office, then he went to all their LPs and convinced them to redirect toward apartments. While building our own business—brokering, recruiting brokers, writing the blog, managing properties, and raising capital—we helped deploy his entire fund. We ended up doing about twenty buildings for him and another ten for other clients.

Your blog was a key tool for you. What made you start it, and did you have to promote it?

I started it because I didn't want to cold call. I had read *Permission Marketing* by Seth Godin. The idea of which is that you provide free education, enriching the lives of your readers. You build credibility in their eyes, such that when you actually have something to sell, it's an educational sale. They're often happy to buy from you because you've provided so much value over the years. That really resonated with me.

All these blogging sites had similar suggestions about writing regularly, having email capture forms, building backlinks. I followed maybe three of their recommendations, pretty half-heartedly, and it still worked. Then I read Barbara Corcoran's memoir, and there's this amazing story where she leverages limited data from her tiny brokerage to position herself as an expert through media. That was eye-opening.

At the time, no one was publishing rental market data for our areas of Los Angeles. The main platform was just Craigslist. There was no quantitative anything. So I spent weekends manually going through every single Craigslist entry for each neighborhood, tracking one-bedrooms, two-bedrooms, amenities, everything in a spreadsheet. I grouped them all and calculated medians for each unit type by neighborhood. Then I reached out to local real estate publications offering this data in exchange for mentions and backlinks to my blog. That's what really boosted our visibility.

What a great idea. It's funny how one little thing sometimes can trigger an entire path to open up.

My M&A banking background helped. I had researched internet companies and understood backlinks and SEO* before it was huge. I think for young people, reading widely and broadly in business is

* **SEO** (Search Engine Optimization): The process of improving a website's visibility in search engine results to attract more organic (unpaid) traffic.

incredibly valuable because you start making these unexpected connections.

So you ended up helping put out all this guy's fund. Does that lay the foundation for you guys to start raising your own capital?

We were raising our own money simultaneously. We had a differentiated view of apartment buildings in Los Angeles. Deals looked different to us than to everyone else, so we could buy right off the MLS. There was plenty of opportunity. The problem wasn't deal flow, it was capital.

How did you come to have that differentiated view?

When a normal real estate syndicator buys a deal, they've got debt and equity and a budget. They're trying to solve for IRR*, so they want to get in and out as quickly as possible with maximum debt to maximize returns. We had no debt and no exit timeline. We just maximized unlevered yield with unlimited capital, thinking carefully about spending that capital in accretive ways.

Being forced to use permits led to comprehensive renovations. If you're putting in washer/dryers, you have to re-pipe, which means opening walls, so you might as well rewire. And once the walls are open, why not reconfigure the space? The building may be really inefficiently laid out 'cause it was built in the '20s when people had different expectations.

We'd buy these $2 million buildings and put in another $1.5 million. Totally insane to normal investors. From their perspective, they'd be like, "What the fuck are you doing?" But we saw these buildings as raw material. With full renovation, modern amenities, and proper reconfiguration, you could get premium rents from quality tenants in great locations. You'd end up with impressive yields on buildings that couldn't be replicated due to zoning, with all-new systems, new roof, everything

* **IRR** (Internal Rate of Return): A metric used to measure the profitability of a real estate investment, expressed as the annual rate at which cash flows break even with the initial investment.

perfect. That's the differentiated view—seeing buildings as raw material for what they could become, not what they were.

Now you guys start fundraising, but don't have the experience doing that. How did you start? Did you have a pitch deck based on what you just told me?

Yeah, though I don't know that it was that well-articulated yet. I made a list of all the rich people I knew. My friend who had funded our original deals really wanted to be done, but I was like, look, I need you to come in for a reasonably large chunk for signaling reasons. If I tell everyone that we did deals together, but you're not putting money into this new one, no one's going to invest. So he did this final, amazing solid for me with a $500,000 check into Adaptive Realty Fund I. Then I had friends from Andover, people's parents. It was embarrassing to call people's parents I'd never really talked to before, but that's what I had to do. I had about $100,000 from my grandmother who had passed away to put into Fund I. We ended up raising about $1.6 million or $1.8 million that way.

That's the grand total?

At first, yeah. $50,000 here, $100,000 there. This was after putting out $14 million the previous few years, so it was extremely painful. I went to our CPA asking if he knew anyone interested in investing. He introduced me to this family that owned real estate. I was so green. I showed up at their Santa Monica offices shaved, hair cut short, wearing a sport coat, while the senior non-family member was in jeans and sneakers. I was so nervous, I'm shaking, trying to make conversation.

This was around 2012 when everyone was refinancing their buildings because interest rates were so low. I made this rookie mistake asking if they were taking advantage of the rates to refinance their portfolio. The look he gave me. When you're that wealthy and own that much real estate, your biggest problem is having so much cash coming in that you don't know where to deploy it. The idea of refinancing to pull more cash showed such a profound misunderstanding on my part.

That's so interesting, I never thought of it that way.

Yeah, it was very instructive for me. That guy has turned out to be an incredible partner for me and shaped a lot of my thinking. So I explained our model and he basically said, "Look, if you want a couple hundred thousand dollars, I'll write you a check today. But if you want a material amount, we'll have to negotiate the docs." When I asked what's material, he offered to match everything we'd raised from friends and family. They just wanted veto rights on deals to prevent anything really stupid.

I was worried about how our other investors would react to this new family coming in with significant influence. But when I called our friends and family saying, "Hey, there's this extraordinarily sophisticated and wealthy third-generation California real estate family that wants to invest alongside you, and all they're asking for is a bit of control over what the investment goes into," they were thrilled. They were like, "That sounds fantastic. Sign those docs immediately."

That became Adaptive Realty Fund I, about $3.6 million. We bought and renovated four four-plexes all cash. The idea was to sell them to people who would use 30-year conventional loans at insanely low rates. We did incredibly well.

So half of Fund I came from a random meeting through your CPA?

Well, the CPA had been doing our taxes for years, and that family trusted him. They had happened to be specifically looking for young operators to capitalize. I'm now close with both the senior non-family member and the senior family member. They're incredibly sharp but so humble. Even when I probably said and did dumb stuff, they never made me feel stupid. They educated me without me realizing I was being educated. I had a certain amount of arrogance, but also some humility, and they managed to teach me in such a gentle way that I never felt talked down to. It's what we're trying to do now with ReSeed. I'm not sure if I'm emotionally mature enough to do for others what they did for me, but I'm trying.

When people talk about real estate being a relationship business, this seems to be exactly what they mean.

Yeah, I would go very far to make things right for them. We've acted with integrity toward each other for a long time. That's incredibly powerful when you're an operator and have a deep-pocketed capital allocator who gets what you're trying to do and has a similar long-term mindset and trusts you.

Did this give you a blueprint of the kind of people you wanted to raise capital from later?

Yes. What ended up happening is all our capital has been inbound since then. Through the blog, Twitter, and referrals. I've learned an enormous amount from these people, and what I learned is reflected in what I write publicly. That writing attracts people who align with that vision and repels those who don't. So our investor base was shaped in that image and mediated through my writing.

Was Fund II easier to raise money for?

Yes, but first that family came to us midway through fund one wanting to give us more money. Around 2012 to 2013, they mentioned their partners in Phoenix and Chicago were buying foreclosed single-family homes and doing well. They asked if we wanted to do the same in Los Angeles. Like an idiot, I said no because I had this other strategy. They still put $10 million in fund two, but in retrospect, one of the most important lessons was—when really smart people come to you with capital and a strategy, say yes! That portfolio would easily be worth $30 million today.

Fund three was another lesson. I told them I didn't want to give them veto rights anymore. They just gave us $100,000 and wished us luck. Fund III was only $2.5 million but ended up great. We started growing relationships with other families who could write larger checks, doing fee deals and joint ventures with them instead.

Then I found a commercial deal in Highland Park and pitched it to the original family. While showing them around, they saw all these buildings we were doing for other people. They realized we were doing well and turned the spigot back on. We went from having around $15 million in assets under management around 2015 to about $100 million very rapidly.

Did you finally start to feel some relief now that you're making a living, like things are working, that you're going to be okay?

Good question. It was around 2016 to 2017 when we hit real scale. I remember looking up when we were at $15 million thinking, if only we could get to $100 million. And suddenly we were there. Then it was $200 million. In retrospect, it happened very fast. By 2018, about ten years into my career and six to seven years into Adaptive, I was like, okay, this is gonna work.

At a certain point, my financial situation surpassed where I would have been on my original track. I don't make as much as a corporate lawyer, but my life is infinitely better. I have financial freedom, my time is free, and it's a great life. Around 2017 to 2018 is when it really started to sink in that I'd exceed the expectations I had for myself before.

So now you have this great inbound lead generator and established capital base, and you eventually launched ReSeed in 2023. It has been described as the Y-Combinator for real estate. Can you tell me more about it?

I can't take credit for the model. My partner Rhett Bennett brought it to me. We had met through Twitter, and he came to Reconvene for a couple years. The problem he identified was capacity constraint. Any single operator can only take so much money at once, not enough for serious capital to get involved. If you're trying to deploy $100 million, you can't do a bunch of little million-dollar deals.

The insight was that you could train and incentivize multiple operators to do this business in different markets. While any individual might only use $10 to $15 million a year, with 20 operators you have a significant mechanism for deploying capital. Every market has its local quirks—rent control, property taxes, zoning, tenants. Rather than try to cover all these different geographies ourselves, we help you build your own business in your market.

The big roadblock was if you're not going to sell, you're never going to be that liquid. Therefore, if your investors keep requiring that you do a large co-invest, you're going to run out of money. This happened to me early on. The investors eventually wanted to do more deals, but I had to tell them we have to figure out a way to do this because I don't have any more money to put up a co-invest.

And they were like, well, we've seen you do a bunch of stuff, you have behaved honorably, and therefore we don't care if you have skin in the game. For a GP, your reputation is so much more valuable than the capital that you put in any one deal. It all depends on maintaining the trust of your investors. So properly understood, the skin in the game is your reputation and who cares about $100,000.

So we designed the economic incentives so operators can steadily build a portfolio while basically acting independently building their own business. You get fees along the way and build up control but minority stakes in building after building. When we modeled it out, we realized these operators would do very well.

How many people did you end up with in the first ReSeed class?

We had 2,000 operators express interest, then around 700 actually completed an application and we cut that down to eight groups.

Did most of those come from Twitter?

Oh yeah. They either came directly from Twitter or they had a friend who was on Twitter who was like, hey, this would be perfect for you, you should apply.

You were one of the first people in the "Real Estate Twitter" community. Has the platform been transformative?

Completely life changing. We've raised about $50 million from Twitter connections. Then there's Reconvene, the conference my wife and I run, not a big business, but we make money from it, and it's been incredible with the people we've met. That's how I met Rhett and started ReSeed. I've made really close friends too. I mean, how would I have ever met Chris Powers, who lives in Fort Worth, where I had never been before. We have no crossover, and he's turned out to be a really good friend. And I could say the same about a bunch of other people too. I just never would have met them in a million years, but they've really changed my life in various ways.

Today, from that unassuming Echo Park storefront, Moses runs a portfolio worth north of $200 million. The numbers tell only part of the story, however. His operation stands apart because of the principles guiding it. When city inspectors delivered that painful early lesson, Moses transformed meticulous permitting into a standard practice. He builds properties with renovations that are thorough and completely by-the-book.

This long-view approach attracted a particular kind of investor. Rather than chasing quarterly returns, Moses's backers often represent multi-generational wealth seeking steady, principled growth. The connections forged through his writing proved far more valuable than conventional networking ever could have.

As co-founder of ReSeed Partners, Moses now mentors and funds emerging operators nationwide, sharing both technical knowledge and the patient mindset that served him well through difficult times. His philosophy emphasizes becoming a definitive expert in specific neighborhoods rather than chasing deals across scattered markets.

What Moses built shows how developing a clear, differentiated perspective in real estate can create lasting value. His consistent focus on quality and depth of market knowledge has enabled him to build a sustainable business that continues to grow even in challenging market conditions.

Connect

- Websites:
    - adaptiverealty.com
    - kagansblog.com
- X: @moseskagan
- LinkedIn: Moses Kagan

Part Three
Developers

Some see vacant land or aging buildings as problems, but these professionals see potential. They're the ones who turn empty lots and outdated structures into landmarks that shape our cities. Their approaches vary. Some manage the entire process, others coordinate specialized teams, but all share a knack for spotting value where others don't.

The developers featured here reflect the full range of the field, from hands-on builder-developers to expert repositioners and strategic project managers. Talk to any of them, and common themes emerge: calculated risk-taking, expansive networks spanning city halls to capital markets, and an ability to envision spaces that endure through shifting market cycles. They're the puzzle-solvers who coordinate architects, contractors, regulators, and investors to create the built environment we live in every day.

Sean Sweeney

Co-Founder, Hall Sweeney Properties

Minneapolis, MN

- Co-founded Hall Sweeney Properties in 2017 as a General Partner, growing from a single boutique project to more than $200 million in design-forward multifamily developments across nine award-winning properties in Minneapolis.
- Successfully implemented the "attainable luxury" strategy in multifamily housing, combining premium amenities with accessible price points to drive exceptional lease-up velocity.
- Sourced and executed acquisitions of over 2,500 multifamily units valued at more than $300 million during his tenure at Timberland Partners.
- Started as a $40,000-a-year receptionist at a California development firm and became a successful developer through strategic networking, mentorship, and a willingness to start at the bottom.
- Leverages social media to share knowledge, source deals, attract capital, and grow The Bright Build platform, now with over 10,000 subscribers and a mission to mentor 1,000 future developers.

Like many others, Sean Sweeney bounced around for a bit before finding his calling in real estate. He came to it through a winding path that included acting, paralegal work, and a brief stint selling mortgages. His real entry came in 2006, when he landed a receptionist job at a California development firm. Instead of just answering phones, he turned the position into a crash course in development, absorbing everything from entitlements to pro formas. Within a year, he'd moved up to project management, only to have the 2008 financial collapse bring the industry to a near standstill, prompting him to reassess and explore new directions.

After moving to Minnesota in 2009, Sean joined Artspace Projects, managing housing for artists, which immersed him in mission-driven development focused on community impact rather than just financial returns. This experience would later influence his approach to building. His next move to Timberland Partners proved challenging at first. Nine months without landing a single deal had him questioning his future in acquisitions. But persistence paid off. Once he found his rhythm, Sean went on to source and acquire more than 2,500 multifamily units valued at over $300 million across seven states. Within five years, he was earning enough to build savings, giving him the runway and confidence to strike out on his own.

That independence came in 2017 when he partnered with Jeff Hall on Kolo, a 41-unit building that filled up in just six weeks without a dollar spent on advertising. The project's success convinced them to formalize their partnership as Hall Sweeney Properties, which has since completed nine multifamily developments valued at over $200 million. Each building has served as an opportunity to refine their approach to construction methods, unit layouts, and amenity packages based on what tenants actually want.

Their formula breaks from convention: slightly smaller units with premium finishes and standout amenities, priced $100-200 below comparable properties. The buildings don't feel like value plays. They offer fully equipped gyms, saunas, smart home technology, and carefully selected art. Their properties have particularly resonated with young professionals who want design-forward spaces without paying top-of-market rents.

Sean has also cultivated something unexpected: a following. He regularly shares detailed breakdowns of his projects and development insights online, attracting aspiring developers and real estate professionals looking to learn from his experience. During our lunch in Minneapolis, a young man approached our table specifically to thank Sean for the knowledge he freely shares. A small moment that revealed how his impact stretches beyond the buildings themselves.

This conversation digs into Sean's distinctive approach to development, his strategies for navigating community dynamics, and the mindset that has helped him spot value where others see risk.

Date of Interview: November 10, 2023

Thanks for doing this, Sean. We're sitting here at your current project on Nicollet Avenue, Akin. What drew you to this spot, and what made you see the potential here?

My business partner Jeff Hall and I had been watching this area for years. We saw how Minneapolis was growing eastward from Edina, which is the wealthiest suburb about two miles west of here. Growth follows people looking for more reasonable housing. When one area gets expensive, people start moving. For apartment renters especially, you're often not looking to live in the most expensive area, but rather somewhere cool with walkability and good transit options.

The city's 2040 plan really helped make this possible. They went through every parcel in Minneapolis and designated where they wanted dense development. As a developer, knowing exactly where the city will be supportive gives you tremendous clarity. They rezoned this whole corridor for 6-story development, which was a huge change from the previous mix of single-family homes and small retail.

Then in 2020, we had both COVID and the George Floyd situation just eight blocks from here. During the unrest, this 1-acre retail site, where there had been a Dollar General and an auto parts store, burned down. Two young finance guys owned it as a triple-net investment. They joked, "It was great for six months, then we woke up one day with a problem." They tried marketing it, but nobody wanted to buy at their price. About six to nine months later, they called back saying they'd heard I might be interested. By then, they'd been sitting on it long enough that I was able to get a very good price.

Before we dive deeper into your development career, I'd like to learn a little more about your background growing up, I understand it wasn't always exactly easy.

I was born in Chicago to an interesting mix. My mom was an Israeli immigrant whose parents had walked from Yemen to Israel, and my dad was Irish-Catholic. We moved to Madison, Wisconsin when I was young. It was a reasonably normal lower-middle-class childhood in the '80s and early '90s. We could afford for me to play baseball and hockey, but we drove rather than flew for vacations.

Looking back now at 45, I can see how my mom's trauma from growing up in the Middle East affected things. Both my parents were yellers. There was constant energy and chaos. When I was 14, they split up. That was particularly hard because they didn't handle it well. As they say, some parents keep it together for the kids, but mine were the opposite.

That must have been tough during your high school years. How did it affect your education?

The really pivotal moment came in my junior year of high school. My dad had always promised they'd figure out how to pay for whatever college I got into. But then he had to tell me they couldn't help after all. That just took all the wind out of my sails. I had a 3.9 GPA my first two years, but after that news, I stopped trying as hard and graduated with around a 3.5.

So what happened next with college?

I applied to Notre Dame and Michigan, determined to get as far from Madison as possible. I got waitlisted at both but ended up getting a full scholarship to Wisconsin. Notre Dame eventually offered me a spot two weeks before school started, but when I saw it would cost $200,000, I realized Wisconsin was the better choice.

What was it like going to school there?

I ended up at Wisconsin with no idea what I wanted to study. I was basically free from my family for the first time after all our struggles, and I just went loose. The first six months, I was just drinking and partying. I got a 2.5 GPA my first semester. I had to maintain a 3.0 to keep my scholarship, so second semester I buckled down and got a 3.7. My transcripts are just this roller coaster of ups and downs. I graduated with a 3.06.

I had to work twenty to thirty hours a week at bars and clothing stores to pay for room and board since my scholarship only covered tuition. Seeing my friends who didn't have to work, who could focus on school and having fun, was the first time in my life I really understood money as a tool.

Your career path took some interesting turns before real estate. What drew you to explore acting as a career option?

Senior year, I got into this directed study program where this guy who had produced *Honey, I Shrunk the Kids* came to Madison. They were making four movies to show at the Wisconsin Film Festival. I auditioned on a whim and got one of the lead roles. It was way more fun than regular school, so I started taking theater classes. I had some natural ability to be in front of people, it just felt easy.

The pivotal moment came in my third year pursuing acting in Chicago. I got into this prestigious theater workshop run by Byrne Piven. After a few weeks, he took me aside and asked if I really wanted to be an actor. He said I seemed too normal, that it's a terrible profession to choose, the profession chooses you. He told me if there's anything else in the world I could see myself doing, I should do that. His son Jeremy (Jeremy Piven of *Entourage)* was sleeping on couches trying to make it.

Around the same time, I reconnected with Kim, who I had met in college and who'd later become my wife. She had just moved from L.A. and was clear she didn't want to make a life with someone who'd be constantly chasing acting roles. Then Byrne passed away suddenly from leukemia. Something about his presence in my life and that conversation, combined with Kim's perspective, it just shook me. I woke up the next day and it was crystal clear: I was done. I needed to move on.

Years later, when Jeremy won his Emmy, he dedicated it to his dad, saying, "This is all I ever wanted to do." It brought me right back to that conversation with Byrne, and I was just a puddle on the floor. It showed me how life isn't always logical, there's more to it than meets the eye.

After your acting experience, you considered a legal career. What motivated that potential direction, and how did it ultimately lead you toward real estate development?

My dad was a lawyer in Madison for the state of Wisconsin, but he worked forty hours per week. I thought lawyers had a good life balance, but later found out it was reflected in his pay. My wife's dad was actually a big-time lawyer in Minneapolis. I figured I was a good talker, I could wear suits, make some money. A buddy got me a job as a law clerk at his old firm. Started at the bottom, just filing documents at the courthouse, but it gave me time to study for the LSAT and research law schools.

You were working at a law firm and seemingly on track for law school. What triggered your shift toward real estate?

I was working in a huge law firm's bankruptcy department, doing paralegal work and writing briefs. Looking around, I saw seventy-year-old partners working 80-hour weeks with more money than they needed but couldn't get off the hamster wheel. The wake-up call came during lunch with some paralegals. I was making $27,000 while carrying student loan debt, and paralegals working under me were making $65,000 to $70,000 just because of seniority.

Around this time, I read *Rich Dad, Poor Dad*. While the book has its issues, the basic framework about assets versus liabilities opened my mind. Growing up, my parents never made investments, money wasn't something we talked about. The concept of passive income was revolutionary to me. In law, the better you get, the more you have to work. But with assets, the better you get, the less you have to do.

When Kim and I both got into schools in the Bay Area, me for law school, her for psychology, I kept having this feeling that I couldn't go through with it. I was terrified to tell my dad and Kim. But when I told Kim, she just said, "That's cool. You've got to do you. I hope you're still coming because I'd really like us to stay together." That was one of the reasons I fell in love with her.

How did that realization lead you to real estate specifically?

Real estate seemed more approachable than other investments. You buy a house for this much, the mortgage is this much, find someone to pay you this much. I started by taking a job at a mortgage company in 2003 when mortgages were flying. The work showed me I was good at sales and people seemed to trust me naturally.

After exploring different aspects of real estate, I started calling everyone I knew to learn more. My uncle in Minnesota was actually doing development, converting a prison to condos and building apartments. When he described his role, I realized he was like a movie producer but for buildings. Something clicked. I'd always been into design. In high school, I'd make my girlfriend drive around looking at houses.

So once you had this realization about development, what did you do next?

At 26, I decided I was going to be a developer. I sent out hundreds of resumes and cover letters to development companies. With one year of mortgage sales and four years of acting on my resume, unsurprisingly no one called back. Finally, this woman named Boo called about a receptionist position at Thompson Dorfman Partners, two guys who had previously run Trammell Crow's West Coast office. I didn't know what that was.

When I met with Bruce, I laid it all out. I knew I had a lot to learn, but I was smart and would work incredibly hard. The pay was terrible—$40,000 in the Bay Area—and it was an hour and a half commute each way. But Boo told me, "These guys are the best of the best. You would learn so much. If they offer you anything, just take it." And I ended up taking it.

What was your experience like in that first role, and what did you do to eventually progress?

I was the first one there every day, did anything they wanted. Making copies, coffee, whatever. After three months, they noticed my commitment. The fact that I was driving an hour and a half each way really showed them I wanted it. They started giving me a car allowance to help with gas.

When Keith, one of the VPs, asked if I knew Excel, I lied and said yes, but I had no idea what Microsoft Excel even was. I went home and studied online at night until I figured it out. About a year in, they had this nonprofit deal, a second phase of an existing housing project. Bruce called me into his office and asked if I wanted to be a project manager. I kept doing the receptionist duties but started taking finance and real estate courses at night.

How did you learn the actual job of project management?

My boss told me, "Take everything as far as you can, but know when to ask questions. I'd rather you ask too many questions on the first project than try to fake it and make mistakes." I kept ongoing lists of questions. Bruce was the principal and would oversee things, but Keith became more of a mentor. He wasn't an owner, so it was easier to go to lunch with him, shoot the shit. I'd ask him all the basic questions. With Bruce, I'd save up my questions and run through them when we had time, like during car rides. They were patient, even when we had to rip out an entire stairwell once because of my mistake. They just said, "That's part of the process."

It sounds like you were building momentum in your career there. How did things progress over the next few years?

By 2008, I was managing multiple projects. The day before Lehman Brothers collapsed, Bruce had called me in to say they were giving me a $20,000 bonus and would start paying me like a real developer, meaning I'd get a cut when deals made money. Next day I came in hungover to news about Lehman failing. Our deals started slowing down. On one condo project, I noticed the construction crews weren't working unless I was there. Then it hit me. They had no next job lined up. They were dragging it out because they'd be unemployed when it finished.

So at some point you and Kim decided California wasn't working anymore. What was it like leaving that job and making the move to Minnesota?

It was tough leaving California. I didn't sleep for about a week before telling them. I was terrified about the conversation. We had decided California was just too expensive for us. We sat on a bench and literally cried as we made the decision to leave.

I flew to Minnesota first for what I called a scouting trip. Met with six people in one day trying to find opportunities. During lunch with a fraternity brother, he went to the bathroom and came back saying he'd just gotten an email about an asset management job at Artspace. They develop housing for artists and musicians.

When I interviewed, I showed up in a suit while everyone was wearing Birkenstocks. Asset management meant overseeing operations of six to ten existing buildings, reviewing financials and supervising property managers. With Artspace's tax credit properties, there was an added political dimension, managing relationships with funding sources like chambers of commerce and mayors. They offered me the job a few days later.

When I finally gave my two weeks' notice back in California, it was incredibly difficult. I told Bruce first, and we only talked about five minutes. I heard him call his wife right after. Will, my other boss, didn't speak to me for three days. When he finally did, all he said was "I'm sorry to lose you. I don't really understand it." That was all he ever said to me the rest of my time there. On my last day, I cried the whole drive home. I made Kim come pick me up because I was so emotional.

How did the transition to Minnesota work out financially?

A big part of the reason we decided to move there was because my wife's mom was selling her big house, and we could live in it for free until it sold, and the market was super dead. We had a two-year plan to see if we liked Minnesota, and if after two years we decided we didn't like it, we'd move.

I was just grateful to have a job in real estate during 2009 when the industry was imploding. The salary was only $50,000, which was tough after making $90,000 in California. But Minnesota's cost of living meant we could actually afford to live in nice neighborhoods that were completely out of reach in San Francisco.

What I didn't expect was the culture shock. My first day, I showed up at 8:30 a.m. but no one else arrived until 9:30. Then everyone went for coffee for an hour. I realized most people there were independently wealthy or former artists who didn't need the money, it was more of a passion project for them. Coming from a different environment, that was a huge adjustment. But it ended up being valuable experience in stakeholder management and community relationships.

So at that point, what was your strategy for building connections in this new city?

When I arrived in Minnesota, I immediately looked for industry groups to join. There was the Urban Land Institute. I'd been part of their Young Leaders Group in San Francisco, which did happy hours and project tours. When I found they had a chapter here, I joined right away. This woman I met thought I had more experience than most members and suggested I join the steering committee. Through that, I met five or six people my age who I'm still friends with today.

My approach was simple. After every meeting I'd ask, "Who else should I meet?" It played to my strengths. I could sit down with someone for coffee, and they'd leave thinking, "I like that guy, seems genuine and eager to help." Of course, there were plenty of misses too. One woman stood me up four different times. And I had this mortifying meeting where I cut myself shaving, forgot about it, and had tissue on my face the whole time.

As the market started showing signs of recovery, one of my contacts called about a Director of Development role at Ryan Companies, this huge developer and construction company. I was excited but also surprised since I only had about six years of experience. The phone screen went great, but weeks passed with no follow-up. I was devastated when they decided not to bring me in for an interview.

A few months later, I asked Rick, my contact there, to lunch just to understand what went wrong. He told me, "Sean, you almost pulled off a miracle. When we posted the job, we didn't realize 75 percent of developers in town wanted the job. We had guys with twenty-five years of experience applying. Everyone loved your phone screen. You were the only candidate with less than twenty years of experience we even considered. You should be incredibly proud."

That conversation completely transformed my outlook. I went from feeling defeated to energized. Within three months, I had multiple job offers, including one from Timberland Partners to handle acquisitions across the country. The role offered unlimited earning potential through commissions rather than just a salary. While other jobs offered $90,000 to $100,000, Timberland's founder said he'd be disappointed if I wasn't making at least $150,000. I took the risk on the commission-based role, and it proved to be transformative for my career.

Looking back, those tough moments—acing the Ryan phone screen but never getting a call back, struggling financially, questioning my path—they were critical. You have to stay persistent and put yourself in position for luck to find you. But equally important is being emotionally aware enough to recognize pivotal moments when they happen. That conversation with Rick was one of those moments that changed everything.

During those first few months at Timberland, how did you manage the pressure of performing in a commission-based role?

I got off to a terrible start. They basically said, "Here's a computer, here's a phone, go find deals." No guidance on what deals or where. They were busy, introverted guys. I've always been a quick study, but they weren't telling me anything. After five or six months without closing a single deal, I started panicking. This was a production role, where if you don't produce, you get fired.

We made some questionable decisions too. Kim and I bought a house and furniture before I'd even made any money. You have to understand, we were in our thirties, a decade behind our peers. We had one car because that's all we could afford.

They said, "Here's what we own, but we want you to find new opportunities in new markets." They wanted expansion beyond their existing footprint. I had to get on broker lists and figure out which markets made sense. St. Louis, Ohio, Michigan, Cincinnati. I'd analyze deals and pitch them in meetings. They'd explain why they liked or didn't like certain deals, which helped me learn.

I worked alongside the owner's son, who had the same job but was technically my boss. He was a good guy and nice, but we had very different styles. It wasn't like my previous mentor Keith where we could grab a burger and discuss everything.

Every time Bob, the owner, would walk past my office and shut his door, I thought, "This is it." But I finally got that first deal done, and things started clicking. Bob was actually fair about commissions. He'd pay me even if Matt, the other acquisitions guy, got his deals picked over mine. But that also worried me when Matt was closing a bunch of deals before I got one.

What turned things around for you at Timberland?

Eventually, I figured out the game. I realized I needed to make offers to show brokers we were serious, even if we might not win the deal. The breakthrough came when I found a property in St. Louis near a Whole Foods in July 2012, about nine months after starting. I followed that with an off-market deal in Omaha. I started understanding what it took: getting brokers to want you as the buyer and selling deals internally. It helped that I was looking at new markets rather than competing for deals in existing ones.

Then I found this deal in Nashville. I kept visiting and could feel the market was about to pop. There was always more people, busier bars, worse traffic. When I brought it to Bob, he initially passed. I had to stand up and say, "Look, you hired me to find deals in new markets. I'm telling you this is going to be your biggest market. If you don't buy this deal, there's no reason for me to work here."

Bob was introverted. When he makes decisions, he shuts his door for a day or two and emerges with an answer. A day and a half later, he said, "Okay." We bought it, and I ended up buying seven more deals there between 2012 and 2015. They all appreciated three to five times. We almost opened a regional office there.

Things really took off after that. I made $160,000 my second year, $200,000 my third year, and $350,000 my fourth and fifth years. We had kids, my wife stopped working, we had a beautiful house. But four years in, I realized something was missing. I wasn't getting any equity in these deals. At first, that wasn't even on my radar. My mantra was just, "don't get fired." But watching deals refinance for $7 million gains while I only got my $30,000 acquisition fee started to hurt. Every year I was starting over at zero, with nothing building up asset-wise to help me long-term.

I went to Bob and said, "Look, I'm not asking for more compensation, you've been great there. But I need to understand what the future looks like. I need some equity in these deals for my family's future." I wanted to be part of the whole pie. Acquisition fees, property management fees, asset management fees, refinance fees, disposition fees. I felt like I'd earned a seat at the table.

To his credit, Bob was direct. He said I could invest in their fund as an accredited investor, but I'd have to write checks like any other investor. When I pointed out that others in the company got pieces of deals without writing checks, he said he'd think about it. He came back and still wanted me to write checks. Over six years and thousands of units acquired, I was only able to invest $20,000 twice. Those investments are worth over $100,000 each now, which just proved my point about missing out on the real upside.

Was that what eventually led to your decision to leave the firm?

It was a combination of things. Bob and I saw things very differently. We're on opposite sides politically, he's a small-town farm kid from North Dakota, and we just had different perspectives. I suggested they make me COO because my people skills combined with their analytical skills would make us unstoppable. Instead, he brought in his daughter from Target to be COO. As my wife Kim reminded me, it's his company and his name on the door, he gets to do what he wants.

Then in mid-2016, several major life events happened in quick succession. My mom was diagnosed with systemic scleroderma and got really sick. We had our second child. My college roommate died, and the Cubs won the World Series. I'd been a huge Cubs fan forever, first time in 108 years.

All of this happened in a ninety-day period. My mom's death at 76 really hit me. I was 38, exactly halfway to that age. It made me realize I might only have thirty more years left. I didn't want to be working until I was 92 unless I was truly loving what I did.

I got to the point where the pain of staying outweighed the fear of leaving. I would drive to work, just a ten-minute ride from my house, and though I'd start the day feeling positive, by the time I pulled into my parking spot, I couldn't physically get out of the car. I'd sit there looking in the rearview mirror telling myself, "You're going to make $350,000 this year. Five years ago, you would have killed to be here. Be grateful." Some days it would take an hour just to get out of the car.

What made you realize development might be your path forward?

When we renovated our house, people would come over and say, "This looks like it's from California!" They'd ask who made these choices, and I'd explain that while I worked with great artists and interior designers, many decisions were mine. For three months straight, every single person who walked in was amazed by how it felt and looked. I always had a hunch I had a good eye for design, but this really cemented that feeling.

I started putting pieces in place. I had a gut feeling there were opportunities in smaller development deals while everyone else was chasing 200-unit projects. I found a small site through a friend. We ended up flipping it to another developer and made good money. During that process, my wife noticed how energized I was and said, "For the month you were working on that, I haven't seen you that alive in a long time."

That was eye-opening. Here I was, dealing with my mom's death and a new baby, but I couldn't wait to work on that site. It showed me what I really wanted to be doing. Before I quit, I made sure we had nearly a year's worth of living expenses saved, and I got another site under contract. I realized at my age, with our spending, I might never have another chance at a year's runway. It was time to take the leap.

And this is when you started working with your current business partner, Jeff Hall, who was key to your initial success. Could you walk us through how that relationship evolved?

On Kolo, our first project, Jeff wasn't initially my business partner, he was just my partner on that specific deal. He had been a friend and mentor who encouraged me to go solo. When I brought him Kolo, he decided to come in as the primary investor. He took about ninety percent of the deal, I got six percent, and we had a third partner, Alex, who got the remainder.

After we got Kolo going, I quickly found another site. I took it to Jeff first but explained that I wanted better terms. I told him, "We've been working together for several months now, and you can see how I guide this process. I'd like to do this with you, but I can't do another 90/10 split, I know I can get better terms elsewhere." He immediately offered a 50/50 partnership, which worked perfectly.

How does the developer fee and equity structure typically work in your deals?

The developer fee is typically 4 to 5 percent of the budget. For example, on a $45 million project, we might get a $33 million bank loan, leaving us to raise $12 million in equity. If our developer fee is $2 million and we roll that back into the project, we only need to raise $10 million from investors.

We pay a 7 percent preferred return to the limited partners, which Jeff and I are also part of through our reinvested developer fees. Any returns above seven percent not only provide additional investor returns but also pay down their capital accounts. Once their capital is fully returned, the preferred return goes away, and it becomes a 70/30 split forever. So while I might start with 9 to 10 percent ownership, over fifteen to twenty years that could grow to 20 to 25 percent as investor capital gets paid down.

How has your capital raising evolved, particularly with social media?

Initially, it was all traditional networking—coffees, lunches, dinners. When we started our later projects, I had been on Twitter for about four months with around 1,000 followers. I was fortunate to join Real Estate Twitter when it was just getting started, and I found myself regularly listed among the top accounts in the space.

For our Wakpada project, we needed to raise $7 million. After just mentioning an investor call on Twitter, I started getting DMs from potential investors worldwide. A million dollars of that raise came through Twitter connections. By our next project, I had about 25,000 followers, and we raised $4 million through those relationships. Some were fraternity brothers I hadn't talked to in twenty years who saw my work online, while others were completely new connections making $500,000 investments.

The challenge is that development is inherently riskier than stabilized assets, and Minneapolis has had some perception challenges. But Twitter has been such a net positive that I've had mayors and city council members from across the country reaching out about bringing deals to their cities.

You've built a significant following on social media. How else has it affected your business?

Having an online platform gives you built-in credibility. I now have over 10,000 people reading my newsletter simply because I've been consistently tweeting for three years. There's a skill to it. You need to be focused on one specific thing and talk about that consistently. Most people don't realize you have to repeat yourself frequently. Analytics show only about ten percent of your audience sees any given post.

If you'd asked us all five years ago about social media, we might have dismissed it, but the proof is in the pudding.

Your buildings have a distinctive style that stands out in the market. How did you arrive at your development philosophy?

I heard Rick Rubin say once, "I get paid to know what I like." That really resonated with me. I realized if I design spaces that I want, my taste seems to connect with what people think is cool. So I just decided to build what I would want if I were the target resident.

Jeff was understandably skeptical on the first project since I hadn't proven my design instincts yet. I told him, "I have this idea that good design will pay more. It will get better residents, better lease-up, more press. Let me drive the design just this once. If my hypothesis is wrong, we can build basic boxes after this."

My target tenant is typically someone twenty-two to thirty, in their first or second job out of college. They want cool amenities and good design, but they can't afford luxury prices. So we offer slightly smaller units but pack in premium amenities. The units might be compact, but when your rent is $1,300 instead of $1,700 market average, and you get access to things like a fully equipped gym with free weights and Rogue equipment, it becomes a no-brainer.

I noticed you have some unconventional amenities like saunas. How did that decision come about?

Everyone pushed back on certain features. I've learned most of my good ideas get resistance initially and I don't take it personally. But in my partnership, I have the final say on design. And at this point, I trust my gut 100 percent. The gym and saunas were the two things people tried to talk me out of, but they've become our biggest selling points. We focused on creating great common spaces since the units are smaller. We have smart building technology, showcase local art throughout the building, and every unit has in-unit laundry.

How did you arrive at this development approach?

Most developers are finance professionals who rely entirely on architects and interior designers. I take a different approach. I spend an enormous amount of time making sure every inch of space works exactly right. When you combine that attention to detail with transit access, walkability, and the right amenities, it creates an incredibly attractive package for our target market.

When we started Kolo, I had been collecting design inspiration for years. I showed the architects a bunch of reference images to convey the vibe I wanted. When their initial plans didn't capture it, I actually drew what I wanted myself. The lead architect told me, "You're either going to be my favorite client of all time, or we're going to be one and done."

Throughout construction, I told my wife we might be the only ones who care how cool it looks. But then we leased all forty-one units in a month and a half, many months ahead of schedule. The project was named one of the best fifty developments across all asset classes in the state of Minnesota and got nominated for Best Urban Development of the year in the city. We had other developers stopping to take pictures, asking who was behind it. That's when I knew I was onto something, and my partner said, "Okay, I don't need to come to design meetings anymore. You've got this."

Have you seen your buildings have an effect on the neighborhoods?

It's had a real ripple effect. Look at the restaurant scene that's developed here. We've got chefs who trained under James Beard winners opening innovative concepts. The whole area is transforming. I even have ideas about bringing in more high-end dining concepts, though I don't want to own restaurants myself. The key is creating spaces that attract the right tenants and help build a vibrant community.

Successfully navigating the development approval process seems to be one of your strengths. Could you break down your strategy for working with local government and community stakeholders, particularly how you approach the various stages of approval?

The process typically takes six months to a year, sometimes more. When we identify a site, before we tie it up, I first do quick gut checks with my architect and builder. For example, with our Wakpada project, I knew we could do about 100 units, it ended up being 126.

Once those initial checks look good, my first call is to the city planner. I've built relationships, so I know exactly who to call. I'll say, "Hey Andrew, we have this site tied up, it's zoned for 6 stories, looking at 120 to 130 units. See any issues?" They'll typically ask to see schematic plans.

We'll develop basic plans and meet with the planner. We walk through everything—our vision, commercial space, parking layout. I'm always trying to get feedback as early as possible because every day I spend designing, I'm spending money. If something needs to be cut, I want to know immediately.

My philosophy is simple: I will work and negotiate with the neighbors, but I'm not going to fight the city. If city planning staff says no, that's it. It's not a good use of my time or money. You're going to have to work with the neighbors no matter what, so you want the city behind you.

After getting initial support from planning, I'll reach out to the city council person: "We've met with the city, they seem supportive. I'd like twenty minutes to share our plans with you." They usually appreciate being informed before the community. It's about giving them political cover.

How do you handle community engagement?

For community engagement, we start by connecting with the neighborhood organization and scheduling a community meeting. While that's being arranged, and before it happens, we identify the most immediately affected neighbors and meet with them individually. By the time we get to the big meeting, I know who my vocal opponents will be because I've already had coffee with them. They may not agree with what I'm doing, but they know I've listened and that I'm reasonable.

At the neighborhood meeting, I address concerns head-on. I learned from my wife, she always reminds me: "Empathy, empathy, empathy. You do not argue." When someone says something like," You're ruining our neighborhood," my response has to be, "Help me understand your concern further." Often, when people say things out loud, it becomes so obviously unreasonable that it turns the crowd against them.

Our goal is to get as many people as possible to vent at the neighborhood meeting because it saves them a trip to the planning commission hearing. If I can isolate 100 out of 103 potential opponents at the neighborhood meeting, and only three show up to yell at the planning commission. That's manageable. I take the brunt of it early to make the approval process smoother.

As you look to the future, you've mentioned potential diversification beyond multifamily development. How are you evaluating different asset classes, particularly retail opportunities, and what factors influence your thinking about portfolio expansion?

I'm starting to think about branching out. While I'm really proud of our multifamily work, I'm realizing I might not be creatively inspired to just keep doing the same thing forever. I'm not a "print and repeat for three years" kind of guy. Even some of the media content creation has been fun because it's a new outlet for ideas and learning something new. I can already envision potential retail projects. Like there's this old tire station that I can see perfectly as a food hall with garage doors.

How do you view each development project?

Each project is like its own company, and I'm the CEO directing what needs to happen to make this building come to fruition. The creation process really drives me. I'm still passionate about our newest building because it's fresh, but I've realized something interesting about myself. I don't visit our year-old projects much anymore. When we're developing, it's all I think about. It's my blood, sweat, and tears for two to four years. But once it's done, my focus shifts. I used to think they'd all be my babies forever, but I've realized I'm really a builder. I want to create the thing.

How are you and Jeff navigating the current market environment?

This is the first time since we started that I haven't had an active construction project. Costs have gone up dramatically, rates have increased significantly, and rents here haven't moved in four years. We pulled out of deals last year even before the rate increases because costs alone made them infeasible.

If I knew everything would snap back in early 2025, I'd just take it easy for a year. But I think we might be looking at two or three years where we can't build. I'm equity-rich but would need some cash flow planning. I haven't made any money in over two years, and with kids in private school and other commitments, we're having to make some adjustments. You can try to nickel and dime your way through it, or you can get creative about finding new ways to generate income. I prefer the latter approach.

We actually had three additional projects in our pipeline last year that we were actively pursuing. If we had built all three, we'd be in a really tough position right now with the market changes. That experience has made me realize I probably need to develop another line of business that's more conservative. I can't just keep going all-in every time.

How has that affected your thoughts on risk and future opportunity?

Looking ahead, I need to find the right balance between staying creative and managing risk. I used to joke that if I was going to go bankrupt, I wanted it to be before 50 so I'd have time to rebuild. Now that I'm 47, with kids who are 11 and 8, that perspective is shifting. Though I'm comfortable with uncertainty. I know what it feels like to have seventeen cents in your checking account.

This whole journey really highlights what's possible in America. My grandparents emigrated from Yemen to Israel on foot in the 1930s, my mother came here by boat, and now, two generations later, I have these incredible opportunities. That's not just about me, that's about the structure of our country and what it makes possible.

You've gone from receptionist to project manager to acquisitions to developer, learning different aspects of the business at each step. What advice would you give someone looking to pursue a career in development today?

If you want to do development specifically, I would go get a job for somebody like me, come work for me for five years. Let's go through three or four deals together. You're going to get paid okay, and yes, some of it will be grunt work, but that's the path. If you're older, like 45, you have two choices: either convince somebody like me to hire you, or figure out another way in.

The best thing somebody can do to add value is to bring me opportunities I wouldn't have otherwise seen. Find a site that fits what I'm trying to do, spend the time making calls, get the owner interested in selling. But you have to be careful, there are people who might take the deal if you just call them about it. So what I tell people is to get it under an LOI or purchase agreement first, then approach a developer and say, "I've got this site, and I want a seat at the table to understand how you do this deal."

The hard part for people who do project management is they don't see the deal-making piece. Even when I finished in California, I understood the development process—how to get the deal designed, approved, under construction, built, and then leased or sold. What I didn't know was how to find deals, how to negotiate them, what price to pay, what metrics people were looking for on returns, and how to find the money. That's a huge piece of it.

Someone needs to pay the pre-development costs, which can add up to hundreds of thousands. We were at $900,000 by the time we broke ground on one project. Plus, if you're 27 and your net worth is minimal, you can't sign a $5 million personal guarantee. You need established partners to back you. That's why it's really hard to do development too soon.

Whether you're fresh out of school feeling like you don't know what to do, or mid-career feeling like you're just in the wrong place, Sean's story can serve as inspiration. If you keep plugging away, maybe take a chance here or there, good things can happen.

Sean carved out his niche in the middle market with a simple but effective formula: smartly designed smaller units with premium touches that don't command premium prices. His properties hit that sweet spot at $100-200 below comparable rentals while offering amenities that feel like they belong in a higher price bracket. The approach connects especially well with young professionals who want quality spaces without stretching their budgets.

This strategy emerged from his hands-on experience across different property types and markets. Managing housing for artists showed him how thoughtful spaces create community. Sourcing deals across seven states for Timberland taught him which amenities renters actually value versus which ones they'll happily trade for lower rent. By the time Kolo launched in 2017, Sean had developed a keen sense for the gap between what people want and what most developers deliver.

The market response spoke volumes. Those forty-one units at Kolo filled in just six weeks, without spending a penny on advertising. Tenants walked through the door, saw features that felt a tier above the asking price, and signed leases on the spot. It was the first building he developed, and from there, Sean knew he had found his calling.

Each one of his buildings bears Sean's fingerprints, from floor plans to fixture selections. He doesn't delegate the details that shape daily life, creating spaces where design choices reflect a specific vision of how people want to live rather than what's cheapest to build or easiest to maintain. He also goes against the grain and trusts his gut when it comes to implementing features like fully equipped gyms, saunas, and smart home electronics.

Twenty years in, Sean's career offers a straightforward lesson about development. Where you start matters less than what you learn along the way. Success comes from paying attention to what people actually want, persisting through the inevitable setbacks, and having the confidence to trust your judgment even when others follow a different path.

CONNECT

- Websites:
  - thebrightbuild.com
  - hallsweeney.com
- X: @seandsweeney
- Instagram: @seansweeney
- LinkedIn: Sean Sweeney

Susan Miller Gruppi

Co-Founder, M2G Ventures

Fort Worth, TX

- Co-founded M2G Ventures in 2014 with her twin sister, growing from a self-funded startup to a company with 24 employees and 20 properties across Texas.
- Specializes in complex, design-forward industrial projects that achieve premium rents through modest, strategic investments in smart design.
- Led redevelopment efforts for the historic Fort Worth Stockyards since 2016, transforming it from a tourist-centric destination into a vibrant district with 9 million annual visitors.
- Uses a three-pronged business model—investments, advisory, services—diversifying from mixed-use conversions to institutional-scale industrial developments.
- Established a million-dollar mental health research initiative at the University of Texas Southwestern.

ABOUT A MONTH after sitting down with Chris Powers, I flew back to Fort Worth, Texas, this time to talk with Susan Miller Gruppi of M2G Ventures. Our conversation took place at their headquarters in their sleek office space known as the Library—a comfortable, inviting room with classy aesthetics. With black painted walls, well-appointed furniture, and a fireplace adding a touch of warmth, the room is a reflection of the firm's investment philosophy. Susan and her twin sister Jessica have built M2G Ventures around a novel idea for their asset class of choice: industrial real estate deserves some style and thoughtful design.

Unlike many others who stumbled their way into real estate by accident, Susan knew early on it was where she was headed. She grew up around her family's scrappy real estate business, where her parents showed her firsthand what it meant to have grit. Their tenacious drive to keep trying until finding something that works provided her with invaluable lessons. Together with her sister, they would dream of running their own firm someday. Later, she planned her education and career intentionally to gain the background that would prepare her to do just that. While at school, she and her sister started a real estate club, and at their first event, she hand-picked her mentor. This led to her spending eight years at Trademark Property Company, where she learned the details on how to break down real estate deals through financial analysis. This foundation proved especially valuable when markets turned volatile, and when fundamentals and resourcefulness mattered more than ever.

Since its founding, M2G has expanded at its own pace. From just the two sisters to a team of twenty-four across multiple offices, it has maintained complete operational independence by self-funding its growth. Instead of bringing on operating partners, they've funded everything themselves and have scaled by carefully aligning overhead with revenue across its three divisions: investments, advisory, and services. By the time we spoke in late 2023, the construction lending environment had pushed the firm toward acquisitions rather than ground-up development, showing their flexibility.

I learned of the Fort Worth Stockyards when I first started researching Susan and her firm. I hadn't visited on my prior trip to Fort Worth, so I knew I had to visit this time around. The day before our meeting, I spent some time walking around, checked out some of the shops, then had a steak dinner at the Drover Hotel. For anyone who hasn't been, it's definitely worth the visit. Susan's work in Fort Worth's historic Stockyards reveals her and her firm's distinctive approach to place-making. Many of the tenants there hardly have any other locations, if at all. And rather than working with the real estate teams, they worked directly with the founders of those brands, creating a unique mix of concepts for the district. For the project's next phase, they're creating multiple smaller structures with varied designs and enhancing the livestock experiences that already make the area special, including the popular daily cattle drives.

From their first warehouse purchase to the firm's current substantial industrial portfolio, Susan and Jessica remain focused on thoughtful transformation. Their buildings give tenants functional space with identity, proving that warehouse districts can inspire when approached with vision and purpose.

Date of Interview: November 29, 2023

Can you tell me about your family background and how you first got exposed to real estate?

Our parents started with absolutely nothing. On their first date, they split a McDonald's Happy Meal. Dad, born in 1946, and Mom, born in 1950, didn't graduate from college. Dad started as a life insurance salesman in Longview, Texas. He was a natural entrepreneur, and in the 1970s, he looked around our small town thinking about what business didn't exist where he could have a competitive advantage. He realized there weren't any custom pool builders in Longview, so he taught himself the business. He grew it to two or three locations over about fifteen years before eventually burning out.

During that time, they started buying duplexes as investments, living in one side, renting out the other. The real estate investments gradually produced more income than the pool business, so Dad sold his portion to his brother and focused entirely on real estate. They did everything completely self-funded, no partners or outside capital, just rolling our precious family money into each new project.

How did your parents grow their real estate business while raising a family?

They did all kinds of real estate. Buying old industrial buildings, developing land, adding infrastructure to increase value. By 1987, they decided to develop a luxury subdivision called Hunter's Creek. This was while raising five kids, including my oldest brother who's mentally handicapped, two other brothers, and then Jessica and me. When we twins were born, they had four children in diapers while running their own business.

The timing couldn't have been worse. The S&L Crisis hit Longview particularly hard, combined with oil and gas issues in the region. Since they had self-funded the entire subdivision project, we went bankrupt when Jessica and I were four. We had to move from our main house to the guest house while they showed and sold the property. They took that money and rolled it into an apartment complex, Dad's first one. From there, he kept reinvesting, building the portfolio one property at a time. He went from bankruptcy to a meaningful net worth, all self-funded with no employees. It's a different kind of success story than you typically hear today. No outside investors, no formal education, no mentor, just figuring it out in a small market.

What was it like growing up in that environment?

Business was their hobby. They never really had many friends. They were each other's friends and partners. Jessica and I were more comfortable talking about business than anything else, even by college. It's like learning a language when you're young. It becomes innate. You don't even realize you're learning it, as opposed to trying to learn it when you're older.

We saw every different type of real estate project. I remember they bought this 100-year-old farmhouse and moved it down the street. I can still picture it on the truck, thinking how cool it was. We renovated it as a family. Mom was incredibly resourceful. She'd rearrange furniture monthly just to make things look nicer, and she'd painstakingly choose paint schemes for their properties, even the less glamorous ones. They were always finding ways to improve properties with limited resources.

Did you enjoy learning about real estate from an early age?

We absolutely loved it! There wasn't Zillow back then, but we'd ask our parents to drive us around to look at houses. We'd call the numbers on the signs and talk to realtors, asking about bedrooms and square footage. We thought that was fun. Later, they started buying larger pieces of land, and we'd do this interesting cycle. Build a house, live in it briefly, sell it, then move five acres away and build another one. By the time I went to college, we'd lived in nine different houses within a couple-block radius.

How did that early experience shape your approach to business?

Everything I learned about work ethic, resilience, constant pivoting, and problem-solving came from watching them. Dad's still going strong at 78. They had this really interesting way of doing real estate, very different from our institutional approach today. They asked themselves, "How can we make money in real estate while still having a flexible schedule to raise five kids?" They found creative ways to add value through sweat equity and careful project selection.

What's particularly remarkable is how they maintained their focus through the tough times. Even after bankruptcy, they kept reinvesting and building, always self-funded, always hands-on. That showed us you don't need outside investors or formal education if you're willing to work hard and think creatively. Their approach wasn't about getting massive scale. It was about sustainable growth through smart, manageable projects.

Tell me about your early days at Texas Christian University (TCU). How did you begin developing your path into real estate?

When I was a sophomore at TCU, I looked around for a real estate club where I could meet mentors and people with companies who could give advice or jobs. When I found out TCU didn't have one, Jessica and I started it ourselves. The Real Estate Club today is the single largest student-led organization on campus.

For our first event, I asked all the professors who the prominent company leaders were in the industry that could do roundtables with students. Terry (from Trademark) was one of them. Jessica and I went in thinking, "We're going to find a boss here today." We scoped everyone out—they didn't know what we were doing—and decided he was the right mentor for us. Because his dad was a twin himself, he connected with us. We've stayed in touch for almost twenty years now.

How did you approach building that mentorship relationship?

When you're asking someone to be your mentor, you're really giving them a compliment, saying, "I respect what you're doing, I think you're super smart." A lot of people are afraid to ask because it feels awkward, but if they're open to teaching and helping others grow, they'll usually lean into it. We were also strategic. We'd always prepare specific questions and make the most of the time. Even now, I rarely meet with mentors without a clear agenda. When someone's opinion is that valuable to you, you want to make every session count.

After graduating, you and Jessica both started at Trademark Property Company. Was that a deliberate choice?

Yes and no. We're entrepreneurs by DNA, and real estate is all we've ever known. When we graduated in 2008, mixed-use development was incredibly popular. Lifestyle centers and malls were thriving. As smart females, we naturally gravitated toward it. Plus, we'd already built that relationship with Terry through the Real Estate Club, and since his dad was an identical twin, he understood our dynamic.

Jessica and I made a strategic decision early on to develop different skill sets, knowing we'd eventually start our own business. I focused on finance and development, while she specialized in leasing. We didn't want to have the same specialties when we came back together.

Can you tell me about your early years as an analyst? How did you develop your financial skills?

I spent a lot of time working with Excel and Argus, particularly during the GFC. While I wasn't naturally the "overly smart one," I was a hard worker. I worked directly with the CFO, who was a CPA by trade. He taught me to think about deals in a very fundamental way. He would make me print everything out and literally check the math with a ruler, line by line.

What I learned was invaluable about how real estate actually generates money. When you're young, you don't naturally think about how a tenant's check breaks down into base rent, CAM* charges, tax reimbursements, and so on. You don't automatically understand NOI † growth or how to factor in rent rolls. But doing those analyses over and over, especially during the GFC, really ingrained the mechanics of investment.

How did that experience shape your approach to real estate?

Learning during the GFC taught me a more defensive way to operate. We were constantly working on loan refinances, updating valuations, and loan workouts. That experience was incredibly formative. I still think about risk management on the front end rather than the back end.

I remember one mall project where I told the CFO, "I don't see how we're ever going to make money on this deal." Five or six years later, we sold it and the promote was $50 million. Watching that as a young analyst was eye-opening. You're running all these conservative analyses based on current variables, but then the market turns, and suddenly you see how much value can be created over time.

What would you say was your biggest strength from that period?

I became really good at making complex things seem simple. In the finance world, people often try to make things more complicated than they need to be. But real estate is fundamentally about addition and subtraction. I learned to focus on the four or five things that really matter in a deal, which allowed me to evaluate opportunities quickly and solve problems efficiently.

I was in the office by five a.m. most days, grinding through complex analyses. Sometimes I'd stare at problems for hours before figuring them out. But that experience was crucial. It impacts so much of how I

---

* **CAM** (Common Area Maintenance): Charges tenants pay for the upkeep of shared spaces in a property, like lobbies, parking lots, or landscaping. Also called CAM charges.

† **NOI** (Net Operating Income): The profit a property generates from operations, calculated as revenue minus operating expenses (like maintenance and utilities), before debt or taxes.

approach business decisions today. Those years as an analyst weren't always enjoyable, but they gave me the foundation I needed to eventually run my own company.

What finally made you decide to leave Trademark and start your own business?

By then I was 28 or 29, and I had been obsessed with having my own business for years. It was all I thought about. Your good days just aren't as good anymore, and your bad days are worse because you're always thinking about something else you should be doing. It starts like a yellow light, goes to orange, then red. There's just nothing you can do about it other than say, "I think I need to do this."

I had no business plan, didn't even know what type of real estate I was going to focus on, no investors, no office. I think I had $200,000 saved up. We didn't have any kids at that point, so I thought, "I'll just see what it's like, give it a year." I took about a month and a half off first because even at that young age, I still had almost ten years where my identity was wrapped up in being the hard-charging, hardworking young lady. I hadn't gotten to just be a regular person.

How did you find your first deal?

I started talking to brokers in town and had lunch with Chris (Chris Powers of Fort Capital) one day. He had started his own business several years prior, so I asked him who the top brokers were since I was trying to get back into the local scene. He mentioned he'd passed on this off-market industrial deal that I might want to look at. I liked it because it was a well-located asset that could be transformed into something else and maybe work for Tesla.

We put it under contract, and by then Jessica had left her job to join me. We put together the investment summary. I need to find and frame it because it was terrible! I mean, it was good enough, I knew what I needed to say, but graphics-wise it took forever. We did a hit list of about fifty people, mostly mentors and contacts I'd developed. Not people I'd done business with at Trademark, but partners of Trademark who had taken an interest in me because I was always so interested in excelling and improving. Also my friends' dads, my dad's old business partners, friends of friends. We closed the deal with nineteen investors.

How did that deal turn out?

Two months after we bought it for $3.7 million, we were touring another car guy for the other half of the building. He said he didn't want to lease it, he wanted to buy it. We told him $5.9 million, which was what we had projected selling it for five years later. He countered at $5 million, which was still insane, but we held firm at $5.9 million. Thirty minutes later, we got a call from the title company saying somebody had just wired them a million dollars, and then he sent us a signed contract at $5.9 million. The guy was just incredible.

So our first deal made $2.1 million in profit in thirty days. My dad said, "This is not how it works, just so we're clear. This is not going to be a repeat!" But it gave us momentum. We did a 1031 exchange, which lets you reinvest up to 200 percent of the sales price. So in a period of six months, we needed to buy about $12 million worth of property. That doesn't sound like a lot now, but at the time in Fort Worth, there weren't many people doing anything.

All our initial investors were excited. These nineteen people thinking, "These ladies are smart, they just made us a lot of money." I tried to stay humble: "Well, I do work very hard, and I did get lucky on this one." Within seven or eight months, we had already sold our first deal, made good money, and bought several other properties. That version of M2G stayed that way—just me, Jessica, and an intern—until we started having kids and realized you can't grind the same way with children. We also recognized that our goals were bigger than two people could handle. You can buy a building once a year and flip it, but it's a whole other thing if you want seven or eight active projects going at once, you need to scale yourself.

How did the business evolve from there?

Initially, we were doing more mixed-use stuff, converting industrial buildings into retail and office. The deal sizes were around $5 to $6 million at most, using friends and family capital. By 2018, we wanted to get into larger deals and add pure industrial as a specific focus. That led us to institutional investors because those are larger deals. We started growing the company and adding the right team members. Right around that time, we were kicking off construction of the Stockyards project, which would become another major turning point for us.

Your company has developed a unique approach to industrial real estate with a strong design focus. How did that evolve?

It came from a combination of factors. Jessica and I started in mixed-use and retail at Trademark Property Company, where I focused on finance and development while she specialized in leasing. After Trademark, Jessica went to Open Realty where she represented tenants like Tesla, J.Crew, Restoration Hardware, and Apple. This exposed her to the best projects around the country since everyone wanted to talk to representatives of those premium tenants.

When we started M2G, we were primarily doing mixed-use, typically buying older industrial buildings with character and converting them. The way our minds work is always thinking about what exists and how we can make it better. We're very iterative thinkers. Through Jessica's work with Tesla, we noticed more tenants needing industrial space but wanting some branded expression of who they are. There was this growing convergence, especially in urban industrial product, driven by e-commerce and companies having some consumer-facing component to their business.

How did you translate that insight into your business model?

In 2018, we were looking at our long-term strategy and asked ourselves what asset classes would be crucial for the future. We had invested in industrial properties before, but always with the intent to convert them to something else. We decided to add pure industrial as a specific investment focus, but with our unique approach.

Our background in mixed-use and retail meant we were used to thinking more intentionally than typical industrial developers.

We're very disciplined about implementation. For industrial properties, we keep the office component under 10 percent. This is important because we're not trying to develop assets that confuse the next buyer. Everything needs to fit within the industrial box. From a capital markets risk standpoint, we want Blackstone to be able to look at our properties and say, "I'll buy this, it fits within my portfolio." Our North Quarter 35 project is a perfect example. It's a 650,000-square-foot industrial park we built from the ground up. The enhancements that make it unique aren't actually that expensive. The black storefront cost $26,000 more over 600,000 square feet. Inconsequential really. The enhanced landscaping was maybe $20,000 more. We might spend 5 to 10 percent more on a project than our peers, focusing on details like paint, landscaping, and lighting. But our rents are typically 56 percent higher than our competition for shallow-bay industrial* product.

The challenge is finding the right properties because we're very location-focused. We don't go out to the suburbs. We're typically looking for warehouses in the middle of Dallas that can be easily repositioned. We do some ground-up development, but it's few and far between because we're so focused on urban locations where it's difficult to find land that you can build something of scale.

What types of projects do you find most rewarding?

There are certain companies that are really good at finding their exact niche and the most frictionless way to execute it repeatedly. That's not us. We are problem solvers who take on complex projects. That's our core competency. While it might be a smarter business model to just rinse and repeat something simple, we love creating.

---

* **Shallow-Bay Industrial**: A type of industrial real estate, typically 15,000 to 50,000 square feet, designed for multiple tenants with shallow building depths, often used for local distribution, light manufacturing, or last-mile logistics.

So do you intentionally seek out these types of projects?

Yes, we specifically look for opportunities where we can solve complex problems and add value through thoughtful repositioning. We're usually focused on urban locations rather than suburban sites, which naturally adds complexity. But that's where we excel, by taking existing properties with good bones and transforming them through strategic improvements.

Right now we're looking at about an 8-to-1 ratio of acquisitions to development projects, though development is particularly challenging right now because construction lending is next to impossible to come by. We're still looking at land. We closed on a deal two or three months ago that we'll eventually develop. We bought it because it was at a great basis and we love the location, but we're not building on it today. It's about being strategic and patient while maintaining our standards for location and quality.

How do you define adaptive reuse in your projects?

We use the term broadly. Beyond the obvious conversion of industrial to other uses, we consider it adaptive reuse even when we're going from industrial to industrial, if the renovation and positioning completely transforms the project. We might take a Class C industrial property bought from a mechanic and adapt it into Class B+ showroom industrial space. It's about seeing the potential for evolution in every property.

How do you balance design ambitions with practical constraints?

For our developments, we focus on thoughtful improvements that don't break the bank. Things like strategic paint choices, enhanced landscaping, cohesive signage, intentional branding. We need opportunistic-type returns of 20 percent-plus IRR, with typical hold periods around 2.7 to 3 years. So while we emphasize design, it has to make financial sense.

Can you tell me about how you got involved with the Fort Worth Stockyards project?

In 2016, we were approached by Majestic about the Stockyards. The Hickman family owned about 77 acres of the 250-acre historic district. Their dad had bought it over time and left the holdings to his kids. They partnered with Majestic, contributing the land while Majestic would handle development and vertical construction. Initially, they were just looking for someone to lease a small retail building, but Jessica, who's usually more selective than I am, said we'd only be interested in leasing all the buildings. We weren't just brokers, we were principals with specialized experience in Fort Worth and adaptive reuse.

What was your approach to bringing in the right mix of businesses?

We spent about 12 to 18 months on strategy and visioning. If you notice, many of those tenants don't exist anywhere else. We created a "wonder wall" of dream tenants and reached out directly to founders and owners rather than real estate teams. I'd literally go hang out at places until I could meet the owner, get them a custom cowboy hat, and convince them to come meet with us at the Stockyards. It was very hands-on.

For each type of concept—whether it was a steakhouse, Italian restaurant, or burger place—we'd identify our top choice and pursue them intensively. Take Wrangler, for instance. They were our top choice for denim retail, and we talked to them for about a year before securing the deal. The hit ratio was high because we were only going after our "A" group.

With so many different tenants and historic spaces, how did you ensure the designs aligned with your overall vision?

We were deeply involved in the tenant design process. After negotiating the lease, we'd work directly with their designers to ensure they built something we'd approve. When you're dealing with historic structures, you can't just let tenants do whatever they want. We were very specific about things like, "How are you highlighting the beams? What are you doing with this wall? Don't cover up that feature." We stayed involved all the way through opening.

The project seems to have transformed the area's reputation. How did that evolution happen?

When we started, the Stockyards had a stigma as just a tourist spot. Locals wouldn't go there because it felt tired and hokey. Post-development, with the sophistication we added, it's become a destination for everyone. The latest stats show 9 million visitors annually, which is more than the Eiffel Tower. It's where locals take visitors now, and it's really part of Fort Worth's broader renaissance.

What's planned for Phase 2 of the project?

Phase 2 covers 20 acres east of the Drover Hotel. It will include 300,000 to 400,000 square feet of commercial space and about 500 hotel rooms. What's interesting is our approach to new construction. It's actually more challenging to build something totally new that fits in than it is to work with existing historic structures. Instead of creating large, uniform buildings like you see in most modern developments, we're designing multiple smaller buildings, each 3,500 to 5,000 square feet, arranged more like a historic town.

We'll have five or six basic building designs but twenty different variations in terms of skins, windows, and details. The goal is to create that organic feeling you get in the current Stockyards, where each building has its own character. We're also integrating more animal experiences, like the twice-daily cattle drive with the Longhorns, into Phase 2, adding both an educational component and authenticity to the experience.

It's more expensive to build this way, but it's a legacy project. We're real estate nerds at heart, and getting to work on something with so many possibilities where we can really focus on the details and create layers of experience is incredibly rewarding. Fort Worth itself has gone through quite a renaissance over the last ten years, and I think we've only seen maybe 20 to 30 percent of what it's capable of.

You do development, but you also do huge design projects like the Stockyards. How do you organize your business around these different types of projects?

We've structured our business into three arms: investments, advisory, and services. The investment side owns about twenty properties, mostly industrial except for one office building. The advisory arm handles projects like the Stockyards, and our services arm covers development, property management, asset management, and leasing, primarily servicing our own investments.

We've grown from just Jessica and me to twenty-four employees now. The growth has been intentional but challenging. We initially said we'd never be more than fifteen people. Then when we got close to that, we thought we'd never be larger than fifty. Having a large company with lots of bureaucracy was never attractive to us. Most groups take on operating partners when they want to scale. We didn't do that. It was all self-funded. From 2019 through the end of 2020, we added people as we built more business, trying to keep our overhead aligned with revenue. When we made the decision to really grow the team, there were a couple of years where we got ahead of ourselves, hiring people before the revenue was there to cover it.

We designed our operations to stay flexible as we scaled. Mondays are headquarter days in Fort Worth, and the rest of the week people work from whichever office is closer to them or from home.

What do you look for when hiring new team members?

When hiring, we focus more on personality attributes than specific skills or education. If somebody is curious, highly resilient, has a positive attitude, and is just ready to work really hard, those are the people that succeed. Most people who work here say they want to be part of creating something. We look for people who have seen what we haven't seen.

Maybe they've worked at big companies but have the resilience and curiosity we need. They've experienced how sophisticated operations work but aren't naturally formal people themselves. That combination works really well in our high-pressure but informal culture. Did I think we'd reach twenty-four people? Maybe, but I thought that would be our size when I was sixty or seventy, not now.

How have you managed geographic expansion?

We expanded into Austin about 15 to 16 months ago. We've always been intrigued by Austin. It has a lot of the type of product we're good at, with cool street retail and industrial conversions. We brought on someone I used to work with to open our Austin office. We've closed one deal there and have another under contract.

What's interesting about Austin is that it's actually quite small, about a tenth the size of Dallas-Fort Worth from an industrial perspective. It still runs a bit like Fort Worth, which is surprising. It's more of a sleepy broker town, which creates opportunities for those willing to work hard. You'd think with Google everywhere and international competition it would be more sophisticated, but that's not necessarily the case.

As self-described introverts, how do you approach networking and relationship building?

We're both more introverted than people might think, but having each other gives us confidence because we're never really doing anything alone. What's important is authentic networking. Not going to huge conferences, but making really close connections with difference-maker relationships. I focus on one-on-one meetings where I can be genuinely curious and learn about someone's business. The hardest thing is when you're in a room and see someone you think is impressive and want to meet. That initial connection is tough. But once you have it, you can build from there: "Who else do you think I should meet?" Then it's not a cold introduction anymore.

Can you tell me about your work with mental health research and advocacy?

This initiative came from a deeply personal place. Jessica's ex-husband was diagnosed with extreme bipolar disorder, and within three years of his diagnosis, he was hit by a car during a manic episode and passed away. Through his treatment journey, Jessica and I saw firsthand the limitations of current care options. Even with the best available treatments and facilities, it often felt like nothing was enough.

After he passed in 2016, we knew we had to do something. We're not the type of people who just accept tragedy and move on. We have this drive to create change and make an impact. But we weren't philanthropists, we weren't a foundation, we didn't know anything about that space. So we approached it the same way we approach our business: systematically and with purpose.

How did you develop your approach to this initiative?

We spent about six months interviewing top researchers, doctors, and hospitals around the country about their work in mental health and mental illness. We wanted to understand who was doing the most promising work in both research and treatment. Eventually, we connected with Dr. Madhukar Trivedi at UT Southwestern, who runs their Center for Depression Research and Clinical Care. He's doing groundbreaking work. His goal is to develop biomarkers that can identify predisposition to conditions like extreme depression or bipolar disorder before they manifest in severe episodes.

We initially committed to raising $300,000, even though I had no idea how we'd do it. When we asked Dr. Trivedi what he really needed, he said a million dollars. So naturally, we committed to that instead. We just finished raising that million dollars this year, five years after making that commitment.

How has being a business owner influenced your ability to make this kind of impact?

Being a business owner gives you two advantages in philanthropy. First, you're connected to a peer set that's used to being asked for significant contributions. It's different when one business owner approaches another about supporting a cause. Second, you're already comfortable putting yourself out there and taking on ambitious goals.

The most rewarding part is seeing how people with no previous connection to this space, apart from personal experience, can create meaningful change. We approached it with the same mindset we bring to business. Seeing what exists and believing it could be better. We'll probably end up raising tens of millions of dollars over time, and it's both exciting and sobering to see how badly this work is needed.

Our company's mission statement is to inspire evolution through impact and innovation. This initiative perfectly embodies that mission, taking on complex challenges, driving meaningful change, and hopefully inspiring others to do the same.

Together with her sister, Susan Miller Gruppi has built M2G Ventures around a clear investment philosophy: identify properties with untapped potential that require inquisitive problem-solving to realize their value. Intentionally seeking out complex projects provides them with an edge over other firms. Her background in financial analysis and practical real estate experience allows her to spot value in buildings that the market may have missed.

The Fort Worth Stockyards project demonstrates her distinctive development philosophy. While maintaining the area's historical identity through elements like the daily cattle drives, M2G created varied structures that honor the district's heritage. Balancing preservation with modern use required coordinating diverse stakeholders and addressing complex regulatory challenges—exactly the kind of multifaceted project where Susan's skills shine.

As M2G expands into Austin, Susan remains selective about which opportunities they pursue. She's not chasing growth metrics for their own sake but instead applying the same careful analysis that built their reputation. Each potential deal must meet their established criteria, which means saying "no" far more often than "yes." This disciplined approach of focusing on quality rather than quantity has become M2G's hallmark as they move into their next chapter.

CONNECT

- Website: m2gventures.com

Antonia Botero

Founder, Development and Management Principal, MADDPROJECT

New York City and Salt Lake City, UT

- Charted a path from architect to entrepreneur, moving from leadership positions at major firms to founding MADDPROJECT, her boutique development firm specializing in hospitality and multifamily projects.
- Managed $350 million of development work as a third-party development manager and over $1 billion of development work as an in-house project manager for other development companies.
- Led the conversion of the TWA Terminal's historic lobby into a hotel space, drawing on her combined expertise in architecture and development.
- Executed 78 hotel renovations across the U.S. in just 18 months, building and leading a nationwide project management team that traveled over 10,000 miles weekly.

DESPITE BEING BORN INTO IT, Antonia Botero didn't just fall into real estate development. The daughter of Colombian developers, she spent her childhood around construction sites before family reasons prompted their move to Miami when she was nine. Though real estate surrounded her early years as her mother collaborated with developers from back home, Antonia would find her own path to architecture only later in her education.

At the University of Miami, Antonia finished first in her architecture class before heading to MIT for a master's in urban design. New York tested everything she'd learned in school. She cut her teeth on projects like Grand Central Terminal and the Empire State Building, complex historic structures that demanded technical precision and creative problem-solving. Meanwhile, she knocked out her architecture licensing exams in six months, a process that keeps most candidates grinding for two years.

Her career took a meaningful turn at MCR Development. Moving beyond the architect's role, Antonia stepped into directing entire projects. She led the preservation of JFK Airport's TWA Terminal while juggling 78 hotel renovations across the country. Her team logged a staggering 10,000 miles weekly, giving her an education in logistics as thorough as her formal training in design.

When COVID hit the hospitality industry in 2020, Antonia saw opportunity rather than crisis. She launched MADDPROJECT, offering development management for multifamily and hotel projects. In just three years, her firm has overseen $350 million in work and is positioning itself with a development partner for what could become a $100 million Manhattan condominium project.

This conversation explores how Antonia built expertise that crosses traditional boundaries, from preservation to ground-up construction, and shaped a business that leverages her comprehensive understanding of the development process.

Date of Interview: January 27, 2024

Let's go ahead and dive in. I understand both your parents were involved in real estate in Colombia. How did that influence your early years?

My parents were developers in Colombia. I have some really cool pictures of me when I was little on construction sites. I truly grew up around buildings and development. But when I was very young, there was this trade agreement Colombia made with China that opened up the economy to Chinese goods. It basically put a bunch of small developers, including my parents, out of business. That contributed to their divorce when I was about 5.

And after the divorce?

My father stayed in Colombia. After that, it was really just me and my mom. When I was 9, she met somebody who lived in Miami. He moved to Colombia when they got married, but after about a year, he said, "I don't like it here," so we moved to Miami. I ended up at an all-girls Catholic school, which you can imagine how that went. Though actually, I was a rule follower. Growing up like that, watching the ups and downs of the real estate business, it really shaped how I approach my work and reputation in the industry today.

Did your family stay connected to real estate after moving to Miami?

My mom worked in various roles. First in business, then for some Colombian developers in Miami, and later became Vice Consul for the Colombian government. There was always something connected to real estate, going to construction sites, meeting with developers. It was just always there in the background. It's weird because a lot of people say, "Oh, I wanted to grow up to be an architect," but I wasn't like that. It was just sort of this constant presence in my life.

That must have been challenging, navigating between two cultures and living in a new country.

It's really funny, every time I go to Colombia, my cousins are like, "Oh my God, you're so American." And in the U.S., people are like, "Oh, you're so foreign." You're just caught between worlds. The immigration status was a huge undercurrent that affected my life until I was about 30. When my mom became vice consul, you can't be a U.S. permanent resident while being a diplomat for a foreign government. After that role ended, we had to go through this complex process similar to political asylum. Every six months, your driver's license expires, your work permit expires, and your travel permit expires. You have to reapply for everything, and each time it costs a couple grand because the applications are like $300 to $400 each.

How did those early experiences shape your approach to life and work?

You grow up a lot faster. You don't get the chance to try out a bunch of stuff or have your twenties to figure things out. For me, it was super clear. My mom didn't have retirement savings, I didn't have anybody else to rely on. I have a huge family in Colombia, but it's a world I didn't really know. Years later, I hung out with a girl I went to high school with, and she told me, "You were always the adult. You were always this older person who had reason, and we were all just messing around." She said, "You must have hated that," and I said, "Yeah, pretty much."

Looking back now, I realize it set the pace for my life. When I talk to friends in business about aptitude and ambition, I often say that a lot of people have both, but when they actually begin to do really well, some people can't handle it emotionally. They just cannot deal with the speed of how things happen. I've been doing this since I was 12, dealing with that speed of current change, the uncertainty, all of it. That kind of early responsibility shapes how you handle success later.

After high school, what was your plan for college?

Originally, I went to Tufts University to study International Relations and Diplomacy, because that's what my mom had been doing. The idea of government and politics was really interesting to me. But at the end of my first semester, they sent me this bill saying I had to pay full tuition in ten days because I didn't have a Social Security number, even though I'd told them about my immigration status from the beginning. It was like $26,000. I just had to pack up and leave.

That must have been devastating. What did you do next?

I ended up back at my mom's house in Miami at 19, feeling pretty lost. I needed a job, so I started working the front desk at the Hyatt. Looking back, it's crazy because I've ended up working so much in hospitality. That first job taught me a lot about the industry. But at the time, it was just a way to make money while figuring out my next step.

One day, I was sitting in my mom's living room, looking at this city skyline I'd painted, thinking about what to do. My dad had always wanted me to be an architect, which was actually why I'd never considered it before. But I started thinking maybe architecture was the path.

How did you make that happen?

I went to the University of Miami's architecture school. I actually had to hustle to get in. I knew the assistant dean's daughter from high school, so I worked that connection to get a meeting with the associate dean. When I met with him, he suggested I go to community college first. I was like, "No, you don't understand. I'm really smart, I have good grades, and I'll be really good at this." Looking back, I can't believe I was that bold at 19.

Did you end up enjoying architecture school?

I hated every second of the social aspect but loved every second of the work. I was all about it. The history, the design, all of it. After my first year, I got a job at a landscape design firm. My boss was this amazing woman who was only 28, she's still the best boss I've ever had. So much of what I learned about work and treating employees well came from her.

What made her such a great boss?

The subtle things that you don't realize the influence of until much later. Like every day at the end of the day when you were walking out, she would say thank you. Nothing fancy, just part of her routine. I'm very mindful of that now, I do that every day with my team. She was always a huge cheerleader too, always encouraging me. We're still really good friends. Actually, when she went out on her own a few years ago, the relationship kind of flipped. She started asking me questions about running a business, and I got to encourage her the way she had encouraged me.

After graduating, you went on to MIT for graduate studies in urban design?

Yeah, because during undergrad, I did an undergraduate thesis and really got into urbanism and cities. I wanted to teach, which meant I needed a master's degree. MIT had this program in architectural studies focusing on architecture and urbanism, basically how city fabric comes together to create place. It was different from urban planning, more about the physical form of cities.

So teaching your main goal at that point?

Initially yes, but that evolved naturally as I got more involved in practice. I think what's interesting is that I didn't have the typical story of always wanting to be an architect. It was more about following opportunities and discovering what I was good at. A lot of it came from just needing to figure out a path forward given my circumstances.

After getting your architecture degree from Miami, and then your master's at MIT, you joined BBB in New York. What was that early experience like?

I started as an architectural designer at BBB. When you first start out, you're doing a lot of grunt work, like changing presentation fonts and working on tedious details. It's an apprenticeship really. The person higher up understands that if the presentation isn't done correctly, with the right fonts and color schemes, it comes across as sloppy. You're essentially sweeping the floor, and if you want more responsibility, you have to sweep it well.

Were you able to work on significant projects even as a junior person?

Yes, I got to touch some amazing projects. Grand Central Terminal, Empire State Building, World Trade Center site, though initially in minor ways. For the Grand Central work, my boss would say, "Go to Grand Central tomorrow morning before anybody gets there and take pictures." So I'd show up at 5 a.m. walking around taking photos. A principal isn't going to do that kind of work. Later, when I looked at their public presentations for landmarks, all the pictures they used were ones I had taken.

You also pursued your architecture license during this time. What was that process like?

To get registered, you need your professional degree plus about two years of internship hours in different categories. Then there were seven exams. Most people take about two years to complete all the exams, but I made rules. It was two hours minimum study every day, at least eight hours on weekends. No study sessions shorter than two hours because you don't really get into it. If you failed an exam, you had to wait six months to retake it.

I told everyone I was going to finish in eight months. This smarmy kid who worked at BBB looked at me and said, "You're just setting yourself up for failure." But I passed all my exams on the first try in six months. Everyone in the office was shocked. Honestly, I don't think I did anything extraordinary other than actually signing up for the exams and studying consistently.

You seemed particularly drawn to construction administration. How did you pursue that?

I really wanted to do construction administration. Being out in the field, observing construction progress, making sure everything follows the drawings and industry standards. There was this one principal, Carlos, who handled that work. I basically had to stalk him to get his attention. I couldn't get a meeting on his calendar because we weren't working on any projects together. His office was behind this wall where you couldn't really see if he was in. I would walk by multiple times a day trying to catch him. This went on for about two weeks until I finally caught him: "Hey, do you have five minutes?"

How did your role at BBB evolve over time?

I was working with all the partners, taking on more and more responsibility. I was in this unique situation where I didn't really have a direct senior person, I just filled in wherever they needed help. I worked on historic tax credit cases, urban design projects, whatever needed doing. If you can do the work well, people keep giving you more opportunities. I also worked with Richard Southwick on tax cases where we served as expert witnesses for the IRS, explaining why certain tax credit claims weren't valid. You'd work really hard to meet a deadline, then not hear anything for weeks, and suddenly they'd need a response within 48 hours.

These weren't simple cases. The historic tax credit program gives building owners a 20 percent tax credit on qualified rehabilitation expenses, but the requirements are incredibly specific. We'd analyze every element of the project. Whether they preserved the right percentage of internal walls, if their window replacements matched the historic profiles exactly, whether their mechanical systems impacted the building's character-defining features. Sometimes we'd catch developers trying to claim the credit on non-historic additions or modern interior buildouts that didn't qualify. It was fascinating work, and I learned a lot about preservation standards.

That sounds like a lot of context switching.

All the time. You might be writing a detailed brief about contract breaches for lawyers one minute, then get a call about a sprinkler burst in a building the next. You have to stop everything, call the project manager, start calling restoration people. It's triage at that point. Nobody cares that you're writing an important brief. You have to handle the flood in the building because the longer it goes on, the more damage there will be.

At BBB, you eventually got involved with a major project for Extell Development. How did that come about?

We were working on this massive project for Extell Development at 500 East 14th Street. At that time, Extell was the largest client for the firm. The project was this huge building on Avenue A and 14th Street, about 300,000 square feet with multiple buildings because there was a holdout property we had to work around. I had been involved in the design development and presentations, and when my direct boss left the firm, I became the person who had all the project history.

As a relatively young person in the workforce, you were sitting at tables with major players in New York development. Was that normal?

It's normal to the extent that you're sitting there taking notes. It's not normal to the extent that you're the project architect. I became the project architect, partly because I had gotten myself registered. Though the liability stamp would still be the partner's stamp, I could actually call myself the project architect. I wasn't just a coordinator or designer anymore.

How did you navigate getting more responsibility on the Extell project specifically?

When it came time for promotions and reviews, I sat down with Carlos and said, "Look, you guys don't give promotions, you don't give people a shot. That's fine, but that means I'm going to have to go at some point soon because I'm outgrowing this place." That April, I got my New York license and became the first associate at BBB to be promoted in about ten years.

The project was coming to the construction administration phase, and typically they would put a more senior person in charge and the project architect would move on to the next project. I said, "No, I designed this thing. I know the whole history. I want to do construction administration." They said I was too young, but they didn't really have anyone else available.

Finally, the principal in charge, who rarely spoke to me, came over to my cubicle one day, leaned over the partition and said, "I hear you want to do the Extell project." I said yes, and he just said, "Don't fuck it up" and walked away.

That must have been intense. How did it go?

The first meeting was set for the following Tuesday. I was super nervous, this was my first major client meeting as project architect. The construction administration guy who showed up was initially quite difficult to work with, but the situation evolved in an unexpected way. That guy turned out to be Mike, my future husband. Though at the time, we didn't start dating until much later.

Around this time, you also discovered some pay disparities at the firm?

Yes, I accidentally saw a colleague's W-2 and discovered he was making about $90,000 while I was making $65,000. This was particularly frustrating because I was working on all these projects, all the partners wanted some of my time, I was crushing it. Every year when there was a raise, they would give me like $3,000, and I would push back. Then they'd come back with $10,000, and I'd think, "Why couldn't we just start there?"

That led to your transition to the development side?

Yes, I eventually went to work for a developer as a project manager. Overnight, I went from making $65,000 to $120,000. The biggest difference was that now I was the client. I was in charge of hiring the architect, managing the architect, managing the contractor. You're actually in charge of getting the building built. Any design changes you make are going to happen, whereas when you're the architect, they might build something totally different from what you drew.

That's a significant shift in both responsibility and compensation.

Yes, but it wasn't just about the money. When you're on the development side, you have real control over the project. You're actually in charge of making things happen. Though I should mention, the work environment was quite different. I went from BBB, where I had this incredible support system, to a much more challenging situation. My new boss was competent at the work but a difficult person to work for. It was more of a sink-or-swim environment with no mentorship.

Quick side question, just curious how or if speaking Spanish has been an advantage in your work. How has that played out?

Speaking Spanish was absolutely crucial in construction. Still is. Just this past week in Oregon, we had a situation where two guys got on a lift and jumped into a second-floor window of an unsecured building. My project manager ran over trying to talk to them, then looked at me because they only spoke Spanish. I've had projects where if I didn't speak Spanish, things would have been way more challenging.

Being a woman in construction also turned out to be an advantage, though people often assume it's a disadvantage. When I was working on the TWA project with all these union trades, these tough blue-collar guys, I knew what all their wives were getting for Christmas. They'd ask me about anniversary presents or restaurant recommendations. You build these real relationships. But it's not just personal, there's a huge business advantage too. I'd know someone was going on vacation before their boss did, so I could reorganize meetings weeks in advance. You're not creating relationships solely for business purposes, but it also means projects run more smoothly because you have better information and stronger connections.

Tell me more about the TWA Hotel project at JFK. What made this project so special?

The terminal building was commissioned by Howard Hughes and designed by Eero Saarinen. He was this engineer-crazy, mad scientist sort of architect. He had to do all these physical models because there were no engineering programs at the time. The building was completed in 1962, and they didn't even know if it would stand up until they built it. The roof surface of TWA is the same size as Madison Square Garden, and it only has four points of contact with the ground.

The terminal was almost immediately obsolete because by the time it was finished, the Jumbo Jet had come out and the building was too small to support big airliners. Eventually, American Airlines bought TWA, and the building was mothballed. Around 2004 to 2005, when JetBlue was starting up, they were going to tear it down like they had the PanAm building. But Richard Southwick from BBB saved it by getting it landmarked, and it became the youngest landmarked building in New York at 40 years old.

What was the development plan for the building?

JFK put out an RFP saying someone could build two towers mirroring the JetBlue terminal footprint, with the historic terminal becoming the hotel lobby. The two towers ended up having 512 hotel rooms total. We also built 60,000 square feet of conference space below ground. It was a massive project combining the JetBlue terminal, the hotels, the conference center, and the historic TWA terminal.

What was your role in the project?

I specifically managed the lobby portion, repositioning the historic terminal to function as a modern hotel lobby. We had to figure out where to put check-in desks, build out the Paris Cafe, which is Jean-Georges' restaurant operated by Tastes on the Fly, plus two round bars by Gerber Group and an Intelligentsia coffee bar. We worked with multiple design teams. Stonehill Taylor did a lot of the interior design, and Thomas Juul-Hansen did the Jean-Georges restaurant interiors.

That must have been interesting working with BBB again, but now as the client.

It was like coming home. I knew everyone on the project. I'd known them for years at that point. When Jason, my boss at MCR asked Richard Southwick about hiring me, Richard immediately endorsed me. One day I walked into the office for a full audit of everybody—architects, engineers, everyone—and one of the guys I used to work with, just looked at me and said, "What goes around comes around." Now they were working for me.

Beyond TWA, you were also managing hotel renovations across the country?

Yes, we had this massive portfolio of renovations happening simultaneously. At one point, we had 54 active projects. Over eighteen months, I completed 78 renovations. We were doing all these brand standard upgrades for Marriott and Hilton properties. Each brand has incredibly specific requirements. Everything from the color temperature of the bathroom lighting to the height of the desk chair. It's not just carpet and paint, you're replacing all furniture, fixtures, and equipment. Every TV has to be the current model, phones need specific features, desk dimensions must be exact. Even the artwork has strict guidelines about size and content. You have to buy everything that goes in a hotel room, and it all has to meet these precise standards, or you risk losing the flag. What makes it really complex is managing different brand standards simultaneously. What works for a Hilton Garden Inn won't work for a Marriott Courtyard, and the requirements change every few years.

The scale of that operation is remarkable. How did you coordinate such a massive portfolio?

I built a team from scratch. I had five project managers working for me plus a procurement team because of all the FF&E (furniture, fixtures, and equipment). We were traveling 10,000 miles a week. Looking back now, talking with one of my project managers from that time, we honestly don't know how we did it. It was absolutely crazy, I've never worked that much in my life.

Did you have to handle both TWA and all these renovations simultaneously?

Yes, while TWA was going on from 2018 to mid-2019, we were ramping up all these renovations across the country. The nice thing about TWA was that I knew everybody, all my former colleagues, which made the complexity more manageable. And having that deep expertise in historic preservation from my BBB days was crucial. But managing everything simultaneously was intense. You'd be dealing with historic preservation details on TWA one minute, then jumping to handle an urgent issue at a renovation site across the country the next.

How did MADDPROJECT evolve from a side project into your main focus?

In early 2020, I was thinking about leaving MCR and focusing on MADDPROJECT full-time, which I had just started by doing development work on the side. This didn't interfere with MCR because they were basically just doing renovations. Then March came around, and I was sitting on a plane in Dallas when my boss called to tell me he had given his two weeks' notice. By Wednesday of that week, my entire team had been laid off due to COVID. I was the only one left because I had about 35–40 open contracts across the country with vendors and contractors.

But you didn't get laid off?

No, and I stuck around for another year. Not so much out of loyalty to MCR, but because of all the relationships I had built with vendors and contractors. I couldn't just exit stage left. I had to close everything out properly. But I knew this was my opportunity to really start the company. Between April and December 2020, while still at MCR, I made about $80,000 from MADDPROJECT alone. I saved all of it, didn't take anything out of the account because I was just paranoid. Then 2021 went pretty well, and by April 2022, I hired Nick, my former senior project manager from MCR.

Walk me through how you work with clients. When someone finds you and needs a development project manager, what happens?

I get that email or form through my website, or sometimes a DM through Twitter, and I say, "Okay, let's set up a call." In the meantime, I ask them to send everything they have. Title work, underwriting, drawings, sketches, ideas, whatever. I review all the materials and write up questions before we talk. Those initial calls are usually an hour, hour and a half. I ask them to tell their story and then explain what I think they need. Based on their feedback, I write out a draft scope in an email. We go back and forth until we're clear on the scope, then I assign a fee based on the work plan and staffing needs.

Do you have a specific approach to managing client relationships?

The minute I say, "send me everything" and they can't provide basic information, that's data for me. Sometimes people will claim they have this amazing project but then never follow through with basic documents or never get back to scheduling a call. If you tell me you don't have certain information, that's fine, that's also data for me. But if you can't follow through on basic requests, you're probably not serious. I've had to fire clients before. Last summer, I had to end a relationship with a client who had been difficult from day one. I actually gave him such a high fee initially thinking he wouldn't accept it, but he did. After two and a half years, things got too complicated, and I had to end it. That's the advantage of having your own shop. You get to choose who you work with.

What types of projects do you typically work on?

Mostly master planned communities, multifamily, and hospitality, including restaurants. Having worked on TWA and other hotel projects, I gained a lot of hospitality experience. Sometimes I'm just an advisor, checking in weekly to make sure they're not going down a dark path. Other times it's full project management. The fee structure matches the involvement level. They pay the first month in advance, then all other months are 15 days in arrears. I'm flexible if projects need to stop for whatever reason, we'll prorate the work.

How do you manage all these projects?

We structure it so Monday and Tuesday are for standing meetings. Wednesday through Friday we're either on the road or in the field. We try to visit each site once a month. If I need to be there more frequently than that, it usually means someone's about to get fired. The GC should be handling the day-to-day.

I understand you want to shift MADDPROJECT into doing your own developments, not just managing or advising as a third party for others. What's your vision there?

Yes, I'm working on that now. I'm putting together an investment thesis and looking for an analyst to aggregate some data to support it. I want to spend time in New York doing meetings with capital. We're talking family offices, high net worth individuals. I'm not looking for fifty thousand dollar checks on Twitter.

What kind of project are you looking at?

Probably a condo building in Manhattan, likely around $100 million. I've been looking at sites, and they're typically in the $60 to $100 million range.

With these ambitious plans, I'm curious, beyond the business success, what aspects of development work do you find most meaningful? What value do you feel you're contributing?

I know that what we do isn't curing cancer, we're not doing brain surgery, we're not saving lives. But we get to do really fun stuff. We get to do work that doesn't feel like work. When we're on site visits, we end up at dinners with the project team, talking about life and building relationships. You're finding out their stories: how did they get here? What's their background? What does their family do? You get to have these genuine human moments.

How do you think about your impact on the people you work with?

I have a really big impact on the people that work for us. I know none of them hate their lives, at least at work. They all have the balance they're looking for, and each one is different. There's a generosity there with the team and with the work. Not just people who directly work with us, but also the architects, the contractors, everyone else. We could make their lives miserable, but why would we? I know my first boss in development was absolutely awful to me, and I feel like I get the chance to not do that.

Do you see your work having a lasting impact on the built environment?

There's something meaningful about building things that are going to outlive us. I get to walk around Manhattan and say, "I worked on that, I worked on that." There's a source of pride there.

So where do you find the real meaning in what you do?

For me, it comes from getting to live fully and experience all these people and places. I get to see things from a very different perspective than most people do. I get to know the stories of these people because I work with them for three to five years. I get to hear about their family history, their dreams, their challenges. That to me is what life is about.

How do you balance being passionate about the work while maintaining that perspective?

You can take it seriously and be passionate. You'll never find someone more passionate than me about the work, but there has to be context. Is it ruining your life? Are you absolutely miserable doing this job? Because this is optional. We're building buildings, not saving lives. It's about balancing happiness and generosity with the understanding that, while what we do matters, it's not the only thing that defines us.

Antonia Botero's career has been defined by an increasing command over complex projects—from contributing to landmark architecture in New York to leading nationwide redevelopments and launching her own firm. Her early experience in architecture laid the foundation for a move into development, where she gained broader control over project execution and long-term outcomes. At MCR Development, she oversaw the transformation of the TWA Terminal's historic lobby into a functional hotel space while also managing 78 hotel renovations nationwide.

During that intense period, she also laid the foundation for MADDPROJECT, building the business on nights and weekends before taking the leap into entrepreneurship. Today, her firm manages hundreds of millions in development work, drawing on her cross-disciplinary expertise in architecture, construction, and real estate.

Now, Antonia is stepping fully into development. In collaboration with a development partner, she's focused on Manhattan condominium projects in the $60 to $100 million range. As she builds out this next phase of her career, she brings the same discipline, foresight, and hands-on approach that have shaped her journey from the start.

Connect

- Websites: maddproject.com
- X: @antonia_mdprjct
- LinkedIn: Antonia Botero, RA, NCARB

Eric Weatherholtz

Founder and Managing Partner, Healey Weatherholtz Properties

Atlanta, GA

- Co-founded Healey Weatherholtz Properties in 2005, leading high-impact projects like Atlanta's Shops Around Lenox, Collier Village, and Summerhill, using a "catalytic development" model to spark neighborhood-wide revitalization.
- Developed expertise across all facets of real estate over three decades, managing more than 100 properties spanning everything from modest neighborhood retail to upscale urban destinations.
- Built a value-creation strategy that extends beyond property lines, placing carefully selected local businesses that energize entire districts and drive up surrounding values, turning strategic tenant selection into lucrative partnerships with cities and major developers.
- Launched Automatic with his wife, who leads the initiative connecting emerging retail brands with developers to boost property value through tenant mixes that reflect and strengthen the local community.

Eric Weatherholtz met me at Muchacho, a buzzing coffee and taco spot in Atlanta that embodies his development philosophy: small, independently run spaces that draw people into the neighborhood and help spark broader revitalization. He calls this process "catalytic development." It has been his specialty for the past twenty or so years.

He began with little more than a history degree and a knack for figuring things out. He found his first role in the industry by flipping through the phone book. This would launch a career that has touched nearly every aspect of commercial real estate. He's worked on construction crews, managed distressed assets, and developed high-end retail in prime locations. This range of experience has given him deep insight into how property value is created, lost, and reimagined over time.

Eric's career has coincided with significant market shifts. When he first started out, he witnessed the aftermath of 1980s tax law changes that devastated previously successful real estate businesses. He then saw quality properties offered at fractions of their eventual worth during market downturns, and observed how neighborhood dynamics can dramatically shift property values. These experiences shaped his approach to development, where value creation is measured across cities rather than individual properties.

In 2005, Eric co-founded Healey Weatherholtz Properties, where he put his catalytic development philosophy into practice. He and his partner have been a part of some of Atlanta's most notable revitalization projects, transforming once unlivable areas into thriving districts. His work shows how small, independent businesses can create economic ripple effects that extend well beyond their immediate locations.

Together with his wife, who leads the venture, Automatic connects influential independent retail brands with property owners and developers who can benefit from their presence. This business model builds on years of observing how certain small businesses can drive foot traffic and be the catalyst that sits at the core of his development work. He talks a lot about the philosophy behind his work through his excellent newsletter, *Asphalt Jungle*, which I highly recommend. Not only is he a gifted developer, but a gifted writer as well.

Our conversation, which moved from Muchacho to locations along the Atlanta BeltLine and finally to Superica restaurant, revealed a developer focused on how people instinctively respond to spaces. Eric methodically analyzes what makes certain locations successful, from the materials used in construction to the specific operators chosen for each space.

In this interview, Eric discusses how he went from novice leasing agent to developer, the formation of his partnership and business philosophy, and specific examples of how small-scale retail projects have transformed neighborhoods. His perspectives offer practical guidance for real estate professionals, urban planners, and anyone interested in the economic and social factors that shape our cities.

Date of Interview: October 24, 2023

Let's dive into your early career. You're based out of Atlanta now, but this isn't where you started, right?

Right. The first gig I had was in Nashville, which was kind of an interesting situation where I found a job by looking through the phone book. I had a history degree, knew nothing about nothing. I was trying to think of people that I knew that made some money, and after I realized I couldn't be a doctor or a lawyer or anything like that, real estate seemed like one path.

What was happening in the market at that time?

This was early 1990s. The tax laws had changed in the late '80s, and this guy had created a company that went out and purchased fantastic properties around Nashville, really well located, super little assets. He had put decades of work into creating this portfolio playing under the rules and tax regime at the time. He had raised money from individuals based on both the real estate and the tax benefits that came along with it. Then the laws changed, almost as if 1031 exchanges became retroactive. It kind of put him in a really tough spot. He was in a position where they couldn't raise any additional capital, and that combined with the general downturn in the real estate industry, I watched how everything collapsed. This was a business that had been working well under one set of rules, but when those rules changed, it all fell apart. I was there for maybe only six months.

What were you doing during those six months?

He needed space leased in these little shopping centers really quickly because a lot of the problems had come from vacancy, reduced income. The deal was, "If you can lease space, I'll pay you the first month's rent," which to me was amazing. I had zero idea what I was doing. I just went out door to door and said, "Would you like to move from here across the street?" And it was amazing how it worked. I leased a lot of space very quickly—when I say quickly, I mean within weeks—just kind of going face-to-face, door-to-door, because he was able to offer lower rents and people would move.

What did you learn from being there during the collapse?

I had a front row seat to see someone's life unravel. This cat had about 20 really terrific properties, had guaranteed all the loans personally, couldn't raise capital. I watched the moving trucks come to his house in the best part of town. It was sort of a jarring welcome to the industry, to see, like, this is what happens, this is what can happen. This guy had done everything kind of right, bought really good properties, but things shifted in a way that didn't seem plausible at the time. He was a thoughtful guy, thoughtful manager, and it just took him down.

The other thing that happened was bankers started coming up to me, asking if I'd buy these properties. They were so desperate to get out that they were offering me properties, which have since sold for $5 or $10 million, for something like $50,000. I remember one meeting with a banker where he was pitching me the whole time about buying this property for $50,000, get it off their balance sheet, and I was just hoping he was gonna pay for lunch. $50,000 to me at the time might as well have been $50 million. But then over the years I saw pretty quickly how that $50,000 property a few years later was worth half a million, and then that half-a-million-dollar property over the next ten or twenty years became $3, $4, $5, or $10 million.

What happened after that first position?

One introduction led to another, and I found another opportunity with a company. The market was horrible, just devastating, war-torn. A group of really bright people had created a company that worked on behalf of lenders as these lenders were foreclosing on primarily retail properties. We would salvage and patch them up, get them back on their feet. The lenders were all life insurance companies, big, really big companies, and they had a lot of capital. They were getting properties back almost daily.

They needed help because they had so much business. With almost no experience, just months of experience, I got thrown into failed shopping centers with life insurance companies' instructions on what to do with it. Wash, rinse, repeat, did that many times. You got to see how somebody first screwed it up, and then you had to try things on somebody else's nickel. It was like an open checkbook to use your own ideas, with little or no supervision.

It was a small company, but I spent a couple of years traveling across the country, touring properties in different markets. It was a high-density learning experience packed into a short period of time.

So you were there for a couple of years. Where did your career take you after that?

That led to working for an individual, this real hustler and deal guy, and I sort of saw how one person with little or no capital can kind of create situations to be in the way of money moving around. He was a broker, slash manager, slash syndicator. He had created relationships with lenders, would get put in a position to help them work out properties, and the lenders would hire him as a third party to make that happen. Then in certain instances, he was able to recruit outside investors where he would put together a group to acquire the property. He would sometimes be working from within the seller organization, so the seller was paying him to solve a problem, and he was going out the back door finding capital, participating on both sides.

He didn't always operate in a way that sat right with me, so I wanted to get out. It had left a bit of a bad taste in my mouth about how he operated the business. And as the market was healing, those distressed opportunities were getting fewer and far between.

You got to work really closely with this guy, though, and see how to raise money and talk to investors, so a great learning experi-

ence. But you wanted to get out, so you started looking for something else?

Right. I found a company that was sort of a blue-chip firm in the Atlanta area, doing really high-quality work, acquiring top-tier properties and working with ultra-high-net-worth folks from around the world. It was a first-class organization. I think that's when I really started seeing properties through a longer-term lens. Their assets were truly top-shelf stuff.

What were you doing with them day-to-day?

Financial analysis, property management, leasing—what they call asset management—which meant being the intermediary between the investors and the specific projects, handling communication and oversight. I was working with European royalty types who had a 50-year outlook on properties. They thought about property through a very different lens. The takeaway was how good properties can outperform, and the idea that buying really high-quality properties can be very lucrative, because the very top-tier assets end up having good things happen to them.

This was also when I started using things like Argus, which is a software program, and learning how those kinds of financial models work. I'd been working directly with probably 60 or more properties over the years, seeing things play out, seeing how you can influence properties for the better and seeing it at scale.

Then the company grew, and I found myself in more of a low-level managerial role. I realized that I got much more of a kick out of being involved, working with a small team on a project, as opposed to general management. So I left that and went to work for a developer out on the West Coast.

Wow, so you really got to see how the industry works. From starting at a small shop with a guy who was doing all the right things but

eventually blew up, to flying around the country working on retail deals, to seeing firsthand how one person can raise money and generate deal flow, to working with a top-tier, sophisticated organization. And now you're about to start working for a developer, which feels like the real beginning of your development career. But before we dive into that, I remember you mentioned spending some time working on a ranch before getting into real estate, and I wanted to touch on that. How did that experience shape your perspective?

Yeah, I spent some time working on one really large ranch in Texas as a guide. This ranch was about 800,000 acres owned by a family, and simply through the ownership of that, they had revenue coming from oil and gas, water rights, cattle, hunting. They had a financial stake in these by lending out access to their land. Someone raised horses there. Oil was the big one, but they had probably 20 different income streams supporting a huge family lavishly.

I think I remember you talking about crossing paths with some interesting people out there, didn't you?

Yeah, a lot of the visitors were oil and gas people, like Exxon folks, businesspeople coming out there as a getaway to talk about business. I'd be in a position of spending a day or two or three with each group as they came through. We'd be on this truck moving very slowly through these huge grass prairies, stadium seating type situation on the back. But one day, these four guys show up who you could tell weren't like the others. They were completely alive in every way. Really funny, really smart, really engaged. As opposed to being waved off by the business guys, these guys were super engaging with me. We talked and laughed about everything from Russian literature to politics.

One night they invited me back to the cabin, and the head guy talked to me about how you can spend your life doing things that you want to do, or things that other people want you to do. That's just sort of the crux of the decision. Each of these guys was remarkably talented in the arts. Jim Harrison was one of the great novelists in American history, Russell Chatham was one of the great landscape artists, and the other guys were a filmmaker and an author. They had all, through singular, passionate focus on those things, created unique success. Jim ended up spending his summers in Montana and his winters in a place down in Southern Arizona, writing for The New Yorker and writing novels. What they really beat into me at a time where I was trying to figure out what my next move was. It doesn't matter what it is, but you got to figure out if you want to do it for yourself or somebody else.

I only spent a few days with them, but the fact that I'm still talking about it 30 years later tells you something. That moment stuck with me. Even if life pulls you into paying bills and raising kids and just keeping your head above water, it planted a seed that never really went away.

What a pivotal moment. I can see why that left such an impression. Okay, back to your career. So you moved out to the west coast to work for a developer. Was this an intentional move to learn more about development?

It was more about wanting to do something entrepreneurial. This West Coast developer role was more of a mid-level position in a small company doing big things. I was sort of sitting behind the pilot, getting to look at all the dials and everything. That was a great experience because we were working on really large-scale projects, but it was still somebody else's gig.

By the early 2000s, I'd worked on everything from really low-quality stuff that had been foreclosed on to really high-quality things in some of the best neighborhoods in the country. At that point, I was like, "Man, I can do this." I'd kind of seen it enough from every angle to justify it to myself, that I had some semblance of know-how.

And some of that confidence came from way earlier. Back in high school, I worked on construction crews. I worked as an electrician's apprentice, did framing labor—physically learning how you built stuff. Then I worked in maintenance, learning how the floors get mopped, what it takes to maintain landscape. I learned about backflow preventers, fire sprinkler systems, even what each clause of a lease means.

So by the time I started thinking I could do this on my own, I had this foundation. From a construction standpoint, from a maintenance standpoint, from a property management standpoint, from a leasing standpoint, all the way to development. That gave me a kind of confidence that I knew what I was doing.

When a specific opportunity came along, one that I could structure in a way where I had some income coming in, I decided it was time to get started.

How did your first development opportunity come about?

A previous boss found out about this opportunity with a wealthy landowner who wanted to develop their property. I was able to structure it in a way where there was an element of fee associated with it, and I was able to structure for a portion of the fee to be paid upfront as a credit against the backend. It worked out for everybody. Got me dollars coming in the door, and the owner got somebody that was completely, thoroughly, absolutely dedicated to successfully executing the project.

Can you walk me through what you actually did as the principal?

At this point, I'd been in the business for eight to ten years and had worked hands-on with at least 100 properties of all sorts and types and geographies. I knew this was a really terrific property and had a very clear point of view as to what could and should be done. The landowner wanted an active role but not hands-on. He had a casual interest in real estate, had a good nose for things as a person. What he needed was someone that could handle the day-to-day grind. Working with architects, coordinating with civil engineers to figure out how the thing works, getting buy-in from the city, finding tenants.

Did you already know all these different players you needed to work with?

I had a lot of conviction about it. I knew all the players that actually needed to be involved because I'd done it many, many times. We had a joint venture arrangement that basically provided the land with the capital, and I provided the expertise. We got the plans together, got some initial tenant interest, and sold the thing. By then, the training wheels were off. I had a little bit of money in my pocket. Enough to say, "Hey, I can stay in the building, and I've got enough oxygen here for another six months or a year. Now let's go find the next one."

That sounds like a really smart way to make the leap, structuring the deal to bring in some upfront income while proving your value through execution. And while it wasn't a massive payday, it gave you the experience, credibility, and breathing room to keep going on your own. Would you recommend that kind of approach to others looking to break into development?

I think this is a good way for anybody that's starting out. There's a big difference between talking about doing something and actually doing it. I think other people could do it much faster than I did. Again, I had already seen it from every angle, which made me feel like I could actually pull it off. It might have been actually too much experience, but that's what it took for me. When you're ready, the opportunity finds you. I had been open to it, looked at a couple of other things that didn't pan out. When this opportunity came up, it just worked.

So this project was out west somewhere? What happened after that?

This was in Phoenix. I worked out there for probably another year or two, working on various projects. Something in Chicago, something in San Francisco, like, you're desperate for oxygen, wherever a deal can pop up. Then I moved to Atlanta and set up a little shop here.

That must have kept you busy. What was happening in your personal life during this time?

I had two young children, both with health challenges, one more severe than the other. My then-wife was from here in Atlanta, so this was a great situation to get here and have a support network.

I then set up a little office, and my attorney says, "You should meet this guy, you're doing the same thing." At first it was, you know, one of the perks was that he had a copier, which I didn't. So we started working on a deal together, and that led to another deal.

Did you and your partner have a specific vision from the start?

My point of view began with any property I would see. I would be thinking what you can do to it. Almost subconsciously, I'd drive by something and think, "That should do this, you can add this piece, change the color." That was decades of seeing those things, so that script was etched into my brain. My partner's background was he was dialed into how to identify scarcity, how to find things that people want and are hard to get.

We started working on projects together and saw how you can use design and tenancy and redeveloping properties to create a whole lot. We could make things way more desirable by implementing certain design techniques, adding certain types of retail and hospitality, repositioning properties to make them more valuable. That led to a series of projects where we just went out and looked for those kinds of deals.

Can you give a high-level overview of what it means to be a developer doing what you guys are doing? How do you find properties and make the business work?

Our business evolved with a shared sensibility of what made a high-quality opportunity. We would always agree on what properties we should be excited about. Our business became finding really high-quality locations, but we needed three key things: the right location, enough time to put it together, and sufficient capital. Those three things are pretty rare to find together, if not impossible.

How would you find these opportunities?

Any way we could, but a lot of it was talking to others active in the industry. Brokers, other property owners, creating as big of a footprint as we could conversationally. We were able to find some opportunities, but they were more serendipitous than following a repeatable process. It's kind of like when you get a new car, suddenly you see that model everywhere on the road. We developed a specific lens we were looking through, and opportunities arose that we could execute on. But they were hard to find, and as the market got hotter after the financial crisis, opportunities became scarcer.

The big thing about our business, which for me started many years before, was the idea that if you improve a property, it has an impact on what's around it. We became students of what makes that happen. When an area becomes newly valuable and desirable, what are the things that made that happen? What generated change and made those places where people wanted to go?

How did you start capturing that broader value creation?

We saw that when we did really terrific projects, everything around them became more valuable. Hotel room rates went up, office rents went up, retail rents went way up. But we had no participation in that broader value creation. We were doing this service to others, in a way. It became really hard to make these projects work within their four walls as things became pricier, but what you're doing is creating a huge increase in value. You do all this work on one project, everybody else benefits around it, without having to do anything.

So we started looking at how to capture that value by opening the aperture a little bit. We found that with catalytic retail components, you could influence the value of surrounding areas. The key became getting involved with all the surroundings. We were able to do that in a couple of instances, and that really changed how we saw the world.

How do you structure these broader development partnerships?

There are really two approaches. In some cases, you might be able to go out and buy a bigger piece of property, use some catalytic retail and hospitality to make it more desirable, and participate in the upside. Or you can team up with somebody that already has the larger property and do this with a smaller component while participating with them.

Our approach has been to minimize team size and take all the key functions in-house. We have a contractor who either does the contracting or interfaces with larger contractors, depending on the project size. We've been his only client for the past 15 years. We've got a creative director in a similar situation who either executes or manages the execution of design-related work. We maintain the same kind of dedicated relationships with our controller, CFO, and leasing team.

I understand you're also working with municipalities now?

Yes, we've got several projects now with municipalities where they want to create their own identity and something unique about their place. They want to have one of these catalytic projects in their neighborhoods. Since they benefit from a visibility standpoint, from a tax base standpoint, from putting their town on the map, a reasonable trade for them is helping underwrite the project we do.

If there's not pervasive public support, we tend to go the other way or partner with someone who specializes in making that happen. For us, the opportunities are wide now, but they have to be the right fit.

Our role now has evolved. We're often teaming up with much larger developers where we play a small but crucial role within larger projects. We're typically a minority partner handling the narrow sort of retail and ground floor retail aspects, and how that comes together, how it gets executed as a catalyst. We'll handle this small project with their help, and then we'll have some sort of arrangement tied to the whole project.

How does that work with the larger developers?

Well, think about it this way. You might have a million-square-foot office building, but the public perception is all about that 20,000 square feet of commercial space on the ground floor. That can help you lease a million square feet at a couple more dollars per foot or six months faster. That's a very valuable tool. You can speed up velocity or enhance value significantly with the right ground floor execution.

What scale of project does it take to transform an area?

What we found is this little niche of small retail commercial projects, maybe 10,000 to 40,000 square feet, can transform an area if you get the right energy and the right operators. You can create something really powerful out of a small space. The key is understanding the specific context and how to create that catalytic effect in each situation.

If you can do something with enough scale, make it big enough, you can create your own location. Take Ponce City Market. With that amount of scale, you could create enough energy to help the neighborhood overcome challenges. If you only have one small building, it's not enough to change the tide. So you see things on a spectrum, you can have 1,000 square feet on Fifth Avenue with a lot of value, or 70 acres in a challenged part of town with awesome upside potential.

What's the economic calculation between going with established chains versus independent operators?

If you have only one building, then maybe you just get the highest rate you can. But if you have multiple buildings and I put in something that negatively influences the values of my other buildings, is that right? For example, this place we're sitting in now, Muchacho, is oozing with energy and vibe. This could be a Starbucks and Chipotle combined. They could probably pay some price premium. They're not negatives, but it would be a bit of a wet blanket on the surroundings. Whereas this has a very energizing effect.

What makes independent operators so special in terms of creating that energy?

It's really hard for large companies to create this sort of energy because to grow these types of companies, you have to become formulaic. If you were to grow Muchacho, it starts to become repetitive as you systematize things. Over time, that energy gets dampened. Look at something like the original Chili's. It was a super killer place in this old funky building with a great hamburger menu. Same with the original Longhorn Steakhouse here in Atlanta, it was fantastic, in this super funky building, almost like a dive bar steakhouse. Through repetition, they lose that energy. It doesn't make them worse companies. They became wildly successful, but from the standpoint of enhancing neighborhood value, they lose that spark that starts the forest fire around them.

Would you say restaurants and bars are the biggest catalysts for neighborhood transformation?

Independent food and beverage are definitely the main thing. Sometimes there are precursors in the retail world. Maybe an art gallery or certain kinds of unique retail can start to initiate change, but for the most part, it's food and beverage.

The interesting thing is it's a positive-sum game. Again, take Muchacho as an example, if you put that outside your apartment building, and then a killer sushi spot opens next to it, instead of having a zero-sum feeling of competition, it actually works the other way. The area becomes even more desirable. "Oh, now there's a sushi place AND Muchacho?" That's cool too. Three becomes six, and then all of a sudden, you've got a thriving district.

The other way to think about it is, imagine you own an apartment building and want to increase the value. The typical approach is to renovate each unit. New backsplash, LED lighting, smart thermostats, updated bath fixtures. That affects each space a little bit. Instead, imagine if you've got your building, and I opened up Muchacho next door. Every year it becomes more desirable, and I didn't touch a single unit or spend a dime on renovations. And it's not just that apartment building. Every building within a five-minute walk has become more desirable. It's an incredibly powerful dynamic.

How do you find and vet these independent operators who can create that transformative effect?

We spend a lot of time identifying folks that have done it at least once. There's a huge difference between someone who's done it zero times versus once. When you can find those that want to do another location while maintaining their authenticity, that's really valuable.

Can you walk me through a specific example of how a small retail tenant can influence a major development project?

Ponce City Market in Atlanta is a great example. Jamestown Properties, the owners of Chelsea Market in New York, announced they were going to redo this 1.6-million-square-foot old Sears warehouse. It was in a part of town that wasn't at all what you would think of as an office location. A little sketchy from a residential standpoint. They had this plan of embracing this wonderful multi-story brick building, using the bones of it to create a leisure destination.

When they were kicking off the project, one of the first things they announced was that King of Pops would take 250 square feet. That's an infinitesimally small amount of space within this massive development. But I remember hearing this and thinking, "King of Pops is going to open at Ponce City Market. It's going to be that kind of place, it's going to be cool." They didn't announce the JP Morgan and McKenzie offices taking hundreds of thousands of square feet. People were talking about this 250-square-foot popsicle stand. It framed in your mind what kind of place it was going to be.

That's fascinating. I spent some time in Austin and noticed similar patterns there. There's got to be a good example of that somewhere.

Absolutely. There's actually a cool documentary about the Broken Spoke in Austin. It was a husband and wife who created this live music venue, this country western joint in a nowhere area. But because of them, that specific area, and really Austin at large, became something different. All that multifamily was built right up to the door of Broken Spoke. It hasn't been torn down yet, hopefully it won't. The idea that this super quirky country western dance hall became a catalyst for hipster apartments is amazing.

Another great example is Hotel San Jose in Austin, which went from being a drug den to becoming one of the coolest hotels in America. These places can completely transform an area's trajectory.

The Continental Club on South Congress seems similar. It's now one of the only old places left, with everything else having developed around it.

Yes, exactly. And what's fascinating is how these principles work across different cities. These simple elements—the right wood for a patio, proper lighting, getting the scale right—they work universally. The best projects use real, lasting materials and are designed to feel welcoming and appropriately scaled for people.

As we're walking here along the BeltLine, I'm reminded of places like Austin, or neighborhoods in Seattle like Fremont and Ballard. I know you've mentioned Europe before and how you'd take pictures in front of their local grocery stores or food markets, which isn't something we really do here in the U.S. I mean, nobody's snapping photos in front of a Whole Foods. Do you think America is starting to develop its own authentic vibe with projects like this?

For sure. I think America is developing its own version of what historically made European cities so appealing. If you look at what we're walking on here, it's basically a road without cars. So many European streets have the same energy. These buildings are four and five stories, which creates a very different energy than 50-story buildings.

What's interesting is that none of this is like some grand striking piece of large-scale development. It's all these tiny little components. A few chairs outside a bakery, the area underneath trees. It's nothing grand, it's all super small-scale with very fine detail. These simplistic things work in Atlanta, Seattle, Austin, Omaha, Paris—everywhere. We're learning how to create these authentic, walkable spaces that have their own character, but with an American twist that reflects our culture and communities.

How have you seen these transformations play out over longer periods of time?

These transformations often happen in ways you wouldn't expect. I grew up in rural Loudoun County, west of Washington, and I remember my dad telling me when I was 16 to try to avoid D.C. Now, if you look at how that area has transformed, particularly in the last decade, it's remarkable. A lot of that value change has happened through this compounding effect where a few things start to change, and then suddenly you have a whole new neighborhood emerging.

The key lesson is that these changes often start small and build momentum over time. You might have one authentic place open up, then another follows, and suddenly the energy shifts. Like I mentioned earlier with the example of Muchacho and the sushi place, these additions don't just compete, they amplify each other, creating a ripple effect that reshapes the entire neighborhood.

How many projects do you typically work on at a time?

A company like ours can handle no more than a handful at a time. Right now we've got probably six projects underway. Everything ebbs and flows in terms of involvement. Something will take a lot of work for a period, then less.

How do you approach working in different cities?

It's all about understanding the universal components that make places work, while recognizing each city's unique character. We focus on the building forms and how people interact with spaces. Whether it's Atlanta, or anywhere else, there are certain fundamentals that work everywhere. But you have to spend time in these places, observe how people use them, and understand what makes them special.

Tell me about how you're evolving your business approach through Automatic.

My wife is leading this new venture called Automatic, which is really striking a nerve in the industry. We're connecting influential retail brands with property owners and developers who can benefit from their presence. So many folks are coming to us saying, "I get it, I see how that works. How can I participate with my property?" It's becoming a game-changer. We're seeing opportunities everywhere. It's an ocean of possibilities that we can't even begin to fully address.

How do you see your role evolving in the future?

The charge I get now comes in a couple of ways. One is identifying meaningfully innovative companies and helping them on their journey, either working with them directly or building relationships. For small companies and innovators, helping make introductions is something I really get a kick out of. I love seeing these places succeed and helping create the connections that make that possible.

Do you see yourself ever retiring?

Right now we spend about a third of our time in Idaho, and I'd like to keep expanding that. I love traveling to see how development is done elsewhere, seeking out the universal components of what makes places work, and then bringing that knowledge back to our projects. If I could write the script, it would be balancing the urban development work with spending significant time in nature. Being able to separate from urban stuff and be in the middle of nowhere in Idaho for months at a time. That's the ideal balance I'm working toward. That contrast, between building cities and being out in nature, is what keeps me energized and inspired.

A chance conversation with a group of independent artists would have a profound impact on Eric. The advice he gained from them would spur him to create a life where not only does he help create the world around him, but also helps others bring their vision into the world as well. Through his company, Eric has figured out a way to make our cities and neighborhoods into places where people gather to enjoy the independent restaurants, coffee shops, and retail that make people want to live and work nearby. Part art, part financial engineering, and part everything else that goes into large development projects, Eric has created his own canvas that enables him to turn his vision into reality.

After finding his first real estate job through the Nashville phone book in the early '90s, which happened to be during a market crash, he saw properties selling for $50,000 that would later be worth millions. Those market conditions gave him a crash course in value creation, and those early lessons would stick with him throughout his career.

As he gained more experience working in markets around the country, Eric noticed something interesting: small, independent businesses often sparked neighborhood renewal more effectively than national chains. He watched as carefully chosen local operators drew people in and created energy that spilled over to surrounding properties. This observation became the foundation of what he calls "catalytic development." The trick is, how do you make something that seems to just happen by accident, into something you intentionally create? In 2005, he and his partner launched their company to do exactly that.

His business evolved from developing single properties to capturing value across entire neighborhoods. Eric now partners with cities that want distinctive character and larger developers that need retail expertise. He's proven that the right ground-floor activation matters more than maximizing immediate rental income. The value they bring creates a flywheel of revitalization far beyond the single property.

These days, Eric splits his time between development projects and Idaho's mountains. Through Automatic, he and his wife connect promising independent retailers with developers who understand their value-creation potential. His projects emphasize human-scale buildings, quality materials, and the right mix of local tenants. Their work bridges the gap between global real estate capital and the local operators who create genuine places.

Between his development work and his writing, I've come to believe that the conversation he had with those artists thirty years ago had more of an impact than I originally thought. I think Eric became an artist himself. After thirty years in the business, his work shows that there's still room for creativity and that a small number of people can have a huge impact on the built environment around us. Creating the change you want to see in the world takes commitment to learn how things work, and then using that to mold the world into the place you want to live in.

Connect

- Websites:
    - hwproperties.com
    - automaticmeetup.com
- Podcast: realestateanonymous.buzzsprout.com
- Newsletter: ericweatherholtz.substack.com
- X: @iononrecourse
- LinkedIn: Eric Weatherholtz

Conclusion

Every building tells a story. So does every career in commercial real estate.

Sitting across from these professionals over the five months I spent interviewing them, I found myself struck by how different their paths have been. Yet beneath these varied journeys, certain threads kept surfacing.

What Makes a True Pro

The developers, brokers, and investors I interviewed didn't succeed through secret formulas or inherited advantages. They built their careers through specific, learnable approaches that anyone with persistence can adopt.

They see what others miss

Chris Powers spotted the potential in industrial properties right before warehouse and industrial investments exploded in popularity. Eric Weatherholtz placed small, independent businesses strategically throughout neighborhoods, using what he calls "catalytic development" to transform entire districts rather than just individual buildings. Sean Sweeney recognized an opportunity in slightly smaller layouts with premium fixtures and outstanding building amenities. A decision grounded in careful analysis of local demographics, affordability pressures, and regulatory trends. None of this vision came from mystical intuition, it emerged from obsessive market research, demographic analysis, and a knack for identifying undervalued assets.

They build systems, not just deals

When Bob Knakal divided New York into specialized territories decades ago, it gave him and his team an advantage with detailed, localized knowledge. Later, he would take advantage of the empty streets from COVID to build The Knakal Map Room. Powers and his team created the Fort Operating System to standardize industrial property operations across their portfolio. Kyle Matthews didn't just close transactions; he created training programs that allowed his firm to expand nationally while maintaining consistent service. These weren't just clever ideas, they were practical systems that transformed individual talent into scalable businesses.

They treat relationships as genuine assets

In our conversations, virtually everyone mentioned moments when relationships made all the difference. Bethany Babcock grew her company through partnerships with former competitors. Her expansion from a small property management operation to a firm with over thirty-seven team members happened through documented processes, systematic training, and strategic delegation. Omar Morales leveraged social media to build networks that changed his market position. Moses Kagan maintained transparent communication with investors during both successes and setbacks. Beth Azor, known as "The Canvassing Queen," built her career through persistent relationship cultivation, visiting some potential tenants up to twenty times before securing deals. These weren't just networking tactics; they reflected a fundamental understanding that this business happens through people.

They innovate within tradition

The most successful professionals found new ways to create value without abandoning industry fundamentals. Susan Miller Gruppi transformed industrial properties through design-forward development when conventional wisdom said industrial meant purely functional. Her company intentionally seeks complex projects others avoid, believing these challenges create opportunities for significant value creation. This approach has allowed them to command higher rents through thoughtful but modest investments in design, landscaping, and cohesive signage. Kagan pioneered blog-based capital raising, turning market education into investor relationships before "content marketing" became standard practice. Antonia Botero applied her architectural background to development management, bridging the crucial gap between design vision and successful project execution.

They adapt without panic

Babcock took a commission-only sales job during the 2008 crash when transactions had nearly stopped. Beth Azor spotted an opportunity after COVID by bringing a toy store pop-up into her Florida shopping center when supply chains were broken, turning a $500 monthly agreement into a million-dollar, five-year commitment. Knakal used downturns to deepen research capabilities and expand territory coverage. Instead of freezing during downturns or getting reckless during booms, they adjusted strategies while maintaining core principles.

Starting Points

One pattern that surprised me during these interviews: successful careers began from wildly different entry points. Knakal walked into Coldwell Banker thinking it was a bank. Babcock showed up at a property management company when a temp agency sent her to the wrong address. Powers bought his first student housing property at 17 after stumbling across an article in his school newspaper. Kagan transitioned from M&A banking in London, while Sweeney began as a receptionist.

The common thread wasn't where they started. It was how they maximized learning at each stage. Commercial real estate, more than many fields, rewards results over credentials. What matters isn't your starting point or formal education, but your commitment to mastering fundamentals, building relationships, and developing a reputation for integrity and competence. Early investments in these areas yielded compounding returns over decades.

Industry Evolution

As commercial real estate continues to evolve through technological disruption and shifting market dynamics, new opportunities will emerge for professionals who remain adaptable and innovative while staying grounded in fundamental principles. The industry's future belongs to those who can embrace emerging tools and approaches without losing sight of what truly creates value.

The professionals I interviewed consistently emphasized several success factors that form a practical roadmap for navigating a commercial real estate career:

- **Continuous learning** - Whether through formal education, mentorship, or direct experience, ongoing learning enables adaptation to changing conditions while building deeper expertise. Nearly everyone mentioned specific books, courses, or mentors that shaped their thinking at critical junctures.
- **Focus on fundamentals while embracing innovation** - Master core principles of your chosen specialty while remaining open to new approaches that enhance effectiveness. The most successful professionals weren't necessarily early adopters of every trend, but they recognized opportunities to improve traditional practices through thoughtful innovation.
- **Build lasting relationships** - Strong connections based on trust and mutual benefit provide the foundation for sustained success. Several interviewees described specific relationships that became turning points in their careers, often cultivated over years or even decades.
- **Balance long-term thinking with daily execution** - Maintain focus on long-term goals while ensuring excellent performance on current responsibilities. The professionals who weathered market cycles most effectively combined strategic patience with operational discipline.
- **Create genuine value for others** - Whether through better buildings, smoother transactions, or stronger organizations, focus on creating value rather than just extracting it. The most enduring success stories involved win-win approaches that benefited clients, partners, and communities.

Beyond Financial Success

What stuck with me most wasn't the deal sizes or company valuations. It was how genuinely these professionals enjoy what they do. For some, it's seeing opportunity and bringing it to life. For others, it's the visible impact of transforming neighborhoods. Many described facing obstacles that might have pushed others out of the industry, yet these challenges only deepened their commitment.

Whether this enjoyment comes from the nature of the industry itself or from the satisfaction of mastery remains an open question. What's clear is that these individuals found not just careers, but callings. And that alignment between personal interests and professional focus creates both excellence and contentment. Perhaps this represents one of the most valuable lessons from these conversations: true prosperity includes not just financial success but finding genuine engagement in one's daily work.

The stories in this book represent what I've come to think of as "achievable excellence." That middle ground between everyday business and billion-dollar empires where lasting success is built through discipline, focus, and continuous improvement. None of our interviewees started with extraordinary advantages or relied on unrepeatable circumstances. Instead, they built their success through learnable skills, replicable systems, and unwavering persistence.

A Personal Note

I feel fortunate to have had the opportunity to sit with each of these professionals and have these one-on-one conversations. My hope is that I've been able to convey the feeling as though you, the reader, were right there with us.

As you close this book, remember that every professional featured here started somewhere different from where they ultimately arrived. Their success didn't come from following a formula but from shaping their own paths and learning along the way. No single story holds all the answers, and that's precisely why this collection exists. It offers a range of experiences, strategies, and lessons so you can take what resonates with you and leave the rest.

Every building has a story. Every career has a journey. The principles shared by these professionals can guide you as you chart your own course in commercial real estate, or wherever your ambition takes you.

If you found value in these stories and want to continue hearing from professionals like the ones featured here, there are ways to stay involved. The learning doesn't have to end with the last page.

Whether you're building a career in commercial real estate, exploring it from another field, or simply drawn to the kind of grounded, hard-won wisdom these professionals shared, I've created resources to help you keep growing. And if you're in a completely different industry and find yourself thinking, "We need a version of this for our field," you're not alone. The True Pros project was built with that very idea in mind.

Stay Connected and Get Involved

This book lays the foundation. *True Pros of Commercial Real Estate* began as a way to capture industry wisdom, but it could grow into something broader. A place where professionals might learn across industries and career stages. The ideas that move you forward often come from unexpected places, which is why I wanted to create something that highlights not just what successful people do, but how they think.

Ways to Get Involved:

- **Share your take.** Which interview stuck with you? Did something change how you think about your work? Drop me a line on X (@jakejames), by email (jake@truepros.media), or through the website. I'm genuinely curious what resonated. Was it a specific piece of advice that changed your perspective? A career story that paralleled your own journey? The conversations about these insights often lead to unexpected connections and further learning.
- **Tell me where to go next.** If this initial concept finds an audience, future volumes might dive into other industries. Got

one you're curious about? Someone whose brain you'd love to pick? Let me know. Your suggestions could help shape what comes next. I'm interested in fields that intersect with commercial real estate in interesting ways, as well as completely different domains with transferable lessons. Every industry has its unwritten rules and hard-earned wisdom worth capturing.

- **Potential community.** I'm exploring the idea of a conversation space at truepros.network where people could connect with others who value meaningful conversation without the distractions of mainstream social platforms. Sign up if you'd like to hear about it if and when it takes shape. The vision is for a place where professionals can ask questions, share experiences, and learn from peers at various career stages, all with the same straightforward approach that guided these interviews. If there's enough interest, this could become a valuable extension of the book's conversations.
- **Dig deeper into CRE.** If commercial real estate caught your interest, check out truepros.media/resources for books and tools I've found genuinely useful. This curated collection includes resources for those considering entering the field or simply wanting to understand how the built environment around them comes together. And since I'm no expert, I'm also working with the True Pros featured in this book, and others, to help curate the list.

Support the Project

If you found value here, consider making any future purchases directly through the website. It really makes a difference. Retail platforms take 30 to 60 percent of each sale, while direct purchases provide more support for possible future volumes.

The site also offers bundle options that combine formats at better prices than you'll find elsewhere. And if you simply want to support the project, there's a donation option too.

This started with commercial real estate, but the vision could expand. Many fields have standouts with knowledge worth sharing. Your support might help create additional volumes of professional insight that would otherwise stay locked in individual careers. Each industry has its own language, culture, and accumulated wisdom, all of which deserve to be captured and shared with the next generation of professionals.

What's Next for True Pros?

I'm considering possibilities for where this concept might go next. If you have thoughts on industries that would interest you, reach out. The goal would remain the same. Capturing real stories from people who've mastered their craft, with the authenticity and depth that makes career insights truly valuable.

Thanks for being part of this initial exploration. Your feedback, suggestions, and support will help determine whether True Pros remains a one-time project or grows into something more substantial. Either way, I hope these conversations have provided value and perhaps a new lens through which to view your own professional journey.

Stay connected at ***truepros.media***

Appendix A - CRE Primer

How Commercial Real Estate Works: A Practical Guide

The Industry at a Glance

Commercial real estate operates as an ecosystem where capital, expertise, and opportunity converge to create and manage the built environment. At its core, the industry revolves around a simple concept: creating value through the development, acquisition, or management of income-producing properties. But the execution of this concept involves complex interactions between multiple players, each bringing distinct expertise and motivations to the table.

The industry operates in cycles, typically following broader economic trends but with its own unique dynamics. These cycles influence everything from property values and rent levels to construction costs and capital availability. Understanding these cycles—and how different property types respond to them—is crucial for success in the industry.

Major Asset Classes in Commercial Real Estate

Commercial real estate encompasses several distinct property types, each with its own market dynamics, risk profiles, and operational requirements. Understanding these differences is crucial for anyone looking to invest in or work within the industry.

Office: The Corporate Backbone

Office properties have traditionally been the most visible face of commercial real estate, housing everything from Fortune 500 headquarters to local professional practices. The office market is typically segmented into three classes:

- Class A: Premium buildings offering state-of-the-art systems, high-end finishes, and extensive amenities. These properties command top rents and typically attract the most creditworthy tenants.
- Class B: Well-maintained but older properties, often in good but not prime locations. These buildings offer quality space at more moderate rents.
- Class C: Dated properties typically requiring significant updating. These buildings often serve price-sensitive tenants or present value-add opportunities.

The office sector has evolved significantly in recent years, with growing emphasis on flexibility, amenities, and workplace experience. Modern office properties often feature collaborative spaces, advanced technology infrastructure, and extensive amenities like fitness centers and conference facilities. Lease terms typically range from 5–10 years, with significant tenant improvement allowances often required to attract and retain tenants.

Industrial: The E-commerce Engine

Once considered a relatively straightforward asset class, industrial real estate has become increasingly sophisticated and sought-after, driven largely by e-commerce and supply chain evolution. Major categories include:

Distribution and Logistics

- Modern facilities featuring high clear heights (32 feet and up)
- Extensive loading capabilities and truck courts
- Strategic locations near transportation networks
- Sophisticated material handling systems

Manufacturing

- Built-to-suit facilities for specific users
- Heavy power requirements and specialized infrastructure
- Often in secondary/tertiary markets with skilled labor pools

Flex Space

- Combination of office and warehouse space
- Popular with R&D companies and light manufacturing
- Typically smaller footprints than pure industrial

Industrial properties often feature the simplest operating model among major property types, with many on triple-net leases where tenants handle most operating expenses. This sector has seen strong rent growth and steady demand, particularly in major distribution hubs.

Retail: Evolution and Adaptation

Perhaps no sector has undergone more dramatic change than retail real estate. While online shopping has disrupted traditional retail models, well-positioned retail properties continue to thrive by adapting to changing consumer preferences.

Regional Malls

These large, enclosed shopping centers have faced the greatest challenges but are finding new life through:

- Conversion to mixed-use developments
- Addition of experiential elements
- Integration of healthcare and educational uses

- Focus on food, entertainment, and services

Power Centers

Anchored by category-dominant retailers, these centers typically feature:

- Big-box retailers
- Strong highway visibility
- Extensive parking
- Complementary smaller tenants

Neighborhood and Strip Centers

These properties serve day-to-day consumer needs through:

- Grocery store anchors
- Service-oriented tenants
- Restaurants and convenience retail
- Healthcare and fitness users

Success in retail increasingly depends on location quality, tenant mix, and ability to create compelling customer experiences. Lease structures often include percentage rent provisions, allowing landlords to participate in tenant success.

Multifamily: Housing America's Renters

Multifamily properties—typically defined as apartments with five or more units—are one of commercial real estate's largest and most stable sectors. The asset class includes:

Garden-Style Communities

- Low-rise (1–3 stories) suburban properties
- Extensive grounds and surface parking
- Typically lower density
- Often feature outdoor amenities like pools and playgrounds

Mid-Rise Properties

- 4–8 story urban/suburban properties
- Often in transitioning neighborhoods
- Structured parking components
- Extensive indoor and outdoor amenities

High-Rise Developments

- Vertical urban properties
- Premium locations and amenities
- Often mixed-use components
- Underground or structured parking

Multifamily properties typically feature the shortest lease terms (6–18 months) among major property types but benefit from diversified tenant bases and steady demand drivers. The sector requires intensive management but often provides the most consistent cash flows.

Specialty Sectors: Niche Opportunities

Several specialized property types have emerged as institutional-quality asset classes:

Self-Storage

- Minimal management requirements
- Strong cash flow potential
- Month-to-month leases
- Recession-resistant characteristics

Senior Housing

- Independent living
- Assisted living
- Memory care
- Heavy operational component

Data Centers

- Mission-critical facilities
- High power requirements
- Sophisticated cooling systems
- Significant technical expertise needed

Hotels

- Full-service properties
- Limited-service properties
- Extended stay facilities
- Daily "lease" terms

These specialty sectors often require specific operational expertise but can provide attractive returns and portfolio diversification benefits.

Market Response to Economic Conditions

Different property types respond differently to economic cycles:

Office

- More sensitive to economic conditions
- Longer recovery periods after downturns
- Strong correlation with employment growth

Industrial

- Generally stable through cycles
- Quick recovery after downturns
- Tied to logistics and manufacturing trends

Retail

- Highly location-dependent
- Vulnerable to changing consumer habits

- Strong properties remain recession-resistant

Multifamily

- Generally stable through cycles
- Countercyclical aspects during housing downturns
- Steady demand from demographic trends

Understanding these characteristics helps investors and professionals choose strategies appropriate for different market conditions and investment objectives.

Investment Strategies in Commercial Real Estate

Commercial real estate investments span a spectrum of risk and return profiles, each requiring different expertise, capital structures, and management approaches. Understanding these strategies is crucial for anyone looking to invest in or work within the industry.

Core: The Foundation of Institutional Real Estate

At the most conservative end of the spectrum lies the Core investment strategy. Core investments focus on trophy properties in prime locations —think Class A office towers in Manhattan, luxury apartment buildings in Los Angeles, or premium retail spaces in Chicago's Magnificent Mile. These properties typically feature creditworthy tenants on long-term leases, generating stable, predictable cash flows. Core investors prioritize capital preservation and reliable income over aggressive returns, typically targeting annual returns of 7%–9%. They use relatively low leverage, usually 40%–50% loan-to-value, further reducing risk. While Core properties require sophisticated management, they rarely need significant capital improvements or repositioning.

Core Plus: Enhanced Yield Through Active Management

Core Plus strategies target high-quality properties that need modest improvements to reach their full potential. These might be Class A- or strong Class B buildings in excellent locations with some opportunity for value enhancement. For example, a Core Plus investor might acquire a well-located office building with below-market rents and some vacancy, planning to increase income through active leasing and moderate improvements. Core Plus strategies typically target returns of 9%–12%, using moderate leverage of 50%–65% LTV. The return profile usually combines current income with modest appreciation potential.

Value Add: Creating Worth Through Transformation

Value Add strategies represent a significant step up in both risk and potential return. These investments require substantial property improvements, aggressive leasing efforts, or both. A typical Value Add play might involve purchasing a dated apartment complex, renovating all units, adding modern amenities, and raising rents to market rates. Or it might mean buying a partially vacant office building, investing in major upgrades, and repositioning it to attract higher-paying tenants. Value Add investors target returns of 12%–16% or higher, often using leverage of 65%–75% LTV. Success in value-add investing requires deep market knowledge, strong operational capabilities, and expertise in project management. Returns come primarily through appreciation, with current income often reduced during the improvement period.

Opportunistic: High Risk, High Potential Return

At the highest end of the risk spectrum lies Opportunistic investing. These strategies involve the greatest uncertainty but also the potential for the highest returns. Opportunistic investments might include ground-up development, major property repositioning, or investments in distressed assets or markets. For instance, an opportunistic investor might purchase a failed retail center to redevelop it into a mixed-use property, or acquire a vacant industrial building to convert it into creative office space. These investments often generate no current income—and may require significant ongoing capital investment—until the business plan is executed. Opportunistic strategies typically target returns of 16% or higher, often using high leverage of 70% or more LTV. Success requires deep expertise, strong market timing, and the ability to solve complex problems.

Strategy Selection and Market Conditions

The choice of investment strategy depends on multiple factors: investor goals and risk tolerance, market conditions, available expertise, and capital resources. Many successful real estate investment firms specialize in particular strategies, developing deep expertise in their chosen approach. Others maintain diversified portfolios, allocating capital across the risk spectrum to balance income and appreciation potential.

Market conditions often influence which strategies are most attractive at any given time. During periods of economic uncertainty, Core investments may outperform as investors seek safety. In recovery periods, Value Add and Opportunistic strategies may find abundant opportunities. Similarly, different strategies may work better for different property types or markets. What works for suburban multifamily might not work for urban office, and strategies that succeed in growing markets might fail in declining ones.

The key to success in any strategy lies in maintaining discipline—understanding the risks and requirements of your chosen approach and sticking to your expertise. The costliest mistakes in real estate often come from investors straying from their core competencies or stretching for returns by taking inappropriate risks.

A Comparative Example

Consider this variation in strategy through a concrete example: imagine a 100,000-square-foot office building in a strong suburban market. A Core investor might purchase it fully leased to credit tenants at market rates, focusing on maintaining the quality of the property and tenant relationships. A Core Plus investor might buy the same building with some near-term lease expirations, planning to modernize common areas and gradually increase rents. A value-add investor might acquire it 60% occupied with dated systems, implementing a major renovation to reposition the property in its market. An opportunistic investor might buy it vacant, with plans to completely redevelop it into a life sciences facility—a much more complex and risky undertaking with correspondingly higher return potential.

Understanding these strategies—and their requirements for success—is essential for anyone working in commercial real estate, whether as an investor, developer, broker, or service provider. Each approach requires different skills, resources, and risk management techniques, and success in one strategy doesn't necessarily translate to success in another.

How Deals Actually Happen

Before diving into specific roles, let's understand how a typical commercial real estate deal comes together:

1. Opportunity Identification

- Someone spots potential value: an underutilized piece of land, an underperforming building, or unmet market demand
- This could come from any player: broker, developer, investor, or even you

2. Initial Analysis

- Market research to validate the opportunity
- Preliminary financial analysis (back-of-envelope calculations)
- Initial risk assessment

3. Capital Structure

- Equity: Usually 25%–40% of total project cost
- Debt: Typically 60%–75% of total project cost
- May include multiple capital layers (senior debt, mezzanine, preferred equity)

4. Due Diligence

- Physical inspection
- Financial audit
- Legal review
- Environmental assessment
- Market analysis

5. Execution

- Deal closing
- Implementation of business plan
- Ongoing management and monitoring

THE KEY PLAYERS AND THEIR MOTIVATIONS

DEVELOPERS: THE ENTREPRENEUR-BUILDERS

What They Do:

- Identify development opportunities
- Secure entitlements and approvals
- Coordinate design and construction
- Arrange project financing
- Oversee lease-up or sale

How They Make Money:

- Development fees (2%–4% of project costs)
- Promoted interest in project profits (typically 20%–30% above preferred return)

- Property management fees (3%–5% of gross revenue)
- Construction management fees (5%–7% of hard costs)

Key Motivations:

- Creating value through physical transformation
- Building portfolio and track record
- Achieving outsized returns through development premium

Investors: The Capital Providers

Types:

- High-Net-Worth Individuals
- Private Equity Firms
- REITs
- Pension Funds
- Insurance Companies

How They Make Money:

- Cash flow during ownership (6%–10% annual returns)
- Appreciation upon sale (targeting 15%–20% IRR)
- Fees on assets under management (1%–2% annually)
- Promoted interest above preferred return

Key Motivations:

- Risk-adjusted returns
- Portfolio diversification
- Tax benefits
- Long-term wealth preservation

Brokers: The Market Makers

What They Do:

- Connect buyers and sellers
- Source investment opportunities
- Provide market intelligence
- Structure and negotiate deals

How They Make Money:

- Sales commissions (1%–3% of transaction value)
- Leasing commissions (3%–6% of lease value)
- Advisory fees

Key Motivations:

- Transaction volume
- Building long-term relationships
- Market knowledge and reputation

Appendix B - Case Studies

Stories from the Field: How Deals Come Together

The best way to understand how commercial real estate really works is to follow deals from start to finish. The following three fictional case studies are based on common patterns and real-world dynamics. They illustrate different aspects of the industry, showing how professionals identify opportunities, overcome challenges, and create value.

While the people and situations in these stories are entirely fictional, they're inspired by the kinds of deals and dynamics I've come to understand through studying the industry and interviewing professionals featured in this book.

The Suburban Office Revival
A Value Add Case

The Strip Mall Renaissance
A Retail Transformation

From Vacant Land to Vibrant Community
A Development Story

The Suburban Office Revival: A Value-Add Story

Stella Wilson had driven past the Oakwood Office Center countless times over her fifteen-year career as an office investor. The three-story, 100,000-square-foot building sat at a prime intersection in a growing suburb, but it had clearly seen better days. The once-pristine glass exterior was dulled by years of deferred maintenance, the lobby looked straight out of 1992, and the parking lot was conspicuously empty most days.

But where others saw decay, Stella saw opportunity. She'd been watching the suburb's transformation over the past five years—new luxury apartments rising nearby, trendy restaurants opening, and, most importantly, several tech companies setting up satellite offices to be closer to where their employees lived. The pandemic had accelerated this suburban migration, and Stella knew that while many companies were downsizing their downtown footprints, they were simultaneously looking for high-quality suburban locations.

One morning, her longtime broker, Robbie Parker, called with news: Oakwood was quietly being marketed for sale. The current owner, a family office from out of state, had owned it for 20 years and was ready to exit. The building was only 65% occupied, generating a mere $750,000 in net operating income—a shadow of its potential. The asking price was $15 million ($150 per square foot), well below replacement cost.

The Analysis

Stella spent the next week diving deep into the opportunity. The current rent roll showed a mix of long-term tenants paying below-market rents and newer tenants who had signed during the pandemic at temporary discounts. The largest tenant, an insurance company occupying 20,000 square feet, had been there for 15 years and was paying just $18 per square foot—when market rates for similar space were now $26.

The building's systems were dated but functional. The floor plates were efficient. The parking ratio was excellent at 4 spaces per thousand square feet. Most importantly, there were no major structural issues. The property's problems were largely cosmetic and mechanical—exactly the kind of issues Stella knew how to fix.

She built a detailed financial model. With $2 million in strategic improvements—$500,000 for lobby renovation, $750,000 for common area updates, and $750,000 for building system upgrades—plus another $1.5 million for tenant improvements and leasing commissions, she could transform this tired B-minus building into a desirable B-plus property. Her target was clear: mid-sized tenants seeking high-quality suburban space with modern amenities at a significant discount to new construction.

The Capital Raise

Stella had built strong relationships with several private equity firms over her career. She pitched the deal to Meridian Capital, a firm she'd successfully partnered with on two previous office renovations. Her presentation focused on three key points:

1. Location Strength: The suburb's growing tech presence and demographic shifts
2. Value Creation: Clear path to increasing rents and occupancy
3. Risk Mitigation: Below-replacement-cost basis and diverse tenant mix

Meridian liked the story. They agreed to put up 80% of the required equity ($4.56 million), with Stella's firm contributing the remaining 20% ($1.14 million). Together, they secured a $13.3 million senior loan at a 5.5% interest rate, giving them enough capital to fund the entire business plan.

The Execution Challenges

The real work began after closing. Stella's first surprise came during the lobby demolition—the contractors discovered asbestos in some of the old ceiling tiles. This ate up $200,000 of her contingency budget and delayed the renovation by six weeks. She had to get creative with the remaining improvement budget, finding cost savings in other areas without compromising quality.

The leasing effort proved equally challenging. Just as they were starting to market the vacant space, a competing building nearby dropped their asking rents by 15%. Stella and her leasing team had to adjust their strategy, focusing more on the property's superior location and upcoming improvements rather than competing solely on price.

The biggest test came from the insurance company tenant. Their lease was expiring in eight months, and they initially balked at Stella's proposed 30% rent increase. After several tense negotiations, Stella offered to phase in the increase over three years and provided a more generous tenant improvement allowance. The compromise worked—the tenant signed a new seven-year lease at market rates.

The Turnaround

By month 18, the transformation was visible. The new lobby featured a soaring two-story ceiling, modern finishes, and a coffee bar. The updated building systems had reduced energy costs by 22%. The refreshed exterior with new landscaping had dramatically improved curb appeal.

The market noticed. A local tech company leased 15,000 square feet at $27 per square foot. A healthcare provider took another 10,000 square feet. By month 24, occupancy had reached 85%, and by month 30, they hit 92%—ahead of schedule and at rents slightly above pro forma.

The Exit

As the building stabilized, Stella began receiving unsolicited interest from potential buyers. A California-based REIT was particularly aggressive, looking to expand their suburban office portfolio. After running a competitive process, Stella and Meridian sold the building for $25.5 million—a $10.5 million increase in value over 36 months.

The final returns exceeded everyone's expectations:

- Project-level IRR: 25% (vs. 22% projected)
- Equity multiple: 1.9x (vs. 1.8x projected)
- Stella's promoted interest: $850,000

The Lessons

Stella's success with Oakwood Office Center illustrated several key principles:

1. Vision: The ability to see value where others don't
2. Relationships: Strong partnerships with brokers, capital sources, and tenants
3. Flexibility: Adapting to unexpected challenges without losing sight of the goal
4. Market Knowledge: Understanding tenant needs and market dynamics
5. Execution: Careful attention to detail in implementing the business plan

Most importantly, it showed how value-add real estate is really about solving problems—for tenants who need quality space, for sellers looking to exit, and for communities seeking to revitalize their commercial corridors.

The Strip Mall Renaissance: A Retail Transformation Story

> **Author's Note:** Before diving in, I want to acknowledge that this case study offers just a basic overview of a retail repositioning story. For anyone looking to go deeper, I highly recommend *Investing in Retail Properties* by Gary Rappaport. His book provides detailed, real-world case studies from a true expert in the field—and is a far more comprehensive resource than what I've attempted here.

Cameron Anderson pulled into the half-empty parking lot of Hillside Plaza, a 60,000-square-foot strip mall that had seen better days. As head of acquisitions for New Urban Retail Partners, he'd toured dozens of struggling shopping centers, but something about this one felt different. Despite its tired appearance and 40% vacancy rate, the property's fundamentals were compelling.

The demographics told an interesting story. While the area had struggled in the past decade, recent census data showed a surge of young families moving in, drawn by good schools and relatively affordable housing. Median household income had increased 15% in just three years. New apartment developments were rising nearby. Yet the retail offerings hadn't kept pace with the changing population.

The Opportunity

The plaza's current tenant mix read like a time capsule from 2005: a struggling video rental store, a dated dollar store, a check-cashing service, and a handful of mom-and-pop shops paying well below market rent. The anchor space—once home to a regional grocery chain—had been vacant for two years, its dark windows creating a dead zone that hurt foot traffic to other tenants.

But Cameron saw past the current state. The location was excellent: high visibility at a signalized intersection, easy access from major residential areas, and no competing retail centers within two miles. The building's bones were good, and at an asking price of $8 million ($133 per square foot), it was trading well below replacement cost.

Due Diligence Deep Dive

Cameron's team spent three weeks analyzing every aspect of the opportunity:

- Tenant Analysis: Most existing leases would expire within 24 months, providing flexibility to curate a new tenant mix
- Physical Inspection: Despite deferred maintenance, the structure was sound
- Market Research: Area retailers reported strong sales growth
- Competition: No new retail development planned within 3 miles
- Demographics: Population growth 8% above county average

The seller, a passive investor who had inherited the property, had done little more than collect rent checks for the past decade. The property's neglect was actually an advantage—it meant plenty of low-hanging fruit for improvement.

The Business Plan

Cameron crafted a three-year transformation strategy:

1. Modernize the facade and common areas
2. Upgrade parking lot lighting and landscaping
3. Divide the vacant anchor space into smaller, more leasable units
4. Gradually replace underperforming tenants
5. Create a tenant mix serving the area's changing demographics

The numbers looked promising:

- Purchase Price: $8 million
- Renovation Budget: $2.5 million

- Tenant Improvements: $1.5 million
- Working Capital: $500,000
- Total Project Cost: $12.5 million

Capital Structure

Cameron's firm would contribute 25% of the equity ($3.125 million), with their long-time capital partner, Sequence Investment Group, providing the remaining 75%. They secured a $9.375 million loan from a regional bank at SOFR + 275 basis points, with a three-year term and two one-year extension options.

Early Challenges

The first setback came during permit review. The city's planning department had concerns about the facade renovation's impact on parking requirements. What should have been a 30-day process stretched to three months, forcing Cameron to adjust the construction timeline and negotiate with existing tenants about construction disruption.

Then came the surprise in the anchor space. During demolition, they discovered the previous grocery tenant had removed crucial HVAC components when they left, significantly increasing the cost of subdividing the space. The construction budget quickly grew by $300,000.

The Leasing Strategy

Sarah Taylor, Cameron's head of leasing, developed a clear vision for the new tenant mix:

- Fast-casual restaurants targeting young professionals
- Service-oriented retailers (fitness, salon, medical)
- Experiential retail to drive foot traffic
- Local retailers with strong community ties

Their first win came when "Fresh Life Market," a growing organic grocery chain, leased 15,000 square feet—half the former anchor space. The lease took three months to negotiate but set the tone for the property's repositioning. Fresh Life's presence immediately sparked interest from complementary tenants.

Community Engagement

Cameron's team learned that previous owners had ignored community input, creating lingering resentment. They took a different approach:

- Hosted community meetings to gather feedback
- Created a property Instagram account to share renovation updates
- Organized pop-up events featuring local vendors
- Partnered with nearby schools for community events

The Turnaround Takes Shape

By month 18, the transformation was evident:

- New facade brightened the entire street corner
- Contemporary signage replaced dated marquees
- Improved lighting made the center inviting after dark
- Refreshed landscaping created pleasant outdoor spaces
- New tenants brought energy and foot traffic

The leasing momentum built steadily:

- A popular local coffee shop took 2,000 SF
- A boutique fitness studio leased 4,000 SF
- A fast-casual restaurant chain signed for 3,000 SF
- An urgent care clinic took 5,000 SF

The Numbers Work

By month 30:

- Occupancy reached 92%
- Average rents increased from $14 to $24 per square foot
- Net Operating Income grew from $480,000 to $1,200,000

- Property value reached $20 million (based on 6% cap rate)

The Exit

Rather than sell immediately, Cameron's team refinanced the property with a new $15 million loan, returning 85% of investor equity while maintaining control of the asset. The property continued to appreciate as the area's transformation accelerated, and two years later, they sold to a REIT for $23.5 million.

Final returns exceeded projections:

- Project IRR: 28%
- Equity Multiple: 2.4x
- Cash-on-Cash Return: 12% average

Key Lessons

The Hillside Plaza transformation highlighted several crucial principles of retail property investment:

1. Demographics Drive Retail: Understanding population trends is crucial
2. Community Matters: Local engagement creates long-term value
3. Tenant Mix is Critical: The right retailers create synergy
4. Flexibility Pays: Being able to adapt to market changes and setbacks
5. Patience Required: True transformation takes time

Most importantly, it showed that despite headlines about the "retail apocalypse," well-located retail properties can thrive when properly repositioned to serve their communities' evolving needs.

From Vacant Land to Vibrant Community: A Development Story

Rocky Taylor stood at the edge of the 2.5-acre vacant lot, visualizing what could be. To most people driving down Madison Avenue, this was just another empty parcel in the suburbs, wedged between an aging office park and a small retail center. But Rocky, a veteran multifamily developer, saw something different: the potential for 200 apartments that would help address the area's growing housing shortage.

The Site

The property had everything Rocky looked for:

- Excellent visibility along a major arterial road
- Easy access to major employers and retail
- Proximity to public transit
- Favorable zoning allowing multifamily development
- No environmental issues from previous uses

The owner, the Johnson family, had held the land for three generations, operating a plant nursery there until the late 1990s. They were finally ready to sell, asking $5 million. It wasn't cheap, but Rocky's preliminary analysis suggested the price could work.

Market Analysis

Rocky's team had spent months studying the submarket:

- Vacancy rates below 4% in comparable properties
- Rent growth averaging 5% annually for three years
- Major employers expanding in the area
- Limited new supply in the development pipeline
- Strong demographics in the target renter pool

Similar new apartments were achieving rents of $2.50 per square foot—

a level that could support new construction. The challenge would be getting the project entitled and built before market conditions changed.

Early-Stage Challenges

The first hurdle emerged during initial discussions with the city planning department. While the zoning allowed multifamily, the current height limit would restrict the project to three stories. Rocky needed four stories to make his numbers work.

He hired Kim Miller, a local land use attorney who had successfully negotiated similar variances. Their strategy:

1. Demonstrate how the project supported the city's housing goals
2. Include significant green space and public amenities
3. Design the fourth floor with significant setbacks to minimize visual impact
4. Commit to enhanced landscaping along property boundaries

Community Opposition

As word of the project spread, a group of nearby homeowners organized to oppose it. Their concerns:

- Increased traffic
- Impact on school capacity
- Changes to neighborhood character
- Construction disruption

Rocky's team launched a comprehensive community engagement strategy:

- Hosted multiple town hall meetings
- Created a project website with regular updates
- Conducted traffic and school impact studies
- Modified designs based on feedback

The breakthrough came when Rocky agreed to:

- Reduce the unit count from 200 to 180
- Include a public pocket park
- Fund traffic signal improvements
- Contribute to local school infrastructure

The Capital Stack

With entitlements secured, Rocky assembled the capital structure:

- Total Project Cost: $54 million
    - Land: $5 million
    - Hard Costs: $40 million
    - Soft Costs: $6.5 million
    - Financing: $2.5 million

The capital stack:

- Construction Loan: $37.8 million (70% LTC)
- Interest Rate: SOFR + 3.50%
- Term: 36 months
- Equity: $16.2 million
- Developer: $3.24 million (20%)
- Limited Partners: $12.96 million (80%)

Construction Begins

Construction started in March. By June, they hit their first major obstacle: excavation revealed an underground spring that wasn't identified in the geotechnical report. The solution—additional foundation waterproofing and drainage systems—added $800,000 to the budget.

Then came the supply chain issues. Their window manufacturer announced a 12-week delay. The framing lumber package came in 22% above budget. Rocky's construction team scrambled to find alternatives and revise the schedule.

The Market Shifts

Halfway through construction, a competing project broke ground two miles away. Then interest rates spiked, putting pressure on their construction loan payments. Rocky's team adjusted their strategy:

- Enhanced amenity package to differentiate from competition
- Revised unit mix to include more one-bedrooms
- Increased marketing budget
- Negotiated loan modification to include interest reserve

Lease-Up Challenges

Pre-leasing began three months before completion. Early results were concerning—traffic was good, but conversion rates were below projections. The team discovered their finishes, while nice, didn't pop in photos like the competition's.

Quick adjustments:

- Enhanced model unit merchandising
- Improved virtual tour technology
- Added smart home features
- Introduced aggressive initial lease specials

The Turnaround

By month 6 of lease-up:

- 45% of units leased
- Rents tracking 3% above pro forma
- Strong referral traffic from existing residents
- Positive online reviews building momentum

The property's amenities proved to be a major draw:

- Resort-style pool with private cabanas

- Two-story fitness center with yoga studio
- Pet spa and dog park
- Co-working spaces with private offices
- Package handling system with refrigerated storage

Stabilization

At month 12:

- 93% occupancy achieved
- Average rents $2.65/SF (vs $2.50 projected)
- Operating expenses in line with budget
- Strong retention among early residents

The property was generating $4.5 million in NOI, suggesting a value of $90 million at a 5% cap rate.

The Refinance

Rather than sell immediately, Rocky's team refinanced with a permanent loan:

- $63 million loan amount (65% LTV)
- 10-year term
- 3.85% fixed rate
- 30-year amortization

The refinance returned 85% of investor equity while maintaining long-term upside potential.

Lessons Learned

The project illustrated key principles of successful development:

1. Vision: The ability to see opportunity in raw land
2. Patience: Development timelines always take longer than expected

3. Flexibility: Ability to adapt to changing conditions
4. Relationships: Strong partners help navigate challenges
5. Market Knowledge: Deep understanding of tenant preferences
6. Risk Management: Conservative underwriting and contingency planning

Most importantly, it showed how developers create value not just through physical construction, but by solving problems for multiple stakeholders—providing housing for residents, returns for investors, tax base for the city, and amenities for the community.

Common Threads: What These Stories Tell Us

While each of these stories represents a different type of commercial real estate investment, several common themes emerge:

1. Vision and Patience
   - Successful CRE professionals see potential where others don't
   - Real estate is inherently a long-term game
   - Timing and market cycles matter enormously
2. Relationships and Network
   - Deals often happen through relationships before hitting the open market
   - Strong partnerships help navigate challenges
   - Industry knowledge is often shared through trusted networks
3. Problem Solving and Adaptability
   - Every project faces unexpected challenges
   - Success often comes from creative solutions
   - Flexibility in execution while maintaining core strategy
4. Market Knowledge
   - Deep understanding of local dynamics is crucial
   - Demographic trends drive opportunity
   - Competition must be thoroughly understood

5. Risk Management
    - Conservative underwriting
    - Multiple exit strategies
    - Careful attention to capital structure

Glossary

A

Abated Rent: A lease agreement where rent payments are waived or reduced for a set period.

Adaptive Reuse: The process of repurposing an existing structure for a use other than its original intent.

ADS (Annual Debt Service): The total amount of principal and interest a borrower must pay over a year, typically used when calculating the Debt Service Coverage Ratio (DSCR).

Air Rights: Legal rights to use or sell the space above a property.

APR (Annual Percentage Rate): Annual cost of borrowing expressed as a percentage, including fees.

As of Right Zoning Jurisdiction: Zoning designation that allows a property to be developed or used in specific ways without needing discretionary approvals, as long as it complies with existing codes and regulations.

Assemblage: The process in commercial real estate of acquiring and combining multiple adjacent parcels of land, often with different owners, into a single unified property. This enables a larger-scale development project, such as a shopping center or office complex, which would not be feasible on the smaller, individual lots alone.

Asset Management: The process of overseeing and managing real estate assets to maximize their value and performance.

AUM (Assets Under Management): The total market value of commercial real estate properties or investments that a firm, manager, or fund actively oversees on behalf of investors, reflecting the scale of their portfolio and often used as a metric to gauge expertise, performance, and fee potential in the industry.

B

Basis: In commercial real estate, the original cost of acquiring a property, including purchase price and associated expenses like closing costs or improvements, adjusted over time for factors such as depreciation or capital additions, used primarily for tax purposes to calculate capital gains or losses upon sale.

BBB: A New York-based architecture and planning firm known for historic preservation, adaptive reuse, and urban design projects.

Biotech Space: Facilities tailored for biotechnology research and development.

Blackstone: One of the world's largest alternative investment firms, with significant holdings in real estate, private equity, and credit.

BOV (Broker Opinion of Value): A professional estimate provided by a licensed real estate broker assessing the potential market value of a commercial property, based on factors like comparable sales, current market conditions, and property characteristics, typically less formal and detailed than a full appraisal but useful for quick decision-making by owners or investors.

Brownfield: A property with potential environmental contamination requiring cleanup before development.

Build-to-Suit (BTS): Properties constructed to a tenant's specifications.

C

CAPEX (Capital Expenditures): Funds spent to acquire, upgrade, or maintain physical assets like buildings or equipment in a real estate property. In real estate, CAPEX often covers major repairs (e.g., replacing a roof), renovations, or improvements (e.g., adding a new HVAC system) that extend a property's life or increase its value, distinct from routine operating expenses.

Cap Rate (Capitalization Rate): A metric that estimates the return on investment for a property, calculated as net operating income divided by its current market value.

Capital Preservation: An investment strategy focused on protecting the original investment amount, prioritizing safety over high returns.

Carried Interest: See Promote

CBRE: One of the largest commercial real estate services and investment firms worldwide.

COCR (Cash-on-Cash Return): Measures cash income earned on the cash invested in a property.

COI (Certificate of Insurance): Proof of insurance coverage for tenants or landlords.

CO (Certificate of Occupancy): Confirms a building is safe and complies with codes.

Class A, B, C: Categories used in commercial real estate to classify properties based on quality, location, and condition, where Class A represents the highest tier—newer, well-located buildings with premium finishes and amenities attracting top-tier tenants; Class B includes older, functional properties with moderate appeal and lower rents; and Class C denotes aging, less desirable buildings in secondary locations, often requiring upgrades to compete, reflecting varying investment risk and return profiles.

CRE (Commercial Real Estate): Properties used for business purposes, such as office buildings, retail spaces, industrial facilities, and multifamily housing.

CAM (Common Area Maintenance): Fees paid by tenants for maintaining shared areas, like lobbies and parking lots.

Core Investment Strategy: A low-risk strategy focusing on high-quality, stable properties in prime locations, typically with minimal value improvement needed and lower potential returns.

Core Plus Investment Strategy: A moderate-risk strategy building upon the Core approach, involving properties needing minor improvements to enhance value and generate slightly higher returns than Core investments.

CoStar: A leading commercial real estate information and analytics platform that provides data, market insights, and tools for researching properties, including sales comparables, lease rates, vacancy trends, and tenant information, widely used by brokers, investors, and developers to inform investment decisions and track industry performance.

Covered Land Play: A strategy where an investor acquires a property that already produces steady income—typically from tenants or existing operations—to cover ongoing expenses like taxes, insurance, and maintenance, while positioning the asset for substantial future appreciation through redevelopment.

Cushman & Wakefield: A global real estate services firm providing brokerage, property management, and advisory services.

D

DCF (Discounted Cash Flow): A valuation method using projected cash flows discounted to present value.

DCR: See DSCR

Debt Yield: A lender-focused metric that measures a property's net operating income as a percentage of the loan amount. Used to assess risk independent of interest rates or amortization.

Disposition: The process of selling a property or asset.

DSCR (Debt Service Coverage Ratio): Another term for Debt Coverage Ratio, used interchangeably to measure a property's ability to cover its debt payments through its generated income. Also referred to as Debt Coverage Ratio (DCR).

Due Diligence: A comprehensive investigation and verification of a property's financial, legal, and physical condition before an investment or purchase.

E

Easement: A right to use another person's land for a specific purpose, such as utilities or access.

Entitlements: Government approvals required for property development.

Entitlement Process: The legal procedure of obtaining necessary approvals and permits for real estate development from local government authorities.

ESG (Environmental, Social, and Governance): Investment principles prioritizing sustainability and corporate responsibility.

Equity Stack: The hierarchy of funding sources in a real estate deal, including equity and debt.

Exclusivity Clause (Lease Exclusive): A lease provision that prevents the landlord from renting space to competing businesses in the same property. Common for anchor tenants, these clauses protect against direct competition and, if violated, can result in legal liability for the landlord.

Exit Strategy: The method by which an investor plans to liquidate or divest their investment, such as selling the property or refinancing.

F

Fannie Mae: A government-sponsored enterprise (GSE) that provides liquidity to the housing finance market by buying and guaranteeing mortgages, including multifamily loans.

FAR (Floor-to-Area Ratio): Zoning metric determining allowable building area relative to land area.

FMR (Fair Market Rent): The estimated rent for a property based on comparable market data.

Freddie Mac: A government-sponsored enterprise (GSE) that supports the housing market by purchasing, securitizing, and guaranteeing residential and multifamily mortgages.

Full-Cycle Deal: In commercial real estate, the complete lifespan of an investment from acquisition through disposition. This includes purchasing the property, managing and enhancing its value (such as renovations or lease-ups), and eventually selling it to realize returns—typically over several years depending on strategy and market conditions.

G

GFC (Global Financial Crisis): A severe global economic downturn from 2007 to 2009, triggered by the collapse of the U.S. housing bubble and subsequent failures in financial markets. It led to widespread real estate value declines, tightened credit, and significant shifts in commercial real estate strategies.

GP (General Partner): The party responsible for managing a real estate fund or partnership.

Greystar: A global real estate firm specializing in the development, construction, and management of rental housing, including multifamily, student, and senior living communities.

Gross Lease: A lease agreement where the landlord covers all property expenses.

H

HFF: Formerly a leading commercial real estate capital markets firm specializing in investment sales and financing, fully integrated into JLL's capital markets division following its 2019 acquisition.

High Street Retail: Retail properties in prominent, high-traffic urban areas.

I

ICSC: A global trade association representing the retail real estate industry, now branded simply as ICSC (formerly International Council of Shopping Centers). The organization provides networking, research, and advocacy for professionals involved in the development, leasing, and management of shopping centers and other commercial properties, often influencing market trends and industry standards.

IRR (Internal Rate of Return): A financial metric used to assess investment profitability—or rate of return—representing the discount rate at which the net present value of future cash flows equals zero.

J

JLL: A global commercial real estate services firm offering brokerage, investment, and property management services.

K

Kick Out Clause: A provision in a commercial real estate lease or sales contract that allows one party—typically the landlord or buyer—to terminate the agreement under specific conditions, such as a tenant failing to meet minimum sales thresholds or a buyer securing better financing terms elsewhere, providing flexibility and risk mitigation during the term.

KKR: A global investment firm known for private equity, real estate, infrastructure, and credit strategies.

L

Land Banking: The practice of purchasing undeveloped land for long-term investment or future development.

LEED (Leadership in Energy and Environmental Design): Certification for sustainable and eco-friendly buildings.

LOI (Letter of Intent): A non-binding preliminary agreement that outlines the key terms and framework of a potential real estate transaction, serving as a precursor to a formal Purchase Agreement.

Levered Yield: The return on an investment after accounting for borrowed funds (debt), calculated using cash flows after debt service.

LP (Limited Partner): Investors in a partnership who contribute capital but do not manage the fund.

LTC (Loan-to-Cost): The ratio of the loan amount to total project cost (acquisition and construction).

LTV (Loan-to-Value): The ratio of a loan amount to the appraised property value.

M

Marcus & Millichap: A brokerage firm specializing in investment sales, particularly in the mid-market commercial real estate space.

Market Cycle: The recurring patterns of expansion, peak, contraction, and trough in real estate and economic markets.

Mark to Market: The process of valuing a real estate asset or investment based on its current market value, rather than its purchase price or book value. In real estate, this involves adjusting the recorded value of a property to reflect what it could sell for today, often used for financial reporting or assessing portfolio performance purposes.

Massing Study: A preliminary analysis that examines the three-dimensional shape, size, and placement of a proposed building or development on a site, often to assess its visual impact, spatial relationships, and compliance with zoning regulations, helping developers and planners evaluate design options before detailed plans are finalized.

Mixed-Use Development: Combines residential, commercial, and sometimes industrial spaces within a single development.

Multifamily: Residential properties with five or more units, such as apartments or condominiums.

N

NOI (Net Operating Income): Income generated by a property after subtracting operating expenses, but before accounting for debt service and taxes.

Net Zero Building: A building that produces as much energy as it consumes.

NINJA Loan: A high-risk mortgage loan issued to borrowers with "No Income, No Job, and No Assets," requiring minimal or no documentation of financial stability. Popular during the early 2000s housing boom, these loans contributed to widespread defaults and played a significant role in the 2007-2008 financial crisis.

NNN (Triple Net Lease): A lease structure at the opposite end of the spectrum from a Gross Lease, where tenants pay property taxes, insurance, and maintenance in addition to base rent, thereby assuming most of the property's operating expenses.

O

Occupancy Costs: The total amount a tenant pays to occupy a commercial space. This typically includes base rent, percentage rent if applicable, property taxes, insurance, and common area maintenance (CAM) fees. In retail, occupancy costs are often evaluated as a percentage of gross sales to assess the financial efficiency of a location. A lower occupancy cost ratio generally indicates a more profitable store relative to its fixed real estate expenses.

Opportunistic Investment Strategy: A high-risk investment strategy focused on distressed assets, ground-up development, or complex repositioning projects, offering the potential for significantly higher returns.

Overlay Zone: Special zoning regulations that supplement or modify the underlying base zone.

P

P&L (Profit and Loss): A financial statement summarizing a property's revenues, expenses, and net income over a specific period, used to assess its operational performance and profitability.

Percentage Rent: A lease provision where landlords collect a percentage of tenant sales above a threshold.

Preferred Return (Pref): A minimum return to investors before profits are distributed to sponsors. Often referred to as "pref" or "the pref."

Pro Forma: Financial projections estimating future income, expenses, and cash flow for a property.

Promote: A share of the profits allocated to the general partner as compensation for managing an investment, typically earned only after investors receive their preferred return (the pref) threshold. Also known as Carried Interest.

Purchase Agreement: The legally binding contract that follows the LOI, formally documenting and executing the detailed terms of a real estate sale, with full legal enforceability.

Q

Quiet Enjoyment: The tenant's legal right to use a leased property without landlord interference.

R

Rent Escalation Clause: A lease provision outlining scheduled rent increases, often linked to inflation, market conditions, or fixed percentages.

Risk Mitigation: Strategies used to reduce potential financial risks in real estate investments.

S

Sale-Leaseback: A property owner sells the asset and leases it back from the buyer for capital access.

S&L Crisis (Savings and Loan Crisis): A financial collapse in the late 1980s and early 1990s, where over 1,000 U.S. savings and loan institutions failed due to risky real estate lending and deregulation. It resulted in a $150 billion bailout, tightened regulations, and a major shakeup in real estate financing.

Shallow-Bay Industrial: A category of commercial real estate featuring multi-tenant industrial properties, typically ranging from 15,000 to 150,000 square feet, with shallow building depths and multiple loading bays, designed to accommodate smaller businesses like local distributors, light manufacturers, or last-mile logistics providers, offering flexibility, cost efficiency, and proximity to urban markets.

SOFR (Secured Overnight Financing Rate): A benchmark interest rate used in loan pricing.

Setbacks: The minimum required distance between a building and the property line, as determined by zoning regulations.

Specialty Assets: Includes self-storage, senior housing, data centers, and hotels.

Sponsor: The individual or company leading a real estate investment or development project, typically responsible for identifying, acquiring, and managing the property.

Stakeholder: Any individual, group, or organization with an interest or concern in a real estate project, including investors, tenants, local community, and regulatory bodies.

Sublease: A lease agreement where the original tenant rents out the property to another party.

T

TI (Tenant Improvements): Customizations or modifications made to a rental space to meet a tenant's needs, often funded by the landlord or through a tenant allowance.

TIRR (Target Internal Rate of Return): The desired IRR for an investment project, used in planning and evaluating investment feasibility.

Triple Net Lease: See NNN

1031 Exchange (read and spoken as ten-thirty-one): A tax-deferral strategy allowing investors to reinvest proceeds from a property sale into a similar property.

U

Underwriting: The process of assessing a property's financial viability, risk factors, and potential returns before approving financing or investment.

Unlevered Yield: The return on an investment calculated without considering borrowed funds, representing the property's pure income potential before accounting for financing.

V

Variance: An official exemption allowing a property to deviate from standard zoning regulations, typically granted by local authorities.

Value-Add Investment Strategy: An investment approach targeting underperforming properties that require significant improvements, renovations, or repositioning to boost value and generate higher returns than Core or Core Plus strategies.

Vertical Integration: A business strategy in which a company owns multiple stages of the production or service process, such as development, construction, and property management.

W

Walker & Dunlop: A commercial real estate finance company specializing in multifamily lending, capital markets, and investment sales services.

Y

Yield: The annual income generated by an investment, typically expressed as a percentage of the property's value.

How This Book Was Made

If you've made it this far, thank you. I wanted to share a little about how this book came together. It was an independent project from start to finish, built without publisher support, a production team, or existing industry contacts with the people featured. What follows is a brief overview of how the interviews were conducted, how the content was shaped, and what tools helped bring the final book to life.

But before getting into the details of how this book was made, I should acknowledge something important: I had never interviewed anyone, nor written or edited anything substantial in my life. This is my first attempt at all three. There were certainly moments of frustration. Staring at transcripts, wondering how to shape them, second-guessing editorial decisions, or fumbling through early interviews as I learned to ask better questions. But despite these challenges, I found myself genuinely enjoying the process. The opportunity to sit with accomplished professionals and ask questions I was genuinely interested in became increasingly rewarding with each interview. I feel incredibly lucky that this book provided the vehicle for me to get the opportunity to speak with such interesting people. Since we all can't have these conversations, my hope is that the book provides a bit of a feeling as if we all had them.

While I'm still very much a novice, I hope I'll get the chance to do this again and continue developing these skills.

Independent Production

This project is 100 percent self-funded and independently produced. Unlike traditionally published books, every aspect—from interviews to editing, design, and distribution—was handled without publisher backing. I used Scrivener to organize the manuscript and Vellum to format the print and ebook versions. I also worked with a graphic designer who transformed my rough sketch into the finished cover. The technical side of the editing process used traditional tools such as Microsoft Word and Google Docs for manual revisions, alongside AI assistance, as explained later in this section.

Interview and Selection Process

This book was created through in-depth, in-person interviews conducted over five months with commercial real estate professionals across the United States. Each conversation lasted several hours and took place in the subject's office, home, or a location of their choosing. What may surprise readers is that I had no prior connections to any of the interviewees. Every conversation in this book began with cold outreach. I had followed several of them on social media, but we had never interacted before I contacted them about this project. Their willingness to share their time and insights with someone they'd never met speaks to both their generosity and the collaborative spirit within the industry.

The selection process focused on finding professionals with distinctive approaches and substantial achievements across different industry segments. To provide readers with a comprehensive view of the industry, I sought diversity in market focus, asset types, career paths, geographic regions, and business models.

Editing Approach

The editorial process for this book combined personal, human review with technological assistance. I refined the manuscript through extensive re-reads and, as mentioned in the acknowledgments, received invaluable editing feedback from an exceptionally sharp and skilled reviewer, who also happens to be my girlfriend. Her insights and attention to detail strengthened the final text considerably.

In editing these conversations, I've tried to preserve both the practical knowledge and the human element of each story. The interviews were carefully edited for clarity while maintaining each subject's unique voice and perspective. You'll find detailed discussions of specific deals and strategies, as well as the personal challenges, difficult decisions, and pivotal moments that shaped each career.

Additionally, in this book, the social media platform X is often referred to as Twitter, reflecting its common usage during the period these conversations took place.

A Note on Privacy

While all interviewees appear under their real names and have generously shared their personal stories and expertise, some names of individuals, companies, and specific properties mentioned within their interviews have been changed to protect privacy. These changes do not alter the substance or key lessons of the narratives shared. Rather, they allow our subjects to speak candidly about sensitive deals and relationships that shaped their careers.

AI Assistance

I want to acknowledge the assistance of several AI tools: ChatGPT, Perplexity, Grok, and especially Claude. They helped refine ideas, restructure content, and enhance clarity throughout this book. The technology assisted with brainstorming and polishing, but the voice and vision are mine. While every word and decision ultimately rests with me, these tools served as valuable collaborators, much like a team of human editors or advisors might in a traditional writing process. Further, unlike the rest of the book, the Glossary and Appendices reference sections were largely AI-generated, with my review and editing to ensure accuracy and relevance. I chose this approach to provide readers with good, basic reference materials that are easily accessible right here in the book and, honestly, to save time. This book is an independent work and is not affiliated with, endorsed by, or sponsored by these companies.

This book was created independently, with great care and curiosity, and to the best of my ability. I feel incredibly fortunate to have sat down with these amazing people and to share their stories with you. I'm especially grateful to you for taking the time to read this. I hope you've found it worthwhile. Thank you.

Support this independent project at ***truepros.media***

About the Author

Jake never expected his years on a nuclear submarine would be good training for high-frequency trading. But after almost six years in the Navy and over a decade in trading, he learned that both jobs involved high pressure, quick action, and the very real possibility of something blowing up.

His life and career have taken him from working as a snowboard instructor in Northern California to bartending in San Diego and Seattle to working in Singapore's freezing, air-conditioned offices. He made stops in Boulder, Honolulu, and Austin along the way. This wandering path through industries and cities sparked a fascination with how people build meaningful careers in different fields. Now settled in Washington, D.C., he's channeled that persistent curiosity into *True Pros*.

In *True Pros of Commercial Real Estate*, Jake shares the candid stories behind some of the most respected professionals in the industry, complete with unexpected turns, serendipitous moments, and hard-won wisdom. The book offers readers the kinds of insights that don't show up in corporate bios, LinkedIn profiles, or short-form interviews, capturing what it really takes to build expertise in a profession.

When he's not buried in interview transcripts, Jake is likely hanging with his daughter, spending time with his girlfriend, or being thoroughly manipulated by Duke, his English bulldog. He splits his remaining time between creative projects and technical tinkering.

Find him at:

- truepros.media
- @jakejames
- jake@truepros.media

www.ingramcontent.com/pod-product-compliance
Ingram Content Group UK Ltd.
Pitfield, Milton Keynes, MK11 3LW, UK
UKHW041855031026
15587UKWH00007B/1246/J